Working the Aisles: A Life in Consumption

Working the Aisles: A Life in Consumption

Robert Appelbaum

Winchester, UK
Washington, USA

First published by Zero Books, 2014
Zero Books is an imprint of John Hunt Publishing Ltd., Laurel House, Station Approach,
Alresford, Hants, SO24 9JH, UK
office1@jhpbooks.net
www.johnhuntpublishing.com
www.zero-books.net

For distributor details and how to order please visit the 'Ordering' section on our website.

ISBN: 978 1 78279 357 1

A CIP catalogue record for this book is available from the British Library.

Design: Stuart Davies

Printed in the USA by Edwards Brothers Malloy

CONTENTS

Chapter One

Working the Aisles

The first thing you have to remember when you walk down the aisles of your local supermarket is that *they do not love you.*

Yet it is easy to be mistaken about this. You come through the sliding glass doors of the market and into a vast hangar of a space, brilliantly lighted, open, free, and everywhere you go there is nothing but good things to eat. Oranges. Chocolate milk. Bread. Rows of corn oil, olive oil, mayonnaise, breakfast cereal, meat – whole hunks of it, and chopped up bits of it, sliced bits, soft bits, ready seasoned if you want it that way, or else raw, bloody, ready to be torn into and gnawed. It is easy to think that you have arrived at a sublime and adult version of the time when you would sit in your high chair, in the family kitchen, and they fed you your first pulpy mashes and liquids. All you have to do is move about and load up your basket, as if mom was making like an aeroplane and zooming mouthfuls of pureed bananas and rice into your mouth. Even the commodities there that are not for eating bring you back to earliest infancy. Plates to feed from. Toilet paper. Napkins. Medications. Nostrums for headaches, stomach aches, ear aches, itchy skin, pimply skin, sore gums, insomnia, nightmares – it's all there, to take away the pain, the itch, the fearful feelings. Mom and Dad are missing, but they have their surrogates stationed throughout the store, with uniforms and name tags to point them out. They are at your service. If you are in San Diego, California – where I first learned many of my lessons in supermarket lore – as you leave the store, loaded up with more than you will need in plastic bags the size and colour of birthday balloons (having decided on having plastic rather than paper, a double bagging rather than a single bagging), the clerks will wish you to have a nice day, the scent of suntan oil and hair conditioner smiling from their clean, bronze bodies, and the look of a smiley face in their well meaning grins. How nice! The sun hits you as you leave and ocean air drifts into your nostrils. If you are in Northwest England, where I lived until recently for a number of years, you will get a little 'Bye now!' to send you on your way, and if that isn't enough – if, for example, you haven't made it off from the check-out counter yet, so that although the clerks have said goodbye you are still there and need to be talked to some more, and this is in a part of the world where people find it hard to take leave of one another – you will also get a 'Cheers! Ta! Thanks! Buh-bye! See you now! Bye!', and if your clerk is female and of a certain age you will get a soft 'Bye, luv!' to put you in the mood, and the scent of a spring rain, or a summer rain, or an autumn rain, or a cold blustery winter rain, to greet you outside the door. 'Cheers!' you respond in kind. 'Ta! Buh-bye! See you! Buh-bye now! Bye!'

But they do not love you at the supermarket, and you are going to have to get used to it. Elsewhere in the world of everyday commerce you may still happen upon the possibility of finding something like love: at a lingerie shop, say, or a neighbourhood restaurant with white lace curtains, or a farmer's market set up outside in a gravelly car park, where the actual farmers come, and they're dying for human contact and tax-free income. I once stumbled upon a modest place with outdoor tables in an ancient alleyway in old Nîmes. It was called the Restaurant de Provence. Already you might be a suspicious of the establishment, since Nîmes is in Languedoc, not Provence, and even though Provence is only 20 miles away you may have reason to believe you are being had. But not to worry. The restaurant was run by a middle-aged *patron* and a thirty-something female chef in the spirit of a cultural exchange: come to us with your hometown Languedoc euros, the restaurant suggested, and we will give you something you can't always get in these parts! And in fact, though my dinner started out with a characteristic dish of Nîmes, a *brondade de morue,* offered I suppose in the spirit of ecumenism, my companion ordered a *soupe de poisson,* one of Provence's most famous dishes. It didn't have any fish in it, we were surprised to find out. We thought we were going to get something like a rudimentary *bouillabaisse,* with maybe a couple of mussels or clams and a bit of monkfish idling in a chunky chowder, but it was only a bowl of thick fishy broth, served with a few thin slices of cold toasted bread rounds and a peeled clove of raw garlic. We looked at it, we sniffed it. My companion, a visitor from California, gave me a look so as if to say, 'I didn't fly six thousand miles to the south of France for a cup of Campbell's and a crouton'. But the proprietor, noting our annoyance, came over to the table with the solicitude of kindergarten teacher floating to the side of a fallen five-year-old girl, grimacing over a scraped knee. He ambled up to the side of my companion and whispered to her in French, 'Have you had this before?' Me, I wanted to lie, 'Of course I have, I'm no tourist, you know-'- My companion didn't even know what he was saying. So while I started to mumble my 'Yes, kind of …' and she blinked at me for help, the proprietor reached his arms around my companion, taking a crouton in one hand and the garlic clove in another. '*Regardez*', he said. His arms still around her, his cheek brushing against her hair, he rubbed the garlic clove against the crouton, describing a little circle of garlic juice on the bread. 'Like this', he said – *comme ça,* which even my companion understood. Then he dropped the crouton in my companion's soup, and pointed to the spoon at the side of the soup bowl. It was only after my companion picked up her spoon, paddled into her soup, and placed some broth and a bit of the crouton into her mouth and smiled in return, signifying pleasure, that the proprietor backed away, patting my companion's shoulders and wishing us both a *bon appétit.*

And this, I submit, was love.

The proprietor loved us, unconditionally, not because of who we were but because we were his clients, and not because he needed anything from us, though our patronage was necessary to him in other respects, but because he loved loving his clients. He loved to love. He loved to love through the medium of serving food to strangers. And why not?

Maybe you don't believe that. Maybe you're cynical and you think it was all an act. But it is through little gestures like this that a nation of sixty million continues to try to feed itself and its hoards of tourists as well as it does, with solicitude even to the scrape of a clove of raw garlic on a crouton. The mothers and fathers and waiters and cooks have to love what they are doing, and have to love giving and receiving love in doing what they do, or else that can't do what they're doing at all. And so the proprietor loved us.

Or to put it in less sentimental terms, of necessity the proprietor *desired* us. He desired us to eat. He desired our desire to eat. When we ate with desire we gave him back the desire he was aiming in our direction, returning our pleasure for his pleasure, our gratification for his gratification.

And you're not going to get it at A&P, or Kroger's, or Safeway, or Tesco, or Asda, or Co-Op, or ICA, or Carrefour or Super-U … or at what was my own supermarket, at the time when I most intensely studying this issue, Sainsbury's, in Lancaster, England. And still, nonetheless, you go there looking for it. You go there for love. And you have to keep remembering that you're not going to get it, unless you steal it, surreptitiously, not accommodating but defying the system … if you can.

¤ ¤ ¤

I went to Sainsbury's the first time as I went to Britain, as if on a kind of quest. Life is like that if you're unhappy and you're travelling. You're on a quest. I went to Britain in search of a job but also in search of that other thing I always wanted. Which was what? Happiness? I had grown up despising the idea – that the meaning of life boiled down to something so trivial as *happiness*. I could hear the laughing Olympians in the background sneering at the notion – Jove, up there in the clouds and the snow, along with Bacchus, Caravaggio, Thomas Mann, and Friedrich Nietzsche. Life was strife. Strife was greatness. So there had to be something more than happiness, I insisted to myself. But what? After years of searching for that thing without a name, and years of misery, I started trying to take seriously the idea of Aristotle's, that happiness is the successful exercise of the virtues proper to oneself. And that, I decided, would not be such a bad thing. It would be something like what we call 'doing your own thing', except it also included the notion of excellence. But how does one exercise this virtue? How does one find out what it is? And most important, how does one ensure that one has supplied oneself with the right *conditions* for exercising one's virtue? 'He is happy', says Aristotle, 'who lives in accordance with complete virtue and is sufficiently equipped with external goods'. And me, I was for years either ill-employed, under-employed, or unemployed, and almost always living month to month, in puny low-floor apartments. I was out of joint. Something had gone wrong somewhere. I had been unable to achieve the right conditions.

I needed. Among other things, I was sure, I needed Europe. An American born and bred, wrenched by a surgeon out of my mother's belly in a hospital in New York City at the foot of the Williamsburg Bridge, raised at the first suburban edges of Cleveland and Chicago, spending the greater part of my adulthood in San Francisco, in Russian Hill and Pacific Heights and the bohemian side of the Mission District, I needed conditions. It turned out, eventually, that I had to move on. New York wouldn't have me. Chicago wouldn't have me. San Francisco wouldn't have me. (A lot of other places, from Tampa to Topeka, were out of the question.) Not even San Diego, where I spent three lugubrious years, choosing between plastic and paper, would have me. And anyway, I needed Europe. I needed town squares, cathedrals, outdoor cafes, high speed trains, cobblestones, and the ironic joys of the European joie de vivre. I needed to live in a place where, if you're over thirty, you don't constantly have the whole Ideological State Apparatus looking over your shoulder day and night to make sure that you're not having too much fun. Not that I wanted *fun* per se. Enjoyment was more like it. But I didn't want my having it or not to be an issue.

And so I came to Europe. I came to Lancaster, that ancient city on the River Lune, first founded by the Romans during the first century A.D., and in its greatest day, politically speaking, becoming the seat of the most powerful duchy in all of England. John of Gaunt, the Duke of Lancaster, the leading man in England before Richard II came into his majority, kept his prisoners there. But of course if you arrive somewhere not as a tourist but as an immigrant, looking to settle down, it is not enough to have a castle or a cathedral or a winding river outside your bedroom window. You have to find what only a place like Sainsbury's can offer. You have to live. You have to eat. You have to find desire. And they do not love you there.

Which is not to say they do not care about you in your capacity as a buyer of goods.

As you walk in you recognize that at once; you are confronted with what has by now become the endlessly researched and universal formula for supermarket design, contrived to manipulate your behaviour and encourage excessive spending. A little kiosk to your right, selling newspapers, magazines, cigarettes, soft drinks, sandwiches to go. Straight ahead, a bank of cut flowers, all yellows, reds, pinks and blues. It turns out that the shopping cart you're pushing in front of you has a special holder for your bouquet of flowers, so you can grab the carnations, the daisies, the roses, the lilies, and keep them apart, safely tucked into their holder. And just beyond the cut flowers, in every supermarket throughout the English-speaking world and other places besides, a great hall of produce, piled up lettuce, cabbages, radishes, potatoes and yams, along with tomatoes, apples, grapes, guavas, bananas, persimmons, pomegranates and plums … all the fruits and vegetables in the world, it can seem.

My own Sainsbury's. It was my first English supermarket and in the early days I was worried. I had spent enough time in England before to know that most of the stereotypes about English food were true. I will never forget the first meal I was served when I visited the campus where I was later to be employed, a 'stuffed jacket potato'. Not a meat-eater at the time, I had ordered the cheese and spring onion potato. And on a nice sized porcelain plate, garnished with a pinch of very dry lettuce, a quarter slice of cucumber, and a quarter of a pink tomato, came a split re-heated baked potato piled high with a yellowish, whitish, lumpy paste, flecked with green things: bland rubbery shreds of yellow cheddar mixed with bland shreds of rubbery whitish cheddar, heaps of sweetish oxidized mayonnaise from a jar, and some bits of bitter scallion, all mixed up like a mound of rock-speckled pastel-coloured grout, ready for trowelling, though some of the oil from the mixture was beginning to separate, and runoff down the sides of the potato and onto the plate.

But hope springs eternal. Things had changed in England the past twenty years, everyone said. And it was true, I had had a couple of nice meals, one Chinese, one Southern Indian, in the West End of London. And the newspapers and magazines and even the TV channels were full of items about the new English cuisine; some Londoners, who knew where to go, were claiming that Britain was now the food capital of Northern Europe. I had already had a decent pizza one night in Lancaster, served Continental style – thin and crisp, lightly topped with a spicy tomato sauce and delicate melted buffalo mozzarella, to be eaten off a plate with a knife and fork.

So with cheerfulness and hope as well as desperation I gave Lancaster a go, which meant giving Sainsbury's a go. The store was sited behind a fine old stone Victorian façade, down from a row of tall grey Georgian apartment blocks on one side and across from a row of grey stone business establishments on the other, including the venerable Bobbin, a comfortable Victorian pub, popular among the town's black-clad Goths. A better blending of the old and new, preserving the ancient character of the city while setting inside it an absolutely modern, and huge, supermarket, I had never seen before. And inside – it was the size of an indoor stadium. Yet when you walked in it seemed inviting. I had never visited a handsomer supersized supermarket, all done up with cool orange and royal blue, understated yet dressy, ready for business. It was not like a typical American supermarket, where the customer is battered with harsh lighting, gaudy colour schemes, and incompatibly urgent messages on every side – buy this, buy that, buy some more, no more, no still more – and the goods are arranged in so deliberately irrational a fashion that it is easy to get lost, as in a Las Vegas casino, and find yourself at the opposite end of the store from where you intended to be, and oddly tempted, by the hub bub of commodities in front of you, to pile your cart with something you didn't come for, don't really want and don't really need. An American supermarket – not to mention those horrifying mixed hypermarkets, like Wal-Mart and Meijer's, where the ketchup bottles are next to the athlete's foot powder and the panty-hose, and the beef steaks are set across from a stack of polyester sweaters in shades of grey, blue, and beige; and as you run your trolley filled with cheese, butter, and eggs on the way to a check out counter you're forced to navigate your way past tables stacked with fluorescent striped rubber-scented Nikes and 80% cotton socks, treated with 'odour eater'– an American supermarket is constantly challenging you, defying you to come out of the store with what you really wanted in the first place, or what in any case you really fancy having to eat, barking at you from every corner to step up to some counter you weren't expecting to see and try your luck, throw down your money, and venture for a Peppermint Obsession Barbie doll, a sofa cushion in the form of Tigger from *Winnie the Pooh*, a Christmas-time CD featuring Tin Pan alley standards sung by assorted country and western artists, a portable DVD player with a nine-inch screen, a pink leather cell phone jacket, or some other piece of absolute shit.

Sainsbury's by contrast was orderly, mannerly, respectful – in a word, conventionally (for this was a very old establishment, until recently run for generations by scions of the old Sainsbury family), English. The aisles were straight and wide, the signs on the aisles were informative and calm, the offers and advertisements put to you as you worked your way through the shop are subtle and polite. It was an undemanding space to navigate, however vast and crowded it may have been. You always knew where you were. And an attractive quietness reigned. If there was any music in the background, and usually there wasn't, you didn't notice. Certainly I never felt a pineapple for freshness in Sainsbury's, as I have in Vons, in Southern California, with cymbals crashing in the background and the Pointer Sisters screaming 'Jump!' I never heard announcements from the intercom system, requiring me to pay attention to a special on Pampers down the aisle from the toilet rolls, and I never heard couples arguing in full-throated rage with one another about what brand of toothpaste to buy, where the shop keeps the frozen hamburger patties, how they are going to pay for health insurance, or where they left the kids, making you feel as if you've come to the wrong place, on the wrong day, for the wrong reasons: you're inhabiting, uninvited, a nightmare of someone else's making. No, I was welcome there. It was my shop. It had everything I needed, arranged in a suitable way. Except it didn't. For I was constantly finding myself forced to work the aisles, to contend with obstacles, diversions, and traps, to bypass the unessential, the unappetizing, the unhealthy, and the unaffordable, to find what I needed, at a price I could pay, in an appropriate quantity, and even to discover, in that well-lighted, well-dressed, respectable cavern of capitalism, something akin to my desire. Which is not in fact what Sainsbury's wanted to give me. For remember, they do not love you.

What they love instead is your money. And that's not the same thing, although they might want you to think it is. They might want you to think that you and they are together in this adventure of satisfaction the same way and the restaurateur might be. 'They' – the people in charge, the people working the floor – may take a perverse kind of pleasure in seducing you with their foolery. But it is not the same thing.

You walk in with your shopping cart – the English quaintly call them trollies, as if they were on rails, transporting children from ride to ride in an amusement park. You come by the flowers, the carnations, the lilies, the potted begonias, and the short-stem roses, you come into the produce section, and they want, they love, they beg you for your money. First things first. There is always a stack of fruit, and usually a stack of fruit wrapped in plastic containers, which you are exhorted to buy **TWO FOR ONE.** Two for one! Strawberries in quarter-kilo punnets, full-size Galia melons, medium size Bramley apples, in bags of six: two for one! Three pounds! Of course, you can buy just one for one, and maybe that's all you can use. You live alone, and there's only so much fruit you can eat, or only so much of the same kind of fruit you can eat before it starts to spoil. Or maybe you're shopping for your family, and you're the only one who tears into the strawberries or the melons or the apples. But three pounds fifty, just for one? Or sometimes, it is not **TWO FOR ONE** but **BUY THE SECOND ONE AT HALF PRICE**. So you can buy a single punnet of strawberries–and they are **BRITISH** strawberries the packaging alerts you, maybe even **DEVON** strawberries, with long stems–for a quarter kilo at three pounds, or buy two punnets and a whole half a kilo at four pounds fifty. **SECOND ONE AT HALF PRICE**. Two for four-fifty. Not bad. But wait, last week they were *three* pounds for two, and your family never finished them, although you like them plenty, and your daughter throws a couple berries on top of her breakfast cereal, which is a good thing because otherwise she doesn't voluntarily eat enough fruit, so that you ate *some* of them, maybe one out of the two, and you had to throw the rest of them out! But maybe they weren't from Devon, with the long stems, which the family will like better ... You don't have much of a choice. No really, you don't have any choice. It's buy a second one at half price or don't buy any at all, because you can't be wasting money, and you've got to get your daughter to eat more fruit. So it's four pounds fifty, and now the market has got you. Thirty seconds into the store, and they've wheedled four-and-a-half pounds out of you, and you expected to buy less and pay less, and you're wasting natural resources, and energy, and throwing your money away, or rather, no, you're throwing your money at the Sainsbury's Corporation, and what do you do now?

They do not love you. They love your money, and they have figured out ways of cajoling it from you. The whole economy of the supermarket depends on getting you to spend as much as you can possibly be made to spend every time you walk in, which means getting you to buy more than you can consume, including items that you will never even try to consume. Better to get you to buy two for one at a fictional special price, which is hard to resist even if you know that this special price is a lie, than to have you standing picking out a handful of strawberries (the amount you really need) from an open basket, or not buying any at all because they don't look so good, or because, simply, you're not in the mood. Better to get you to buy too much rather than, simply, enough. It has been estimated that the British public throws away 40% of the food it buys.

And yet, apart from wheedling money out of you that would

be better off keeping in your pocket, the supermarket isn't really *harming* you. The food isn't *killing* you. The extra amount you're spending isn't throwing you into bankruptcy; even if you're spending too much, the cost of food is the lowest it's been as a percentage of income since the Second World War. Waste is the privilege of affluence, and the cost of affluence. And in any case, whether it is harming you, hindering you, enabling you, or regaling you – let's not forget that every once in a blue moon they offer free samples of sickly sweet Irish Creme Liquor and utterly cloying mince pie – this is all you've got. You are a human being. You not only have to eat, you have to like to eat. And there is hardly anywhere else to go. Working the aisles of the supermarket, making your way past the stuff you don't want, don't need, or don't understand, finding your way (if you're me) past all the more popularly British items – ready meals and crisps – to the Turkish figs, the organic Brie, the Italian tagliatelle, the Illy espresso, the French bread flown in the morning from France, or made in-store with genuine French flour and French sourdough starter, the Umbrian cold-pressed unfiltered extra virgin olive oil, the 'Taste the Difference' organic single cream, the blue Cotswold Old Legbar free range eggs, the Côtes du Rhone Villages A.O.C. rouge, and the Pepcid Two fast relief long-acting indigestion tablets, you are constructing for yourself a life of the senses.

¤ ¤ ¤

This book is a memoir but it is also an essay, trying to make a point. The two things, the memoir and the essay, are supposed to work together. I am trying to make a point – but I am myself the point. I am trying to explain what my life has been about – but for the purposes of this book (as it was for many of my predecessors in autobiography, the great and the not so great) my life has been about the point I am trying to make.

So let me continue with a little more about that point. The

supermarket. The institution, the system, the metaphor.

In the United Kingdom, I found, supermarkets were still controversial. I started reading books on the subject – Joanna Blythman, *Shopped: The Shocking Power of British Supermarkets;* William Young, *Sold Out: The True Cost of Supermarket Shopping.* Supermarkets only came to dominate the food business in the UK in the 1980s, I learned, but they succeeded so powerfully that almost all of the food purchased was bought in a shop owned by one of four and only four extremely large and profitable companies: Tesco, Sainsbury's, Morrison's and Asda, the latter a British concern, purchased some years back by the American mega-merchant Wal-Mart. There were a few regional chains and specialty shops here and there in Britain, a few discount operations, a few local markets, the national hybrid high street retailer Marks and Spencer's, which sold packaged food (much of it 'ready to heat and serve') along with shirts and dresses and scarves, and some butchers, greengrocers, and convenience stores (mainly specializing in beer, crisps, frozen pizzas, and sex magazines) outposted in the neighbourhoods. But the big four supermarkets dominated not only the merchandising but even the very growing and producing of food for the nation, and there was no going back. In the space of two decades the production, distribution, and retailing of food had been overtaken, apparently once and for all, by a four-headed hard-hearted monopoly. So supermarkets were controversial. On the one hand, British palates and stomachs and wallets had not done badly by the big-chain monopoly. On the other hand, it was a monopoly, or tetrapoly if you prefer. It caused irreversible damage to *the local,* to local farming and marketing. It emptied city centres of their small-scale and local purveyors, not to mention the customers. It put a virtual end to the autonomy of local farming (as farmers must produce by contract what the supermarkets demand in advance or nothing at all) and local distribution networks. It made people depend on their cars in order to feed themselves, ruined traditional traffic patterns, blocked up roadways with traffic jams going in and out of the big boxes where the all the food is to be found, and undermined the autonomy of local governments by imposing development either outside their jurisdictions or within their jurisdictions in configurations that local planners know to be hostile to neighbourhood community, and architecturally malicious.

But if supermarkets were controversial, so is what they had done to us. *Done to us*. According to the impoverished model of human existence that still governs the dismal science of economics – even after the absolute failure of the dismal science in the crash of 2008, when it was shown, in a word, that mainstream economists didn't know what they were talking about, and never had – supermarkets provide us with choices and nothing more. According to the dismal science, therefore, supermarkets haven't done anything to us at all. They have provided us with freedom. 'Reason is but choosing', as John Milton once said in a more exalted context, and to be able to choose, to exercise one's reason in choosing, is the very essence of freedom. According to mainstream economics, we operate as more or less rational agents, though in complicated ways – game theory is a big part of it – in order to maximize our pleasures and advance our interests. So the supermarkets in this view cannot in any sense be said to have 'done' something to us; they have only given us opportunities for doing something for ourselves. But what if you have no choice but to shop in a supermarket, since the dominance of supermarkets has forced all the alternatives out of business? What about your freedom then, and the freedom of those shopkeepers who are suddenly shopkeepers no more? Or what if, for example, one of the ways you take your pleasure is by shopping, and shopping in a supermarket is unpleasant? What if you like to walk, and the supermarket, by way of its location, forces you to drive? What if you like to shop outside, in a neighbourhood, among purveyors you know by name? And what if the 'freedom of the marketplace' that economics refers to is different in kind (in spite of analogies and homologies) from the freedom or the experience of shopping in a market? Shopping, buying things, constructing for oneself a life of the senses – can that really be identified with the maximization of rational choices that traditional economics insists upon? Is that all there is?

The supermarket has permanently altered our behaviour. It has caused us to change our lives. Add it up as you will, modern capitalism has transformed the way we live, forced us to do one thing rather than another, to organize our time one way rather than another, to structure the space we live in one way rather than another, to socialize among ourselves one way rather than another, and so on ... And in large part it has organized our time *for* us; it has structured our space *for* us; it has provided conditions for socialization *for* us. How did this happen? Who knows. Where were we when this was happening? Who knows. Were we better off before any of this happened? Very likely, although how we could have avoided the onslaught of hyper-capitalism is unclear. Can we in any case do anything about it, that is, alter the very system of hyper-capitalism that has so altered us? Who knows. But if not, or if not now or not yet, how are we to live?

Thinking about these things, I went back to my readings in social theory and considered which among them best explained the new socio-economic order. I mean, not so much how we got into this new order of things – that was a subject for historians – but what it was that we had got to when we had gotten there. What was the *position* of the consumer, of people like me, in the modern order? Where and how was a subject like me been placed, with my shopping basket and my labours in fashioning a style and a life for myself? I wasn't yet thinking about problems of income distribution, the way in which the supermarket economy had institutionalised inequality: the managers and the investors in supermarkets and related businesses made a whole lot of money, and the rest of us, as a result, made less. I wasn't yet thinking about the big picture of hyper-capitalism since the 1970s and 80s, as neo-liberalism triumphed, wealth became concentrated in the hands of the few, and the rest of us became dependent on credit. The Crash and the Great Recession had yet to come. I hadn't been compelled to come to terms yet with my own relation to credit and inequality. But I saw that with or without genuine prosperity, most of us in places like Britain had access to a lot of *stuff,* including foodstuffs, but maybe not so much access to *ourselves*. There was the idea, I recollected, conceived by the French Marxist philosopher Louis Althusser, of interpellation. To be 'interpellated', a French word for being called upon, for being hailed, 'Hey you!', and most significantly (it sounds fancy in English but in French this is an everyday term in the newspapers), for being called to account by the police, for being 'summoned' and 'questioned' as we say in English, which is to say to be subjected to the inspection of authorities, short of being 'arrested'– this is how the Althusserian model suggested we ought to think about the modern consumer. Something is done to us. And in having it done to us, we fess up, we identify ourselves, we become who we are. It is not that, when I paraded down the aisles of my local Sainsbury's, I was expressing my freedom and my rationality, choosing the goods I desired for the sake of my pleasure and my interests; it is rather that I was being summoned and questioned, required to state who I was and what I wanted. Who are you? What are you up to?

You are the person, let us say, who goes for the Galia melon, the organic Parmigiano Reggiano, and the Romaine lettuce, for the purposes of the supermarket world. And more: you are the person who *goes*. You are the person who goes *here*. Your day, your time, your space, your socialized existence is determined by the fact that you are here, and that you have to be here, and that you have no choice but to surrender your identity: the Galia melon, the organic Parmigiano Reggiano, the Romaine lettuce (but not the organic Romaine, which isn't available, or costs too much, not leaving you any enough to spend the extra quid on the organic cheese.) Indeed, almost before the moment when you step into the shop, the supermarket already knows this about you. And while you are in the supermarket it has you constantly under surveillance, even to the hiring of spies, of customer-watchers, and to the placement of closed circuit television monitors to oversee you all the better. As you arrive at the till you encounter a colleague from work, with his own shopping trolley, and you examine each other's purchases, to some extent doing the work of the system for it. Ah, so your colleague … buys sliced bread, but the brown bread, drinks generic Australian Shiraz (a taste for cheap Australian red it is a fatal weakness of Northern Europeans), likes a nice take-home curry, only it is 'Chicken Tikka Masala', a British invention, not the real thing, and can't resist the temptation, and indeed goes out of his way to the far ends of the store in search of Kettle-Fried potato crisps, Hägen Daaz ice cream, and Coca-Cola! Shame on him! But you see, this is who he is. There are no vegetables there! Yet the coffee he's got is Fair Trade Costa Rican. And he likes a Fair Trade banana and a genuine Valencia orange every now and then. And this is who he is. A bad eater, with average tastes, a middling awareness of quality, money to spend, and a social conscience. And of course, he is looking at your own trolley, and thinking this is who you are: a guy too full of himself to openly admit to liking potato crisps, a guy who makes a show of fresh vegetables and foreign cheese, a pretentious, snobbish healthy-eating foodie (yet not, as he sees, when he scans up from the vegetables to your generous torso, an entirely *impressive* healthy-eater). 'This is who he is!', you're both thinking. But you already knew this about him, and he already knew what he knows about you, and you already knew that he already knew that about you, except here is confirmation, here is interpellation, here you been examined, short of being arrested. You've fessed up!

And still the process isn't finished. At the check-out counter the clerk checks you out. Forced by the laws of supermarket etiquette – and the customer is being monitored by management at all times, so that he or she has to follow the etiquette, and again and again reiterate the formula, though each time with a fresh smile and a winning sincerity – the clerk says, 'Hi! Did you find everything all right?' And you have to say 'Hi! Yes! Thank you!' You have to engage in eye contact with this stranger in a shit job with bad pay, irregular hours and no future, and let him see that you haven't stolen anything, that you're old enough to buy the alcohol you've selected, and probably have enough money in your pocket or on your credit card to pay for the ridiculous extravagances you've loaded onto the conveyor. Organic Parmigiano Reggiano. What the hell! 'Do you need any help packing?' the clerk asks. And you're supposed to say 'No', and pack everything yourself (this is democratic Britain!) in those undersized sticky plastic bags they make you pick out of the distributor one by one and won't allow you to double (don't waste! this is green Britain!) 'No, thank you. I'm all right, thanks!'– even though you want to say 'Yes! Please help me! Load me bags!' As the clerk looks away, grateful he doesn't have to do any packing for you, and scans your purchases, each item is immediately entered into the central computer system of the store: one less helping of Romaine lettuce, one less Galia melon, one less chunk of organic Parmigiano. If the computer had a mind, you have to fear, the first thing it would think as it adds up the bill is 'What a sucker!' After all, it is no mean achievement to spend eighteen pounds per kilo for a wedge of grating cheese. And then the computer thinks, 'What an inconsistent son of a bitch!' Organic Parmigiano, and regular, insecticide-raised lettuce? But now, if, after your purchases have been scanned and the bill reckoned, you surrender your 'loyalty card', the card with your name encoded, the use of which entitles you to a discount on this or that, or a small bit of cash back every now and then, then the computer knows you entirely. It has taken your profile before. It has added to your profile now.

ATTENTION SHOPPER 358-9876-021 MALE 53 POSTAL CODE LA 1XX, A SOCIAL CONSCIENCE FOREIGN ITEM SHOPPER, STILL GOING FOR THE POISON LETTUCE BUT JUST ANTIED UP FOR THE FIRST TIME FOR THE ORGANIC PARMESAN. PROGNOSIS POSITIVE. LIKES ROMAINE. LIKELY CAESAR SALAD EATER. CHECK FOR ANCHOVIES. SUPPLY WITH COUPON FOR OLIVE OIL.

And even if you do not hand them a loyalty card (as I don't, on principle) it has got you still: you are registered among the no-loyalty-card holders, you are registered as one of the Caesar salad no-loyalty-card holders, you have been added to the rolls, they know that you are there even if they don't have your name, for God's sake they've got your credit card number and they know where you bank, they've seen you here before, they know where you live, they know what you buy – or rather, having provided the conditions, the encouragement and the options, the only options you have, they know what they have caused you to buy, and what they no doubt will cause you to buy again.

Interpellation. Not arrested but summoned. Caused to fess up. And this is who you are. Some day soon you'll be back in store for the cold-pressed unfiltered Umbrian olive oil, and they know this too, or at least they suspect it. Or rather they suspect you; you are the usual suspect, and they will summon *you* again.

So that was the Althusserian version, and it seemed right. You go through life with the illusion of autonomy, and in reality you are someone who has been summoned into the illusion, and fixed there as if on the threshold of being drawn into prison. You go through life looking for pleasure and love, and you think that you are always really on the way to getting the one and the other, but you are only being allowed to pursue their kind of pleasure, and their kind of illusion of love. Once they have you, there are no other rules to play by than theirs. But there was a second theoretical model which seemed a little more hopeful. *The Practice of Everyday Life,* a translator of the work of Michel de Certeau once called it. *Arts de faire,* de Certeau originally put it. Lurking under the radar of political and economic and even historical thought for centuries there has always been, according to Certeau, this *everyday life,* a life and a system of practices with is own politics and economics and history. Everyday life: my walk from the townhouse where I lived down toward the river, where the Sainsbury's is, a walk I deliberately varied, sometimes diverting myself by walking along the cobblestones on the quiet side of Dalton Square, sneaking a look into the Borough, a pub, to see if any of my friends were sitting by the window, as they were wont to do, and having an afternoon pint; and sometimes going instead along Thurnham Street, the main drag, so I could take a peek into Room 12, a dress shop that like several others in not-so-benighted Lancaster specializes in mid-priced good quality slut wear, of whose window display – very short tight bright dresses on headless mannequins with their plastic tits sticking out – I was always pleased to have a scopophilic gander ... and everyday life: my struggle with the traffic noise from Thurnham Street or the eerie silence along Robert Street, the feel of the wind and the damp against my face, the smell of slick old stones, wet oak trees and diesel fumes in my nostrils ... and everyday life: my knowing that I had a family at home in the safety of central heating and off-road silence, counting on me, awaiting my purchases, the members of the family having entered into the bargaining that is everyday life, the result of which was that I was going down to the store, in the damp early evening, to get what we need for dinner, while my wife Marion was occupied with readying the kitchen, and my stepdaughter Sara was occupied upstairs, as we expected her to be, watching a soap opera depicting the lives of young people in Liverpool or Chester, which are always somehow more *dramatic* than ours, filled with quarrels, break-ups, bang-ups, bankruptcies, and murders ... and everyday life: my taking a diversion to the river, to look down from the parapet at seagulls and ducks, ferreting in the gloom at the water's edge for minnows and water flies, and finally my entering the store, coming the back way to the sliding glass doors and into a vast warm hangar of a space that my Sainsbury's is and telling myself, *they do not love you*.

For resistance was part of the game. When you shopped you tried to outsmart the outsmarters. You tried to buy only what's on sale. You tried to refuse to buy for four pounds fifty what you bought last week for three pounds even. You didn't buy the pre-packed nets of tangerines: you'd only buy them loose (if you can), and purchase only as much as you wanted. You palpated the melons. You snuck a taste of the pre-packed grapes. You looked longingly toward the shelves of salads and greens, bemoaning the fact that you aren't in California anymore and you can't get radicchio or loose baby chard, and settling on the Romaine instead, which didn't look too bad all in all. You only got the proprietary Côtes du Rhone Villages when it was marked down a pound; otherwise it was straight to the cheaper Côtes du Rhone, or even (if you were having something un-ceremonial for dinner) the lonely, bottom shelf £2.99 Corbières, a wine with enough raw tannin to turn your tongue into leather and your oesophagus into a purse. You finagled the selections of toilet rolls, of dinner napkins, of organic and inorganic milk, of free-range versus organic versus free-range organic versus free-range nut-fed tree-sheltered but not organic eggs. And in the process, if resistance was incomplete, rebellion impossible, and the supermarket had you where it wanted you, nevertheless you followed a logic of your own. In a British supermarket, filled to the rafters with British food, pushing chemically-loaded heat-and-serve meals and pre-fried fish and pre-fried chips and overly-sweetened yogurt and trifles and packaged Cheddar, twenty different kinds of cheddar, some of it old, some of it new, some of it tangy, some of it bland, some of it even sweetened, and twenty different kinds of breakfast sausage that all taste the same, and a good fifteen feet of bottled Indian-style cooking sauces (Marsala, Korma, Balti, Vindaloo, Dal, all cloying and gummy and piquant and otherwise tasteless, to serve on 'Easy-Prepare Rice') and another fifteen feet of bland canned beans (to serve on thin naked brown or white toast) and two whole one-hundred-fifty-foot-long aisles of frozen food, from frozen 'fried chicken fingers' to frozen artificially flavoured multi-fruit 'lollies' … in this British supermarket you have nevertheless carved out for yourself the raw materials of a Mediterranean diet. The practice of everyday life.

¤ ¤ ¤

So I thought about social theory and I thought about a pair of models, one depressing and one a little hopeful, which seemed to explain the phenomenon that was me, the consumer doing the best he could in the world of the consumer society, dominated by mega-corporations like Tesco and Wal-Mart. It seemed to me that both models were correct, though from different angles. Maybe with some work they could be reconciled. But there still seemed to be something missing: desire – my desire and yours, not the appetite for things, for acquisitions and sensations, not interpellation in the prison house of commodities, and not the practice of everyday life in the overdetermined spaces of the post-modern city, but desire … the desire that pushes us from behind and lures from the other side of a busy road, the desire that hurls us into each other's arms and threatens to dump us off a cliff, the desire that makes us and breaks us, that digs a hole in us and keeps on digging a hole to the other side of the world, convincing us of the rewards that await us when our digging comes to an end. That desire is a part of consumption too, and a constituent element therefore of cultural production. And it too is part of working the aisles. In fact, it is the main part. It happens when we are stuck in the aisles and it happens when feel that we have escaped them. It happens in spite of the fact that the supermarket chains actually *do not want it* (since they do not love you) and it happens because *it must*. And it ought to happen too. If we cannot be seduced by life, we cannot seduce life either.

To get to the root of the kind of person or agent I had seemed to become, and to get the root too of thinking about how I might become something else (and you too, dear reader), I had to take account not only of interpellation and the practice of everyday life, but also about this less tangible, less controllable and less explicable phenomenon called desire. Our desire, yours and mine. I had to take it into account abstractly, for 'desire' is an idea. But I also had to think of it personally. I was already thinking of it personally, although I didn't know that yet. I had already lived a kind of life where, along with a struggle for economic and emotional survival, I was continually engaged with a quest for desire. I mean that. To satisfy desire was essential, certainly. But first of all, in order to satisfy desire you have to find it, and in order to find it you have to go looking for it, even if you don't know that that is what you are doing, and even if, though the system of global capitalism wants to keep you unsatisfied, wants to keep stimulating with more and more need to go along with the commodities it wants to sell you, it doesn't really want desire.

Desire, not need. That dangerous non-thing. Not a summons, not a practice, not even, really, a choice. But the end and medium of seduction. I saw that to come to terms with the desire that was working within and against this system of hyper-capitalism, the desire I wanted to celebrate and advocate but that I also wanted to specify and analyse, I would have to come to terms with, well *me*. I would have to think about what autobiographers often call 'my story', although I wasn't sure that I had 'my story', only that I had many stories, with many gaps in between … although on the other hand, I might have 'my essay', a single essay making a single point.

But let me begin, then. Let me tell you a story. And let me show you what I mean by desire.

It was in Chicago, 1973. I was a student at the University of Chicago, in Hyde Park, on the city's south side, an island of higher learning and cloistered lifestyles, surrounded on three sides by crumbling crime-ridden slums and on the fourth by a bleak, wind-swept lakefront. Lake Michigan, three hundred miles long, a hundred miles wide. I was studying philosophy and writing a thesis about Plato – that's the kind of thing young people do in Hyde Park. I had recently met a girl from Greece, perhaps coincidentally, perhaps not, whom I had I fallen in love with. That was also the kind of thing young people would do. Elena Voutira, let us call her. She was living in a dormitory room in a mock-medieval college overlooking one of the quads, and she was everything I always supposed I wanted, and she represented everything I always supposed I didn't have: rich and cosmopolitan, elegant in her manners, slim and well dressed, fluent in French (she had studied in France for a year), dark-haired and very white-skinned, with a high forehead, a tiny chin, and thin nail-bitten fingers, a lover of poetry, a writer of poetry, she talked to me about Rimbaud and Verlaine, she wrote poems for me, and she could speak poetically about William James and the stream of consciousness, about Roman mosaics and the rules of ancient perspective, about the mysteries of rocks and sand and 'the sea'. She identified, as apparently all Greek intellectuals did in those days of the Junta, and especially Greek intellectuals who had found reasons to live abroad, with the Alexandrian poet C.P. Cafavy. But Elena was no hedonist. In fact, though I didn't understand this at the time, she was suffering from anorexia. Instead of eating, she smoked cigarettes. ('Si j'ai du goût', she once recited to me from Rimbaud, 'ce n'est guère que pour la terre and les pierres'.) Elegant with her clothes on, she was shockingly slight with them off; her ribs stuck out. Nor was she completely comfortable about her sexuality. She was shy about it, restrained, a bit embarrassed by it, really. The idea of oral sex she found obnoxious. And one thing more: she wouldn't have me, not entirely at least. A Greek in the age of the Junta, of Henry Kissinger and CIA-sponsored repression, she could never seriously couple with an American, she insisted. Her family, prominent members of the left-wing intelligentsia, a beleaguered family, wouldn't hear of it. She had an uncle in jail for the crime of political belief. It was reported that he was being tortured. Her father, a magistrate, had several times been placed on house arrest. And anyway she was already engaged, to another Greek, whom she had followed to Chicago, but who that year had moved on to pursue a graduate degree at Harvard.

I was in love with a woman who insisted she couldn't love me back, although we spent all our spare time together. She resisted me, she slept with me, her slight and bony nakedness against my heft, and then she resisted me again. She said she couldn't see me anymore. She disappeared for a few days, a week. I was despondent. I too lost my ability to eat. And then she saw me again, and we were huddling together in her dorm room again, reading Ezra Pound's *Cantos*, listening to Brahms's concertos, and working over images in our mind of rocks and sand and the sea.

I was only 21, and I had no idea that this was what life was like, what life would almost always be like, this coming and going, this coupling and parting, this ecstasy and despair. I did not know about desire, even if I was already pursuing it. I did not know about what the supermarket world was creating for me to live within. I certainly did not know about women, or about men and women. But I had the sense to seek outside help. I sought out the friendship of another woman. Her name, let us say, was Michelle, and though American and Jewish and Midwestern, and so potentially as akin to me as Elena was not, she too was elusive. We had coffee and donuts a couple of times a week. We talked about – I don't remember what we talked about, but I know it wasn't poetry and William James. She was studying science, chemistry, microbiology. She planning on being a medical doctor. Tall and dark and freckled, with thin hair and dark narrow eyes, she was sturdy, independent, feminist, and no doubt, had I ever had a chance to find this out for myself, an animal in bed. I am quite sure that she never talked to me about her family or about a fiancé. I hardly knew a thing about her, not even her last name. She never really flirted with me, but she never discouraged me either. She was the one asking all the questions. No doubt, she was considering me as a back up, and I suppose that was fair enough because although the concept was well beyond me at the time I must have been doing the same thing with regard to her. Michelle was my backup. And in spite of the elusiveness of her erotic energies, she was reliable. She was always available for coffee when I ran into her in the halls. She liked donuts, although she was careful about her weight. She was concerned about what she took to be my inclination toward gloominess. 'There's no need for that!' she insisted. She had a car. She was doing volunteer work farther south in a poor part of the city, at a school. She worked out at a gym. This in 1973. More athletic than me, apparently, more daring, more at home in the world and more giving of herself to others than I found it possible to be, Michelle had joined a YMCA on East 91st Street, near the school where she tutored, a dangerous area, but one where she was eager to pitch in. Twice a week or more she drove down into the dodgy precincts of the deep south side – an area I knew as well, and feared, since I often travelled through it by bus on the way to a job on the far south side – parked her car in parking lot of the YMCA and lifted weights and ran on treadmills and rode on stationary bicycles, made her self strong and stronger.

In the late winter of 1973, while I was struggling with my

thesis on storytelling in Plato, trying to get on with a woman whom it was impossible to get on with, and yet who was necessary to me, every now and then seeing this other woman whom I could not get it on with either, and overall feeling as if something was freezing inside me, tearing at my guts, I ran into a pair of friends from high school. And this is where my story begins. Stuart and Bill, not among my closest friends, but garrulous, a happy-go-lucky pair of guys, had a proposition. Both of them were pre-law students at Northwestern University, on the north side of Chicago, a school to which members of the University of Chicago community had the same relation as the people of Languedoc to the people of Provence, or rather, more accurately, as Croats have to Serbs, or Sunni to Shia. The north side, Evanston, amidst all those comfortably rich folk, those white folk (though to be fair, Evanston was famous for being the only racially integrated suburb on the North Side), a town with a lot less crime, bordering wealthy suburbs that had even less crime, a town with much more pleasant parks and houses and beaches, and far less serious students (who actually went in for professional training) and a less accomplished professoriate (of this we were certain), and where no doubt the wind off the lake didn't blow so hard, and the sun shone brighter – this was a place for which we self-lacerating monks of Hyde Park had nothing but the greatest contempt and envy. And my friends, Stuart and Bill, bore this out. They had changed. These two straitlaced suburbanites from the good sides of the township where I went to high school, pre-law students for God's sake, far from becoming monastic Brahms-and-Rimbaud mystics, had turned into happy, sloppy dopers. They were late-blooming hippies. Their clothes smelled of marijuana. Their hair was trailing below their ears. Their eyes were glazed. Their faces were fixed in permanent only slightly ironic smiles. And they had a proposition. In a few weeks time, when the spring break came, and all of us were off of school for a week, they would be driving cross-country to San Francisco. I could join them. Stuart's father had transferred to San Francisco, and he needed someone to transport his car, a big four-door Cadillac sedan. This was the deal. The father would pay for the gas to have Stuart and a friend or two, preferably two, for safety, to motor cross-country, and he would pay for one-way fares for each of us to fly back from San Francisco at the end of the trip. 'Apples', Stuart said – that was what he called me, and that was the kind of guy he was, a born nicknamer – 'Apples, you've got to come with us. We've got a Cadillac. We've got a kilo of weed lined up! And speed too!'

I am talking about desire. I am telling you about desire. And I am telling you about an invitation to go looking for it, even if I didn't know that at the time. A trip to that San Francisco I heard so much about, whose embrace I had so much craved for so many of my so few years. I was kept back for only one reason, Elena, my anorexic goddess. She was thinking of spending the spring break, or at least most of it, in Chicago. But she was also thinking of spending it in Boston. She could stay with me, the two of us with a week off, with no obligations except to each other. We could have – each other. Couldn't we? It was what she wanted. Wasn't it? But her fiancé in Boston suspected something was up. How could he not? He was making noises about coming to Chicago for a week. Except he couldn't. He was too busy. This Greek intellectual was studying symbolic logic, language theory, Wittgenstein. He was BUSY. To hear Elena talk about it, the future of Greece depended upon his wrestling match with Wittgenstein. He would have to pin the damn philosopher DOWN. And so Elena would have to come to him.

Elena hesitated to commit herself, or at least she hesitated about telling me whether she had committed herself. I was her poetry boy. She wanted to stay with me. She couldn't stay with me. She didn't know.

I told my friend Stuart that I wanted to go with him on his trip. San Francisco. I had been to California before but never up north. But I didn't know if I could make it. I'd give him a call.

As the last few days before the deadline approached I still hadn't called him. I waited for a word from Elena. And then when I got one from Elena, when she told she simply had to go to Boston, and would be leaving early, before the actual beginning of spring break, I waited for her to change her mind. I waited for her to call to say she was staying in Chicago. With me. And after she called only to say goodbye to me, and she was off to the airport, I waited to get a call from the airport, or from Boston. I waited to hear her say that she had made a mistake, that she was coming back. To be with me. I waited by the phone, and I waited some more, the silence from the phone so loud that it was like listening up close to an explosion going off. Elena had gone to Boston, to Harvard, to her Greek philosopher. To be with him.

Friday night, the official beginning of spring break, and the night before Stuart and Bill were to set off for San Francisco, I was back home with my family, my mother, step-father and sister. They had moved since I left home, and were inhabiting a five-room low-ceilinged flat in a newly built brown brick apartment complex on Golf Road, a wide busy roadway lined with mini-malls and supermarkets, apartment blocks, gas stations, sewage ditches and still-to-be developed plots of gravel and weeds a mile down from the nearest Interstate expressway. Twenty minutes by car to O'Hare Airport, the apartment complex was popular with flight attendants. It was the kind of place where you lived when you wanted to be close to something without actually being there.

In our second floor flat, on a cold Friday night at the end of March, in a neighbourhood that wasn't a neighbourhood at all, I sat with my parents and my sister in front of the television set, watching the news. In 1973 there still may have been items on the news about the Vietnam War, or about Watergate, about Tricky Dick, as we called our President. I had marched for McGovern the year before. I had been issued a lottery number for the draft – twenty-six out of three hundred sixty-five and one quarter possible numbers, meaning that without my college deferment, I would be among the first to be called up and sent off to war. Ehrlichman and Haldeman had resigned in disgrace. Who was next? Who would go to jail? But as I was watching and listening, whatever I was watching and listening that night, there came on an unexpected item:

'Police report finding a young University of Chicago student dead in the parking lot of the East 91st Street YMCA. Michelle Fineman, 22-years-old, was found last night in her automobile, stabbed to death. Police report that she had been sexually assaulted and robbed. No suspects for the case have yet been found.'

I got on the phone.

'Stuart, it's me. Yeah, Apples.'

¤ ¤ ¤

I am talking about desire. I am talking about the long road away, which is also a long toward … something. Of course, there is an allegory here. But Elena's flight was real and Michelle's death was real, and so was the trip. By ten in the morning we were on our way.

The open road from Chicago to California, America's version of the Grand Tour – it used to be Route 66, but now it's Interstate 40 to Los Angeles, and Interstate 80 to San Francisco. Once you're past the Chicago conurbation, whether you're veering off north or south, it's open road. The land is flat, and there is little to be seen (in late March) but empty muddy cornfields and soybean fields and a broad austere sky. When we stopped, for our first break, in Davenport, Iowa, on just the other side of the Mississippi River, I was astonished by the silence. We had parked behind a restaurant. No one else was out. No cars were coming and going. And I could hear – nothing. Not the din of traffic. Not the wind. Not the sound of voices, footsteps, of birds flying about, of physical objects being shifted around. But nothing. I was out in the open, with 2000 miles to go, the complications of my life put behind me. (Years later, on another cross country trip, I made a point of stopping at Davenport and found that it had been built with strip malls and the like and it was no longer a silent town.)

'Apples, what are you doing', either Stuart or Bill must have said to me in my reveries. 'Let's go in and get some coffee and pie.'

Coffee and pie, about the only thing you could eat on the road to California, along with hamburgers and French fries and Coca-Cola. Neither then nor now, I can assure the reader, in the middle of the mightiest corn fields in the world, at a roadside restaurant, are you ever offered a freshly-picked serving of corn. But my boys were hungry. They had been smoking marijuana virtually from the moment we hit the highway. They had an enormous plastic bag of the stuff, dry, twiggy, and pungent, which they kept hidden under the bench of the back seat. Disdaining cigarette papers, these born-again hippies used a small heavy brass hash pipe for their smoke. Stuart, thin, shaggy-haired, and talky, would light it up from a Bic lighter while he was behind the wheel going 70 miles an hour, passing the law-abiding drivers going 65. 'Oh God, oh yeah!' he'd intone after he took it in his lungs.

'Let me have it, let me have it!' Bill would cry out impatiently from the back seat. Square-faced Bill would smoke his weed silently, as if praying.

'Hey Bill', Stuart said, 'show Apples what else we've got!'

What else?

'You've got it', Bill said.

'Oh yeah. Apples. Take a look at this.' From his jacket pocket he fished out a vial of prescription pills, shaking it. 'Speed', he said. 'Copped it from a buddy, a freak. For the journey. Fuck sleeping, you know what I mean?'

I took the bottle and looked inside. About twelve pills in all, in capsule form, in a bottle labelled for antibiotics.

Me, I wasn't having any of any of it, except maybe a chip of speed if I was driving. Only twenty-one years-old, I had already discovered that my drug of choice was alcohol. Marijuana, which I had first experimented with at the age of 16, gave me the willies. I had stopped using it. I wasn't tempted by it. It scared me. And it both scared and irritated me to see these two guys using it so cavalierly, lighting up, and then lighting up again. I would open the window and put my head out to avoid inhaling the smoke filling up the cabin. I would tell them what I thought about the stuff, me in my twenty-one-year-old wisdom. 'Marijuana', I would say, 'it brings you down. It makes you forget things. It makes you dull. It makes you stupid. And the way you smoke it, out in the open …'

'Apples, why don't you shut the fuck up, and hold the pipe for me a minute.'

Apples: the whole trip I was Apples, nothing but Apples. Except for Bill, quiet Bill, a big Polish guy who used to play football, and who now had turned into this other sort of creature, with a big round curly head of hair – quiet Bill would allow himself to call me Bob every now and then.

Stuart, though, was the ringleader. It was his car and his gig and it was his exuberance that was the psychic motor powering this trip. I thought he was funny. I liked the frivolous life in the guy – such a far cry from the dead seriousness of the people I knew in Hyde Park. He scared me a bit. He especially scared me with the way he wielded that hash pipe. It hardly mattered where he was or what he was doing, he would pop the thing out of its hiding place – the glove compartment, the ashtray, his jacket pocket – and let his little Bic lighter have a rip at it. On the road, stopped at a red light next to a truck driver delivering medical equipment, or moving at seventy-miles an hour, passing a station wagon filled with kids, the kids waving to us as the parents scowled, pretending not to see us and what we were doing, whenever the urge took him he'd pop it out, ask for a refill if nothing was left in the bowl, and bending over the steering wheel light up and inhale and give a few groans of exhaling contentment. Scared the shit out of me, he did, at least at first, until I got used to the idea that neither the medical truck nor the station wagon in the next lane over was going to pull us over and arrest us for possession or call the cops on us, and until I saw that Stuart was not only a good driver, but a good driver stoned, and not only a good driver stoned but a good driver stoned leaning over the steering wheel, hugging it tight with his elbows, and using his hands to light up another pipeful. I was in good hands, as it were. And he otherwise kept me amused, with his insane talk about women – 'chicks' – and drugs and rock n' roll. It seemed that he had spent his three years at Northwestern so far neither reading anything nor thinking anything but chicks and drugs and rock n' roll. 'How could a guy like you, how could either of you guys, think of becoming lawyers?' I asked. 'I mean, the law. The Law. Working for the Law.'

'What else are we supposed to do', was Stuart's answer. 'Where else is the money for drugs supposed to come from?'

Surely he was kidding. Surely there was something more substantial to him, but he wasn't letting it on. Even the music he listened to seemed thin. It was all Rod Stewart, again and again, singing 'Maggie May'.

Wake up Maggie I think I've got something to say to you.

It's late September and I really should be back in school.

Again and again, the cassette tape in the dash reiterated this odd anthem. 'I know I keep you amused', the song went on. 'But I feel I'm being used', the singer complained. Bad faith, in other words. Stuart and Bill, these two bourgeois, one of them an ex-football player for God's sake, with their Cadillac and their law school, their pre-law school, with their marijuana and their rock n' roll, filling their heads with a song about a poor boy being victimized by an older, manipulative woman – these two guys with all the advantages and all of their future ahead of them, and nothing in their mind but 'I know I keep you amused', and nothing in their mind but the driving of lyrics about the fear of being exploited that keep stumbling over the most elemental issues of metre, cadence, and rhyme: that was their shtick.

You made a first class fool out of me
But I'm as blind as fool can be
You stole my heart but I love you anyway …
Good God!
I laughed at all of your jokes
My love you didn't need to coax.

Not exactly Rimbaud or Verlaine. Not even Ira Gershwin. Not even Paul McCartney. And had my friends even spent a moment's thought to what the lyrics were saying? Had they noticed how astray and clunky they can go? 'You stole my soul', the singer complains again; 'that's a pain I can do without'; followed by 'All I needed was a friend to lend a guiding hand …'As if the lyricist had misplaced his rhyming dictionary for a few moments, the same dictionary that had earlier served him so well with 'me' and 'be' and 'jokes' and 'coax'.

But the more I listened to it, the more I found myself liking the song in spite of myself. The introductory riffs on the guitar, perhaps a twelve-string, later followed up by a mandolin, were brilliant. And the beat was driving, the bass line precise, the tune compelling, the playing both controlled and energetic. And when all was said and done, the premise of the song was attractively sophisticated. This was 1973, and here was a number one song imagining a young man in bed with an older woman, telling her about his feelings. (I doubt that I was savvy enough to see irony in the fact that this first highly popular rock song openly discussing sexual exploitation had the woman exploiting the man.) 'Wake up Maggie I think I've got something to say to you.' A young man, in bed, interrupting somnolence, hoarse with directness, hoarse with pleading, frustrated, ingenuous wrath. 'Oh Maggie I wish I'd never seen your face!'

Lighten up! I said to myself. Go with the flow. Go with these guys! Maybe you should try some marijuana. For all intents and purposes, shut up in the cabin with them, I was smoking it anyway. Maybe I was getting high …

We drove a short way the first day, stopping at the apartment of another high school friend's in Des Moines. It was the same Des Moines that Jack Kerouac had stopped at, as he discussed it in *On the Road*. Whether the best looking women in the world actually resided in Des Moines, as Kerouac claimed they did, seemed from my experience of the place – I had visited it several times before – to be rather unlikely, but we spent most of the evening shut up anyway, the three guys smoking marijuana and drinking beer, me just drinking beer, and lying back on the hardwood floor of the old flat listening to Rod Stewart complaining about Maggie May.

It went on and on. I liked it more and more, I was beginning to understand the anger the song expressed – though never, no not once as far as I can recall connecting the premise of the song to my own situation – but I was also getting exhausted by it, and as the alcohol took effect along with the ambient marijuana smoke I began remembering Michelle, and thinking about what had happened to her, and I was getting dizzy.

And then, by mid-morning we were on the road again. Mid-morning, a late start. We were behind schedule. We were going to try to drive the next twenty-four hours straight, each of us rotating at the wheel. That would take us, if we went as far as fifteen hundred miles, all the way to Sacramento, and another friend's place to stay at for free, in fact to the home of one of Stuart's chicks, and the hardest part was only the first eight hours, the drive through Iowa and Nebraska, where the road was unerringly flat, wide, and dull. Iowa gave way to Nebraska; the flat land got bleaker. Nebraska City, Lincoln, Grand Island, mere sign posts along the way, towns where it was hard to imagine that any people actually lived, out in the bleakness, we inched past; Hamilton, Kearney, Phelps, North Platte. And drive as we did the same featureless landscape met us everywhere, as if were weren't making any progress. Evening came on, the darkness lowering behind us. Still another two hundred miles before we made it past the border into Wyoming, that promise of variety, at the other side of the Continental Divide, where we would climb into the Rocky Mountains. In the West. In America. Yet already we saw signs of being in the West. The land was getting rocky and sandy. You could see the suggestion of gorges creasing the wide earth. Signs along the highway indicated roadside attractions featuring Indians, real Indians, Lakota Sioux: you could stop at a filling station gift shop that sold fudge, turquoise jewellery, and beaded belts, with designs of silhouetted buffalos running along a white horizon. But it was getting dark.

At around 10:30 at night, weary with driving but knowing we had another fifteen hours to go, we stopped at an all night restaurant just off the exit to Ogallala. The boys were high and hungry. I was high too. I'd taken one of the capsules, and felt myself rushing, rushing, and hardly hungry at all but ready to eat all the same. The restaurant was new, one of the chain restaurants that stood along the Interstate highways with their garish monumental plastic signage like so many oversized balloons from hell, each of them saying, insisting, yeah you've gone another hundred miles and here's another Denny's. It's all Denny's. There's no escape. You may think you are pursuing desire, but what has been built in front of you is an institution to elicit and satisfy need.

But we were enjoying our burgers, our fries, our apple pie, our coffee – or at least Stuart and Bill were, I could still hardly eat – and we were all hopped up. We were in high spirits. We stayed in our booth for nearly an hour, playing with our food, loading up on coffee, smoking cigarettes, talking about the good old days in high school, talking about chicks, talking about rock concerts and who was the best guitarist if it wasn't Eric Clapton, or Jeff Beck, arguing about Watergate, arguing about Tricky Dick, whom my newly baptised hippie friends didn't begin to despise as much as I did, and about whom they didn't even seem to understand what the fuss was, though there was no way either of them was going to allow himself to get drafted, no way, Nixon or no Nixon, Kissinger or no Kissinger ... talking about anything, three loud and elated and contentious long-haired Chicagoans lousing about, attracting attention but not caring, in this ... Denny's, with orange seats and bright lights and thick brown Formica tables and the scent of ketchup, coffee, cigarette smoke, and disinfectant.

In the chill night air we marched back into the car. Stuart was happy to drive for now. Bill said he'd get in the back and in spite of the coffee have a nap. I would ride shotgun for a few hours, until it was my turn to drive. But we were no sooner back on the local frontage road, approaching the on-ramp to the Interstate, when Stuart abruptly pulled over, stopping the car on the shoulder.

'What are you doing!' I shouted, alarmed.

'I need some dope', Stuart shouted back. 'Where's the dope? I'm not getting back on the road until I've had some dope.'

'It's all under the seat', Bill said. 'There's none left anywhere else.'

'Ah shit!'

'It's okay, I can get it. Just wait. I'll have to stand up.'

'Isn't there any dope still in the pipe? Where's the pipe? The glove compartment? Apples?'

'Yeah, it's here', I said, checking.

'Is there any weed left in it?'

'Just a bit.'

'Ouch!' yelled Bill, 'I got my hand stuck. I can't get at it from here. I'll have to get out of the car.'

'All right, then.'

'Aw come on, I can't get out on the road here. Let's just have what's in the pipe. There's got to be plenty of residue there. We'll smoke the residue for now.'

'Fuck.'

'Look, I've got it', I said. 'Just relax. I'll light it up for you.'

Bill sat back down while I took the lighter and for the first time in months and months, who knew how long it was, it felt like years, I put my mouth to a vessel containing the psychotropic cannabis, and clicked on a Bic lighter to set it afire. I would allow myself a taste, a little taste. No, I would just light it up without inhaling, and the smoke in my mouth, all right well the smoke in my mouth I would allow myself. I would be all right. It couldn't hurt. And in any case the glow from the pipe as I set the touch of weed and the residue afire was attractive in the dark, and the smell was not so bad.

'SHIT, COPS!'

A squad car was stopped behind us, its lights flashing red and white. A search beam came hurling into the cabin of the car, light a ray beam from outer space. I was startled at how bright it was.

'Hide the dope! Hide the fucking dope.'

'I'm doing it! I'm doing it!' But where? Where was I going to put it? I tried forcing the hot pipe under the seat but it wouldn't go.

'Aw SHIT!'

'Not there! They'll find it there!'

Oh yeah, so the thing to do was to get out of the car and throw it away in the dark. Get out of the car and don't let them see what you're doing and throw it away. At least open the door and don't let them see what you're doing and let the pipe slip out in the darkness. When they go round to the driver's side to check his driver's licence squeeze open the door, just a little. At least open the door …

There was a rap at the door. At my side of the car. My door. A policeman standing there, with a flashlight. There was no one standing outside on driver's side of the car.

'Open the door!'

He was rapping on the window.

I wedged the pipe under my seat. Good work! And he won't have a search warrant. He'll never find it. Will he? Shit!

'Open the door! You too. Get out of the car.'

The policeman was a young man with close-cropped dark hair and a round face, maybe twenty-eight- years old, standing there with his right shoulder cocked back so we could see the black butt of the big black gun in his holster.

'All of you. Out.'

Bill came out from the back, Stuart came out from around his side. A few cars sped past us.

'Stand to the side, over here', he directed us.

He flashed the light in our faces. Flashed it at us, and looked us over as if we were … criminals.

'Let me see your IDs. One at a time. Take your wallets out of your pocket.'

Interpellated! But the IDs seem to satisfy him. Or did they?

'What are you guys doing out here?'

'We were just on our way back to the freeway, Officer', said Stuart as meek and as earnest as could be. 'We're on our way to visit my father in California. We were just stopping to have something to eat.'

'I saw you boys in the diner. I was following you up the road. What have you got in the car?'

'Nothing, Officer.'

'Stand here, together, where I can see you. Three boys from Illinois, making all that noise in the diner… . You', he said, motioning to me, 'would you please open the car door, please.'

I opened the door.

'Now stand back. There. The three of you.'

We were just behind him as he flashed his light into the car, looking over his shoulder. There on the floor of the car, next to but not under the seat, was the hash pipe.

The interpellation was over: we were now officially under arrest. It didn't help matters that when he had us spread-eagled against the side of the car and searched us, he found the bottle of pills in Stuart's pocket.

¤ ¤ ¤

The compelling structures of modern society – for example, consumerism – are always accompanied by compulsive structures – for example, jail. There are things that you are caused to have: cars, snacks, television, indoor plumbing. There are things that you are encouraged to have: white teeth, a Cadillac, a Big Mac, a large home freezer, a detached house with a large front yard. There are things that you are discouraged from having: bad breath, old clothes, hunger pangs, a crowded home on a dangerous street on the wrong side of the tracks. And there are things that you cannot have, on pain of punishment: marijuana, amphetamine, stolen property, child pornography, a bomb. You are supposed to be the person who has, without complaint, what you are already being caused to have; you are supposed to be enthusiastic about the things you are encouraged to have. You are not supposed to dally with what is not encouraged. And you must not possess what you must not have. The crime itself is called 'possession'.

We were led into the basement of the police station. There were two cells. In the first one an old man in baggy overalls, drunk, with red leathery skin and a large nose, was standing about. 'Hey where you been?' he called out to the police officer as he led us by.

'Shut up, you', said the officer.

'Shut up you', the drunk repeated, clinging to the bars. 'Shut up you.'

The second cell was empty. It had four bunk beds, a toilet bowl without a seat, and a sink with a single cold water spigot. The station was newly built, a small concrete block just off the Main Street of the town; the cells were clean, with a cement floor, bare cinder block walls, and fluorescent lights overhead, out of reach and behind metal cages.

Stuart and Bill were huddled at the front of the cell. I sat on a bunk toward the rear. It was late. I was exhausted.

'We did it this time', Stuart was saying, 'we really did it.'

'Fucked', Bill responded.

'Fucked', Stuart said.

Fucked, I said to myself. And I was thinking: Elena. If Elena only saw me. If she saw me here. And I was thinking: Michelle. And I was thinking, my parents. We had a kilogram of marijuana in the car. And to be in this room, this cell: I hadn't understood it before, what it was like to be incarcerated, locked up, you felt that, you felt it both ways, you were incarcerated, meaning you were institutionalised, you had lost your freedom; and you were locked up, meaning there was a door you couldn't open, a threshold you couldn't cross, you couldn't move.

The officer – Bartley, let us say he said his name was – made a point of walking past our cell several times. He was searching our car, he told us. He had a crow bar in his hands.

Fucked, I said to myself.

'Officer, Bartley', Stuart said to him. 'Could you at least tell us what's going on?'

'Like I said, I'm taking your car apart.'

'But what for?'

'You know what for. Any other questions.'

'Well, yeah one. What's the law here in Nebraska? What's the penalty? For possession.'

'Seven-seven', Bartley said.

'Seven-seven!'

'Yeah, they changed the law just a little while ago. You got lucky.'

'Lucky?'

'For what I've found so far, it's seven-seven. Under an ounce of marijuana, it's seven days and seven months probation. I don't know what they do about probation for out-of-state boys.'

'Seven days, that's it?'

'For what I've found so far. But this stuff ...' He took the bottle of pills out of his pocket and shook it at us. 'This stuff, I'll have to wait until the pharmacy opens at eight o'clock to see what it is. And this stuff could be serious.'

'Yeah, well. We're studying law, we told you. We're pre-law, except if it's serious we'll never get into law school. And we'll never get to practise.'

'You should have thought of that first', said Bartley. 'Anyway, I've got work to do. I'll see you in the morning.'

A door slammed after him when he left, a heavy door, metal against metal.

It hit the two of them hard. They would never get into law school. They would never get to be lawyers. They were going to prison. They stayed on their feet, shuffling and pacing back and forth, muttering to themselves, thinking about the phone calls they would have to make in the morning, thinking about their lost ambitions, every now and then one of them coming out with a curse.

'I can't believe it!'

'What are we going to do?'

'We're good and fucked! We're good and fucked!'

'Apples, who told you to light up the pipe? You could have waited until we got on the road. Son of a bitch!'

'Why don't you settle down', I said, 'and wait to see what happens.'

'Settle down! That's easy for you to say! You're not preparing for fucking law school! What are you studying anyway? Philosophy? What the fuck is that about? Philosophy! I suppose that's what taught you to light up the pipe on the goddam shoulder in the dark, with a cop car behind us!'

'Hey, it wasn't his fault!'

Or was it? I really didn't care. I lay back on my bunk, thinking not so much about what would happen as about where I was, about where I had ended up, the speed still coursing through me in spite of my exhaustion, and riding on top of that speed, an accumulating sense of dread, a pit in my stomach, a burning at my temples, a throbbing in my head, not a fear but a premonition, and not a premonition but a disgust, a nausea, a revolting contempt for the disaster I had brought upon myself. Dread. So that was what Kierkegaard meant. I couldn't stand it, I wouldn't stand it, I had to stand it. And humiliation. I wanted to hide. How was I going to face my parents? What would I say to them? That was what I had made a fuss about going to college for? I went to college so I would end up in jail? For drugs? And wouldn't it be a good one to call Elena on the phone, yeah say hello Elena guess where I am? This is … Well, I wouldn't call anyone. I would just stay in jail. I would hide myself here. I could never face Elena. I would never have to face Elena. I would never see her again. And she would say well, I'm glad that's over, and I am grateful to you, Bob, you showed me what kind of man you really are, you really are just like all these other irresponsible Americans. Our people die for freedom, our people die for an idea, they have their fathers torn away from them, their uncles tortured, their brothers and sisters disappeared, and you, you smoke marijuana, you take speed.

I wanted to cry. I wanted to die. None of this was what I intended. I had meant to do something else. I was meant to have a future.

I lay there in pain. Stuart was still on his feet, pacing. Bill was seated at the edge of the cot opposite mine, biting his nails. It was four o'clock in the morning. It would be another four hours or more before we found out what was in store for us. Stuart seemed to be whispering something to himself. Bill's eyes were glazed over. He had been fighting back the tears. I closed my eyes and fought back my own, and images of Elena, and of my stepfather and mother danced in my head. I remembered Michelle. I remembered that in a way I had been running away. And I fell asleep, and dreamed.

When I woke up about three hours later, Stuart and Bill were still pacing the floor.

'Apples, I can't believe you've been sleeping.'

'You been up all this time? Anything happen?'

'Nothing.'

'I'll bet he hasn't found anything. He's not allowed to break into the car, you know, not without a warrant.'

'He's breaking into it just fine, Apples. Did you see that crowbar?'

'He's just trying to scare us.'

'Well it's worked. What the fuck are we going to do?'

'Seven days', I said. 'We'll be in jail for seven days.' We wouldn't be back in school in time. I wouldn't see Elena in time. Seven days. Only more.

Bill started sobbing.

Seven days. Seven months. Seven years.

At about 7:30 Officer Bartley came down to us again.

'The District Attorney won't be in until ten this morning. We can't do anything until then. You'll just have to wait here.'

Ten o'clock. The beginning of the seven days, or the seven years. Stuart's father was going to have a fit. Bill's mother and father were going to have a fit. Worse than a fit. It was the end.

At eight-fifteen, after the pharmacy was open, Bartley still hadn't come.

At eight-thirty he still hadn't come.

We went silent. None of us said a thing. The cell was a square of dead air. Outside the door to the cell, a heavy metal block with steel bars, it was still nothing but dead air.

A little before nine, Bartley finally came down and stood in front of the bars of the door, with a mischievous look on his face and the bottle of pills in his hand.

'The pharmacist said that these are heart medications. He can't understand what you have them for.'

'That's all right', said Stuart.

'They're not illegal. You can have them back.'

'All right.'

'So I got on the phone to the District Attorney. I told him about you. I told him you law students. I told him what I found. He said just to let you go.'

'What?'

'He said to let you go. To take you off the books and let you go. Only he wants you out of town, and he wants you out of Nebraska.'

¤ ¤ ¤

On the road. The weather had turned fine, chilly and hazy but with the sun overhead. We were out on Interstate 80, on the way to Wyoming, and the road was all but empty in both directions. The marijuana was still under the back seat, we determined. Bill had slipped his fingers under the seat and felt the bag. As for the pills, Stuart told the policeman that he could keep them. He didn't want them.

It was the best morning of our lives. On the road. We told ourselves that we couldn't believe our good luck. Stuart said, 'All I know is I'm driving this fucking car and I'm not stopping until we get the fuck out of Nebraska.'

'And were getting rid of the grass', I said.

'You bet we are', Stuart said, 'as soon as we get to Wyoming'.

'Listen', I said, 'I'm not bullshitting. We're getting rid of the stuff.'

'He's right', Bill said.

'Yeah, I guess', Stuart conceded. 'But not until we're out of Nebraska. They might be following us and I don't want to stop. Not now. Not yet.'

'Well watch your speed', Bill said. 'Let's not get pulled over.'

'I'm watching it! I'm watching!'

In fact, he was driving nerve-rackingly slowly, looking over his shoulder all the time. The land here was brown and yellow and uneven; the road curled through hillocks and declivities, then opened up to a straightaway again, tufts of prairie grass and tumbleweed on both sides of us. We were tired, dead tired. We needed coffee. We needed sleep. Sidney, Nebraska came up. We were lagging at sixty miles an hour. Kimball, Nebraska. A turnoff leading to Scotts Bluff. And then a sign announced Cheyenne, Wyoming, eighty-six miles ahead. The Wyoming border had to be close. Get the grass ready, I said.

'I'm getting it', Bill said. 'As soon as you tell me.'

Welcome to Wyoming, the sign at the edge of the road said.

'All right!' we all chimed together. 'Fucking Wyoming.'

'I've got it out', said Bill, yanking at the seat and pulling up the bench.

'Hand it over.'

I had the full bag of marijuana in my hands.

I opened the window.

'Full speed ahead!' I shouted.

'I'm gunning it', said Stuart.

The road was empty. We were at the edge of the badlands, the earth parched and eroded, the prairie grass struggling against the dry wind, the Cadillac lurching off to the west.

'I'm letting it rip', I said, opening the window.

A cold blast of air came through. The bag almost blew out of my hands and back into the car. I leaned out of the car, got my head and my hands up high, straining against the pull of the car and the cold wind, and let the marijuana rush out of the bag. Then I let go of the bag. We could see it behind us, blowing off. Then it was gone.

'What a relief', Bill said, as I got back into my seat and closed the window.

'Damn straight', said Stuart. 'Apples, good work!'

We were free. Now we were really free.

But when we got to the outskirts of Cheyenne, and pulled off the road for the cup of coffee all of us were longing for, Stuart and Bill were already having second thoughts. 'I can't believe we did that', Stuart said. 'Apples, I can't believe we let you talk us into that. What were we thinking? All the way to California, without any grass. All the way to goddamn California. With nothing. I can't believe it.'

We couldn't manage to go much further that day. We found a motel at Laramie, to be paid for by the credit card Stuart's dad had given him, where we spent a quiet afternoon and night, mostly sleeping. It was another twenty-four hours before we arrived in Sacramento, and all the time Stuart and Bill were complaining. 'We should have kept some, at least a little.' 'We should have kept the whole lot. What were we thinking?' 'I could go for some weed right now. We should have held on to it.' 'How am I going to get to sleep? I need my dope.' 'We should have kept it. Apples, what a fucking brainer! You and your ideas!' 'At least a little, I mean, we should have held on to at least a little.' 'Look in the back, maybe we've still got some seeds back there.' 'I could go for a joint just about now. I could really go for one.' 'God I'd like to get high just about now.' 'Damn straight. We should have held onto it. What were we thinking?'

¤ ¤ ¤

And this, I maintain, was desire. Think of it what you will, this was desire, the guiding the principle, the blind force, and the empty sucking vacuum gasp, motoring us through the byways of consumption and beyond.

Without the marijuana the boys felt listless; they felt unfulfilled; they felt unmotivated. And they wouldn't get off my case about it. Passing through the great range of the Sierra Nevada, the tops of the mountains still frozen white with snow – that was nothing. They didn't have their marijuana. Passing through the Central Valley, green and fertile – that was nothing either, even though a girlfriend awaited Stuart in the midst of it. The landscape was empty, the time passing was empty, the whole trip was a disaster. As for me, I remember an interval when the two boys were asleep, and I was driving past Salt Lake City, along the famous Bonneville Salt Flats, a moon face of a landscape, white, eerie and hot, and I had caught by accident a classical music station. The radio was playing the slow movement from Mahler's Fifth Symphony, and the convergence of the blank desert, the smooth drone of the Cadillac along a mainly empty road, and the lumbering, terrifying chromatics of the music – where Mahler makes you feel as if you and the music together are holding up the universe, if only you can sustain and resolve yourself into something stronger – I felt I finally understood what was beautiful about the sadness of my existence, and what was sad about its beauty. I thought of Michelle, dead. I thought of Elena. She would never know anything about this. And perhaps the boys, too, Stuart and Bill, in their sleep, could sense that something profound had overtaken us, profounder than fear, more essential than a career, or a clean police record, or access to the cool elation of being stoned on marijuana. In any case, the sense of emptiness, of unfulfilment, of opportunities lost continued with us for nearly a thousand miles.

And the general mood didn't change until we arrived at the edge of the San Francisco Bay, and made our way across the San Francisco-Oakland Bay Bridge, way up in the air, where we saw something we hadn't anticipated. San Francisco. An alabaster city. A city of high white towers and vertiginous hills, set in the midst of a great blue sea. Far off, we could see the orange outlines of the Golden Gate Bridge, spanning the edge of the Bay and crossing into high and deep green slopes of land. We Chicago boys had never realized that something like this existed. San Francisco. A city as beautiful as a work of art, but even greater, since it was made as a collective enterprise, and it was bigger than any single mind could encompass. Thousands and thousands of people had been involved in building it, and thousands and thousands kept it kinetic. Everyday. There is no work of art as great as a great city, although there is no work of art that can be treacherously seductive as a city either. When you crossed the second span of the Bridge, you saw the city framed by the great suspension towers and the curving cables, you saw the white stone towers, the streets, the TransAmerica Pyramid, huge and Ptolemaic, you saw the old Ferry Building Tower, like a dream of Seville standing at the head of the city, almost beneath the elevation of the Bridge; you smelled the bay air, the ocean air, you saw yourself rolling beneath an improbably blue and brilliant sky, you felt that you had arrived at America's Jerusalem. The strangest part may have been the roads themselves. You saw them climbing up and down the hills and criss-crossing one another in perfectly straight lines, like regular gaps between stacks of white stone boxes. They were like the aisles of a supermarket. We couldn't wait to get down there, onto dry land and into the city, and work our way through the streets.

But there was a catch. We didn't know it then. I wouldn't know it for quite some time. There was a catch. For whatever you took the city to be, whatever you took the modern world to be, whatever you took your experiences to be, however enjoyable, interesting, challenging or not, *they do not love you*. Moreover, it is easy to be mistaken.

Chapter Two

In the Kitchen

For most people it begins with the mother, or rather with the mother-and-me, the original dialectical pair, where desire opens and closes and still opens up again. So let me begin with my mother-and-me. Only I have to begin in a way which is at once conventional – since a grandmother from the old country is involved – and unconventional. For my mother was different, even though she didn't know it, and never knew where her difference would lead her.

My mother was a rebel.

Her own mother, my grandmother Lena, had come from Ukraine to the United States in the early twentieth century. She spoke Russian and Yiddish as well as English, and read the Bible and prayed in Hebrew. She was a conventional housewife who waited on my grandfather Morris, an umbrella-maker, hand and foot, and cooked traditional meals day after day from scratch: chicken soup with noodles, boiled chicken with dumplings, braised brisket with carrots and potatoes, liver and onions. When Passover came along she did a ritual cleansing of the house and started on a laborious routine of preparing the special foods for the holiday, using only specially approved ingredients and respecting all the demanding rules, including above all the prohibition against *chometz*, leavened or fermented grain – a restriction which brought out in her, if not inventiveness exactly, a kind of creative industriousness. For the soup she prepared her own Passover broth with chicken, onions, carrots and celery and hand-made matzo balls. For desserts and treats she made hard crisp unleavened almond cookies and flourless coconut macaroons and an unleavened orange sponge cake, composed of fine ground matzo meal and sugar and orange peel and blown up with whipped egg whites and salt. I used to watch her, in her brightly lit old-fashioned kitchen, overlooking a busy street in Williamsburg, Brooklyn, mixing her batters, kneading her unkneadable dough, brandishing her long pastry knife. It was probably in her kitchen, watching her among her pots and pans and baking tins and cookie sheets, that I developed my own fascination with the alchemy of cookery. Everything *meant* in Grandma Lena's world, and everything was affected with magic – or so at least it seemed to me. There was immanence in her life, and in all the lives and things she touched, beginning with the home, with food, the rituals of everyday life.

My mother Beverly, however, would have none of it. She had been Americanised – whether in spite of the admonitions or because of the tacit encouragement of her family – from childhood. English first was the new rule, along with Big Band Swing and dating and preparing to be an office worker rather than a homemaker: in high school, in Brooklyn, she studied bookkeeping. She married early, at eighteen, in 1948, out of impatience to get on with it, I suppose. At first she lived with my father in the same apartment building in Brooklyn as my grandparents and her three older married sisters. And she must have felt the pull to revert back to the lifeway of Grandma Lena, even as she also went out into the work world, contributing to the family income, and leaving behind her the kind of household routines my grandmother took for granted. But then she gave birth to me, and her working days were at least temporarily over, and then, after four years of marriage and two years of motherhood, she found herself displaced from Brooklyn to Euclid, Ohio, just outside of Cleveland, a town on the edge of Lake Erie. And she was on her own, then, to experiment with life in the new consumer society of the new suburbia.

My father Leo, an ex-wartime sailor from Brownsville, Brooklyn and a shop floor worker in the Garment District in Manhattan, had been promoted to the position of first a local salesman and then a travelling salesman. In 1954 he was transferred to northern Ohio, with responsibility for selling a line of children's clothing to stores across the eastern half of what in Ohio was called the 'Midwest': Ohio, Indiana, maybe a bit of western Pennsylvania or southern Michigan. We settled in a newly built, red brick, white wood trimmed housing complex, something like what in Britain is called a council estate, with townhouses and apartments set around small yards and open lawns crisscrossed with concrete walkways. There were many other young families living in the complex, including a number of transplanted New Yorkers. And it was there in Euclid, in the new suburbia, that my mother seems to have finished becoming a rebel.

She ended up knowing no language but English. Her childhood Yiddish she allowed herself to forget, until she barely recognised a word of it apart from the occasional profanity or funny-sounding buzzword. *Schmuck, meshugeneh, schmata.* Her religion she forgot too, except that she continued to identify herself as a Jew. She did not know Hebrew and did not go to synagogue. I never knew her to pray. I never heard her express a single religious sentiment, for that matter, except that she continued to respect the authority of rabbis – about which, however, she ended up knowing nothing, and didn't care to know a thing. She found that she didn't care for the role of the traditional housewife either, though for most of the rest of her life, partly for health reasons (in her late twenties she was diagnosed with Lupus disease, and before that she had a gall bladder operation from which she had trouble recovering) and partly because of the expectations that were imposed upon her, she had no alternative but to try to conform to it. She did her housework with the same scruples as her mother – our house was always antiseptically clean, the beds were always made, the laundry fastidiously attended to – but she did it angrily. She was, at least to my ears, a constant screamer, always finding fault, always finding a reason in the course of her housework chores to yell at me or my father or my sister about how careless we were, or thoughtless or stupid or malicious. I never dared leave a cup on a table, a pencil on a bureau or a toy on the floor. As for cooking, she had no taste for it, and not much skill, and spent as little time as possible in the kitchen. She had learned from her mother the rudiments of slow cooking, but she had no patience. She liked things done quickly or not at all. And she found that she was ambivalent about childrearing and marriage. I was often neglected, or, at least, left to my own devices. Although like other healthy children I always woke up early, full of energy and appetite, my mother got into the habit of sleeping until about ten o'clock in the morning, unconcerned about the toddler in the house. From the age of three, past the joys of being strapped in a high chair and fed by someone else's hands, I was left to make my own breakfast, and sometimes, I have been told, I got dressed and went outside and knocked on neighbours' doors, asking them to feed me. Then, for the rest of the day, I was pretty much on my own as well. It wasn't that my mother did not love me with a mother's love. It was that she entertained the convenient belief that male creatures however young or old could fend for themselves if they needed to, and she was happily unnecessary to them, except when nature called; she was to that extent free of a number of obligations to them. And anyway she was tired, she was always tired, she was sick after all, except she usually felt better during the afternoon and evening; she had headaches and dyspepsia and she needed her sleep and her privacy. As for marriage, though she knew that she was supposed to be a dutiful wife, she found that she was interested in men besides her husband. She was a fair-featured, good-looking, buxom woman; she took to dying her thick wavy hair platinum blonde, Jayne Mansfield style, and, until weight gain interfered, she liked to wear very tight brightly coloured Capri pants and busty white tops. Eventually she left my father for a neighbour, with whom she had gotten intimate at Thursday evening bowling parties at a local alley where alcohol and ribaldry were as important as spares and strikes, and from which my dashing dour father usually absented himself.

Several years later, after my mother and father divorced and at about the same time as my mother was getting married to her new man, my father took my sister and me on a consolation trip to Atlantic City, after which he dropped us both off at my grandmother's in Brooklyn, to which my mother was soon to arrive to pick us up and bring us back to Cleveland. My grandmother and father spoke for a little while in my presence, and though I don't remember any part of what my father said I do remember what my grandmother said to him on parting: 'You will always be a son to me.' It brought a lump to my eleven-year-old throat. But the thing is, I don't think my mother or my father by this time were capable of understanding or sincerely using the concept of 'always' as it came so readily from my grandmother's mouth. I don't think that I have ever been capable of it either. 'Always' was turned into 'sometimes', and 'sometimes' was turned into 'never'. For the revolution had taken place, in 1954, and there was no going back. All of my mother's life, and my father's and mine as well, had since been condemned to be experienced, or liberated to be fashioned, in the un-magical evanescence of 'sometimes' and 'never'.

¤ ¤ ¤

My first memory comes from when I was three years-old and I went about the neighbourhood – dressed in underpants and a cowboy hat and a toy gun holster, with toy guns, I am told – knocking on doors and asking people to feed me. I was relaxing near the playground of my housing complex one afternoon, fully dressed I am sure, standing by my tricycle, a foot raised to rest on the ledge between the two back wheels. It was a warm grey afternoon and I looked up at the sky. 'They talk to me like I'm a baby', I thought. Those were probably my exact words, spoken to myself. *They* … meaning my mother, my father and other adults. They talked to me in a high-pitched, musical voice, with unnatural rises and falls, cooing the words, as if otherwise I wouldn't understand them. Even my name, Bobby, was spoken as if it were music, like the *Bah-bah* in 'Bah-bah black sheep, have you any wool?' But what I remember thinking to myself was that *I was thinking*; I was thinking something in words, *I* was, and the words I heard in my head had none of that babyish music that adults used when they spoke to me. No, when I thought to myself, the words in my head sounded like the words adults used when they spoke to each other. There I was, thinking, with the sky above me and my tricycle at my side, standing by the chain link fence surrounding the children's playground. I had a mind, and it was mine. It was here and it was now and it was me.

And so I found myself; and so too I found myself separated from the world around me, separated from other people as well from other things beside myself, frozen into my own 'glassy essence' as Shakespeare puts it once. I was temperamentally a Cartesian. But I was not for that reason less dependent on people and things and the here and now in which I encountered them. With regard to the things of the world I was especially enthusiastic: partly because I was being raised amidst the new unrestricted materialism of post-War America, which my own parents and all their friends embraced; partly because my own mother retained at least as enough of her Jewish upbringing to sustain a sincere respect for abundance; and partly because I was naturally curious, self-absorbed and hungry.

For food we always had, as far as I could tell, plenty of plenty. The new world of suburbia we had moved to featured supermarkets, of course. Instead of the small markets on the streets of Brooklyn, surrounded by the bustle of people and the roar of erratic traffic, Euclid had very large markets in plazas off the main roads, surrounded by rows of mute and stock-still cars, as if by so many gravestones. The market was an end-point rather than a by-way of life. The system encouraged once-weekly shopping (along to which I was *schlepped* until I was old enough for school), where a shopping cart was loaded up with heaps of goods, and the goods were brought home by car and heaped up in our cabinets and refrigerator and freezer. The new abundance, paradoxically, encouraged a kind of hoarding, and our house always felt empty unless it was packed to the bursting with boxes, tins, cartons and cellophane wrappers of food, from cans of Chef Boyardee Spaghetti and Cheese and jars of Motts Apple Sauce and bottles of Wishbone Italian Salad Dressing to packages of Sealtest Vanilla Ice Cream Sandwiches and bags of Wise potato chips, not to mention all kinds of meats (bought fresh and then frozen in our freezer: lamb chops, pork chops [yes pork, we had no time for dietary laws], beef steaks, hamburger patties, chicken portions) and fruits and vegetables kept cold in the refrigerator: apples, oranges, grapes, lettuce and tomato. We had frozen TV dinners too, from Swanson's to Stauffer's, including two favourites of mine, Swanson's Chicken Pot Pie and Stauffer's Lobster Newburg, and we had boxes of food mixes, Betty Crocker's Scalloped Potatoes ('Made with Real Idaho Potatoes'), Duncan Hines Chocolate Cake ('Just Add Water and an Egg') and Jello Chocolate Pudding ('Just Add Milk'). I am not including the brand names of our foodstuffs just for decoration. The brands were part of our experience of consumption. They were part of its governing structure. When you ate Chef Boyardee Ravioli for lunch, you didn't eat ravioli; you ate Chef Boyardee, which was at once a brand, a corporation, and a man with a moustache in a white chef's hat, smiling at you from the label on the can, and who, because he was called 'chef', and because of the anglicised spelling of his name (originally it was 'Boiardi'), I mistakenly took to be French. These brand identities were not just part of the observable structure, of course, but also the hidden structure, which was difficult to figure out, or even to register awareness of.

We had moved on rather quickly, you see: my mother, my father, me, and millions like us, rolling ourselves up like area rugs to exit unobserved from the capitalism of the first half of the century and then unfurling ourselves like wall-to-wall carpets into the capitalism of the second half. We stretched out our hands and we opened our mouths and all these commodities seemed to be raining down upon us. We opened our eyes, we opened our cupboards, we opened the fridge, we sat down to eat, and there was Swanson's and Betty Crocker, Jell-O and Chef Boyardee, all but ready-made, and all of it ready for the taking. The Affluent Society was our society, and we, of course, were its. It was ours, but we had nothing to do with it except to buy what it provided for us. It was ours, but it was dictating terms to us; it was ours, but it was making us live the way it wanted us to live; and it was coming between us and ourselves. Who knew?

Amongst all this plenty, nevertheless, I prospered, for I was a happy eater. The only things I didn't like were cooked green vegetables. And if my mother neglected me in the mornings, and was never a happy cook, I nevertheless flourished. When my mother prepared something to eat, and we ate together, I was always encouraged to do my duty and enjoy myself to the limit. Food was love as well as food, and in both ways food was good for you, the more the better. My mother too liked to eat, even if she couldn't cook, and when we ate together, with or without my father, who was away from home four days a week, selling *schmatas*, we were happy. I have seen many families, especially in Britain, where the meal is not a happy occasion, where adults and children fight over what should be eaten and how, with what gusto or self-restraint, and a feeling of competitive malaise hovers over the experience. That never happened at our table. Food was love and food was fun, even if its powers were only temporary, and both from the example of my elders and from their admonitions I got a message akin to the prescription in François Rabelais's sixteenth century utopian Abbé de Thélème. 'Do what you will' was the law in Rabelais's utopia. And in my own ideal world of the dining table, the law was a traditional Jewish message, sublimated into a godless, carnivalistic invitation to excess: 'Eat! Eat! Eat!' That television ads were constantly saying the same thing; that the commercialisation of everyday life had transformed the nostrums of Jewish epicure-anism into a commercial command – Hey you! – that the food industry from which we took our provisions was as ready to poison us as nourish us so long as a profit was there to be made; that Rabelais's utopianism was turning into an obese nightmare of alienation – of this I was unconscious, or at most indifferent. It wouldn't have mattered. I liked the message: food was love and food was fun.

I ate, therefore. And yet from my mother's inattention, I also learned another lesson. I could not only eat, happily, at the family dining table. But I could also, at just about any time of the day, feed myself. I could go the cupboard and plunge into three or four bowls of Kellogg's Sugar Frosted Flakes, or a carton of Nabisco Oreo Cookies, or a tin of Durkee's Onion Ring crisps, or when I was old enough to manage I could make myself a sandwich of Hebrew National Kosher Salami, a couple of slices of Wonder Bread and Heinz Ketchup, or heat up a can of Campbell's Condensed Tomato Rice Soup (just add water). I could raid the refrigerator for plums and nectarines, or for those ice cream sandwiches of which I was so fond. I could make myself a treat which my mother introduced me to: Philadelphia Cream Cheese spread on a Nabisco Saltine and topped with Welch's Grape Jelly. There were no restrictions, as far as I can remember, except perhaps nuts (Planter's, usually), which my mother regarded as a luxury item, to be consumed on special occasions.

I was a chubby boy as a result, but not cripplingly so, for I was also very active, even athletic, and food was only one of my passions. I loved sports, especially baseball and football. And in those days when parents were pleased to leave their children to go outside and play on their own, unsupervised, for hours at a time, and my mother was particularly adept at the art of leaving a child to run free, I was frequently (when I wasn't eating, or watching TV, or preoccupying myself with comic books or real bound books and tablets of drawing paper and writing paper and pencils) out and about. I played games with playmates and sports with teammates and rivals. I wandered about solitarily, through fields and play-lots and woods. I studied things: the shapes of clouds, the colours of leaves, the smell of freshly cut grass, the taste of strange wild berries, the constellations of the stars that came out at night. The Little Dipper was my favourite and especially the North Star at the end of the Dipper's handle, whose position in the sky I was in the habit of trying to spot at night, so that I could orient myself and pick out a little bit of the order of the heavens. If I was a little bit chubby I was also (as adults were quick to remind me) a handsome imp, a *schöne bubbeleh*, and I was energetic in mind and body. I hungered after experience and knowledge as well as after Oreos and ice cream sandwiches and I was always busy, trying to make sense of things, and I was not discouraged. As the eldest child and the only son of a Jewish couple, I was expected to be ambitious.

But speaking of 'favourites', it is important to note that somehow by the time I was five or six I came upon the idea that I was supposed to have 'favourites' in almost every area of life. So my favourite number was seven, my favourite playing card suit was diamonds, my favourite colour was blue, my favourite baseball player was Mickey Mantle, my favourite football player Jim Brown, my favourite comic book hero the slim blond-haired fast-running Flash. I had learned – which is to say, I had been trained to obey the idea – that I should interest myself in the world by establishing my preferences among the commodities it made available to me, and appropriating them as features of my individuality. I should have 'favourites' therefore, and understand who I was in view of the favourites I stuck to. Baseball and Mickey Mantle, the North Star and Flash, Bumblebee Tuna (never Starkist) mashed up with mayonnaise and served on a long soft roll: they were all part of the configuration of personal identity that had begun when I first realised that I had a mind. I couldn't have understood it at the time, but just as I was busy trying to invent myself, and earnestly arranging the world about me, in my own way, for my own unique purposes, so I was also being tacitly trained to live life as a consumer, according to the rules of consumerism, exploiting the materials that consumer society provided me with. Chubby, athletic, independent, mentally energetic, curious and inventive, and also hungry, self-absorbed, selfish and greedy, I was becoming both my own unique 'I' with my own glassy essence and precisely the common kind of materialistic but well designed 'me' the world of my parents required me to be. I was being trained to become a scrupulous *homo economicus*, with heart, soul and stomach buying into the commercial system of American life and the universal laws of mass production. It is true that while I studied books about astronomy and scientific exploration I did not study books about Sealtest ice cream. Nor, if I ever went to sleep at night thinking about travelling in a space ship to Mars, did I ever pass into my dreams while fantasising about having a mouth full of Duncan Hines instant mashed potatoes. But I did fantasise, having been inspired by *Surfside 6* and James Bond movies and *Flash* and *Batman* – that crap, that substitute for genuine culture I was licensed to devour – about becoming rich when I grew up, and having a houseboat in Miami Beach with a glass and chrome bar from which I could offer sophisticated cocktails to women in low-cut gowns, and dine on exquisite dishes served *à la cloche* by a butler in a black tuxedo. It would all have happened after, in a Monte Carlo casino one night, having doffed my superhero jumper and attired myself in a fine blue suit, I had rolled, in a game of craps, a very lucky number seven.

Fortunately, though my mind was corrupted by popular-culture-inspired fantasies that transported me to Miami Beach and Monte Carlo, I usually could sustain in my mind an ironic distance between the fanciful and the real. I was tarnished, my powers of concentration diminished, my values cheapened, and I often pretended to myself that I was someone I was not, boating on the Biscayne Bay in the evening light, or driving in an open-top Corvette down Sunset Strip, suavely attracting the attention of TV cameras; but I knew a thing or two as well. At the age of seven or eight I started writing stories, which I handed into my grade school teachers and read aloud at show-and-tell sessions to my classmates; and I found myself, as a child writer, committed to realism. I don't know how or why. I don't remember what most of the stories were about, except that they were about people like those I knew and some of the stories were *à clef* and inclined toward gossip and what people did in them were the things of daily life. But I wrote, and that changed everything. I wrote as a way of coming to know the world, of focusing on it as an object. If ever I indulged in fantasy-spinning in my stories, talking about space travel, for example, it was always ironic or satiric. (I had learned about irony and satire from *Mad Magazine*.) Otherwise, however it came about, I was a realist, in spite of the irreality everywhere around me. Cocoa Puffs. Hasbro Toys. Barbie and Ken. The Jolly Green Giant, hawking frozen carrots and peas. Hertz Rent-a-Car, putting you in the driver's seat. Marlboro Cigarettes, making you into a Cowboy and a Man. Father Knows Best, coming to you every Sunday night, teaching you the inevitable and indurate lesson that no matter what, IT WILL ALWAYS WORK OUT FOR THE BETTER, since after all, father knows best. One lie after another, one imposition on the imagination after the other, trying to impress on all of us the superiority of what Jonathan Swift's Houyhnhnms call *the thing which is not*.

We moved house every few years, which made it all the harder to anchor myself in the world, or find a way out of the blind consumerism in which I was being raised. First we moved from an apartment in Euclid to a townhouse in the same complex; then we moved from Euclid to a newly built detached house in the more prosperous and ethnically homogenous suburb of Beechwood, a lawny patch of subdivisions for Jews; then we moved to an apartment in the less prosperous, more crowded and heterogeneous suburb of Mayfield Heights, first to one apartment in a brand new light grey brick complex there and then to a slightly larger one with a better situation, on the second floor, overlooking a baseball diamond; then, when I was fourteen, we picked up roots and moved into a tan brick townhouse in the similarly modest, crowded and heterogeneous suburb of Niles, Illinois, just north of Chicago. Along the way I had acquired a sister and a new father, the original one having moved back to New York City. This new father made my mother much happier. He did not succeed in making my sister and me happier, though.

His own father, an immigrant from Hungary, had been the owner of the largest Jewish delicatessen-restaurant in Cleveland; but when, a prosperous man of fifty, he decided to retire to Southern California, he refused to pass along the business to his only son. Instead he sold the restaurant to a nephew, to whom my stepfather almost never spoke again. Sandy – for that was my stepfather's name – had been a Marine in the Second World War and had fought in the terrible Battle of Tarawa. Living in Beechwood, about a mile away from us, he ran a car repair garage in the slummy Hough section of Cleveland, although he was not himself a mechanic or particularly talented in any capacity that running a car repair garage required. He muddled through, though as the neighbourhood deteriorated and then deteriorated some more his business deteriorated, and when he divorced his first wife to marry my mother, the divorce court, I believe because adultery was involved, dispossessed him of what little money he still had, and pretty much dispossessed him of his children too (a son and daughter about my age). He was left with little but my mother and her passion for him and two strange children to support, who missed their real, far more dashing father. Sandy tried to improve his situation by going into business with a pair of friends, in the used car business, but the business failed within a year. For a while, Sandy was unemployed; then he got a job as a travelling salesman to the Chicago-Milwaukee region for a Cleveland merchant in speciality steels (a corrupt business, which flogged overpriced products to factories whose engineers took kick-backs in return for ordering them) and we were off again, this time another five hundred miles away, to a city that was not New York but at least had the value, to my own estimation, of not being Cleveland, and of being very big and muscular too.

With Sandy, it turned out, we would not, as had earlier seemed our destiny, complete the trajectory from urban working class to the full-fledged suburban middle class. Instead, we would hover in the region of never being wealthy enough to live well, and never poor enough to suffer. We did not reside in houses, like many of our neighbours, but in rented apartments and townhouses, hard by shopping plazas and busy interstates. We did not go on family vacations to a country or a seaside resort, even in the midst of a hot and nasty Chicago summer, but we owned a late model Buick, which drove us back and forth as far as Cleveland and New York now and then, to stay with relatives, and we had a second compact car for my mother, and we were always able to dress as well as my mother thought we ought to dress, with new wardrobes purchased every year. As for food, since Sandy had grown up in the delicatessen business, and was himself a happy and corpulent glutton, we still always had more than enough, and the quality of food in our house actually improved. Old fashioned Jewish foods suddenly appeared on our table with redoubled frequency – smoked salmon and whitefish, cream cheese and bagels, served with sliced Bermuda onions and tomatoes; fresh sliced corned beef, pastrami and salami, brought in from a real deli, served with caraway-seeded rye bread and fat dill pickles sliced in quarters and maybe a bit of American potato salad or coleslaw on the side. Our commitment to branded foods bought from the supermarket was kept up, all the same. It was always Heinz Ketchup in our household, never Hunts Catsup. It was always French's Mustard, Hellman's Mayonnaise, Jiffy Peanut Butter and Lipton Tea. To have bought a different brand would have seemed both an act of infidelity and a danger, lest our house be profaned by the goods of inferior gods. But apart from the fixity of the brands in our life, much else had changed. Sandy spent more evenings at home than my real father had done – an indicator, among other things, that Sandy was not apt to work so hard, keeping himself on the road until money had been earned – and the family meal, at six o'clock at night, was an occasion, if not of festivity, at least of regularity, peace and plenty. My mother tried to take more of an interest in cooking, seeing that her new husband was so fond of food, and we made do, not altogether unenthusiastically, with her experiments. She made a 'potted' dish where she prepared meatballs with unseasoned ground beef and placed the meat in a kettle with quarters of peeled potato, a peeled onion, Heinz Ketchup and water, and simmered the whole for an hour. She made a 'barbecued' chicken dish composed of cut-up chicken pieces placed in a baking pan and covered with Milani 1890 French Dressing and then baked until the dressing had burned off and the extremities of the chicken pieces had begun to blacken. She made beef steaks cooked from frozen to well done under the grill, served with beef flavour Rice-a-Roni on the side; and veal Parmesano from frozen, battered veal patties, Buitoni Marinara Sauce, and dry supermarket mozzarella, the assembled casserole baked in the oven until the edges of cheese, breading and veal had turned brown and started to shrivel. To go along with our meat-based meals, Sandy often made salads, usually composed of iceberg lettuce, tomato wedges and red onion, though sometimes with some green bell pepper or cucumber thrown in. He liked his salads Italian-style, tossed with oil and vinegar and salt and maybe a little Kraft Grated Parmesan Cheese, but I preferred mine drowned in Kraft French Dressing, a sweet, orange and creamy condiment with a sharp vinegary aftertaste which burned the back of your throat.

The move from Cleveland to Chicago was not very good for me. I had for several years been writing stories, as I mentioned, and I had later begun writing poetry too. At the age of twelve, having already learned the rudiments of playing clarinet, thanks to lessons I took from an old Cleveland sideman who called me *boychick,* I had taught myself to play guitar from a Bob Dylan songbook, and by the age of fourteen I was writing songs and singing and playing and reciting poems in public. I had even set the verse of T.S. Eliot's 'The Hollow Men' to music, colouring the despair of the verse with chords in minor sixths and sevenths. I had outgrown the superheroes and Perry Mason and James Bond, and my new heroes, besides Dylan, little though I understood them, were e.e cummings and George Bernard Shaw and Leonard Bernstein, and I was being contacted by adult rock musicians in the Cleveland who had heard about my ability to write music and were interested in finding out if I were the real thing and I could make them money. I was hip with the countercultural movement (it was 1964, 1965), which I read about in *Time* and which I encountered mainly on the radio and in the record stores, but also sometimes in person, as when I was visited by an associate of Paul Revere and the Raiders and given a free ticket to their concert in the city. I was against the War and in favour of The People, and I had bought clothes, with my mother's blessings (for my mother was usually advanced about such things), fashioned after the English mods and the Rolling Stones, including Tattersall bell bottom pants and pastel turtle neck sweaters, to be worn with an open faux-leather vest. And somehow, I had a future. It seemed that I would become the hero of my own life, not only in fantasy but in reality too.

All that changed when we got to Chicago. I was friendless when I got there and for long time after. People made fun of my clothes. In fact, the first day of school, at a big high school named Maine East, I was taunted by the other children, and the adults in charge threatened to send me home, while warning me never to show up in school dressed so outrageously again. My outfit included a pocket comb in the shape of a fish which I had bought in Chicago's Old Town and flaunted as a sign of my avant-garde sense of humour, and I think it was the fish above all that irritated the Marine-trained physical education teacher who threatened to have me removed from school. Within a year or two, to be sure, Maine East would be visited by the counter-cultural movement as well, and such clothes as I wore that first day would seem at worst quaint, a reminder of a more innocent phase of the sixties, which Niles, Morton Grove, Des Plaines, Glenview and Park Ridge, the five very different but equally boring towns which converged at Maine East, had somehow skipped. But I lost my ability to write music and stories and poetry. I lost my sense of belonging anywhere, or having a future. Eventually I was playing in a rock band with some kids from Morton Grove – children of rising middle class Jews with whom my parents were associating – but we were covering other people's songs plus a couple of holdovers from when I was still able to compose; there was nothing exploratory or interesting about us, the rest of my group lacked talent, and I was ambivalent about what we were doing and why. I wanted to do something else but wasn't sure where to begin. School, in comparison to what I had experienced even in suburban Cleveland, was backward, unchallenging and over-institutionalised. Our textbooks seemed behind the times, and the discipline exerted over the students was a kind of dysfunctional totalitarianism. We were always being watched, but we were seldom being seen. We were always being told what to do, but never how, and we seldom did it. Fistfights were common in those first two years, as was a perennial rivalry between 'the greasers' and 'the skins'. Only the coming of the counter-culture and hypnotic drugs would put an end to the mutual aggression. There were four thousand of us baby-boomers crowded into old Maine East, and the institution hardly knew what to do with us except exert itself as an institution and hope for the best. I did well in all my classes, but my teachers and my fellow students had little to give me, and apparently I had little to give to them, except smart answers, disgruntlement and irony. By the age of fifteen I had begun to suffer from depression.

¤ ¤ ¤

I lose sight of my mother around this time. Up to then my mother was frequently on my mind. I went to her when I was in need. And when I wasn't in need, I observed her from afar, or else I kept her in my mind as ghostly presence, a constant observer who could listen to my thoughts, who could oversee what I was doing. I thought about ways that I could please her. I didn't think about doing nice things for her. That simple strategy somehow never occurred to me; it had never been taught to me. And in any case, it seemed unlikely that there was anything I could *do*, exactly. My mother was not very gracious. It was hard for her to say 'Thank you'. It was even hard for her to say 'Please'. And when you did do something nice, her response was to make you feel guilty for not having done it earlier. But I thought about becoming the kind of person, or achieving the kinds of things, that would earn her approval, that would give her something to boast about. I had to be, and I had to become, what she wanted me to be, whatever that was. So I tried to organise myself around the idea of her existence, her expectations, and I never strayed far from her physical presence without thinking that her spirit was watching over me, measuring my merits and demerits, evaluating the quality of my thoughts and the integrity of my deeds.

I never stopped trying to organise myself in this way, until the day of her death. There was always a part of me that kept on the lookout for occasions to grab her attention – even after I moved 2200 miles away from her and dwelled in California, or 4000 miles away to England – and shout to her, 'Hey! Look at me! I know I've been off on my own, but look at what I have done!' Or even worse, there was always a part of me that felt that whatever I did, *she already knew*. Yet soon after we arrived in Chicago, in 1965, the real presence of my mother faded from my consciousness. I wasn't much interested in her. I had reached puberty and I had shot up and sprouted whiskers and sideburns and like most fourteen, fifteen and sixteen year-old boys I was obsessed with girls and the legs, mouths and breasts of girls; I was a diligent if otherwise unremarkable masturbator. My mother and my stepfather, in the face of these urges, were irrelevant. Or rather, they were impediments. Liberal-minded, they appreciated the kinds of needs I was beginning to experience, and allowed me some essential freedoms, and sometimes my stepfather went so far as to coach me in my sexual explorations. It was my stepfather who taught me what a blow job was. For her part, my mother let me know in no uncertain terms that as far as she was concerned sex was beautiful. But even so, as far as I was concerned, my parents were in my way. They were preventing me from getting what I wanted. Which was … what? I didn't know, except that sex was a part of it, and I wasn't getting it, mostly, and not just the sex. Some*thing*, some*one* was getting in the way. And meanwhile, I could feel that, for all their liberalism, my parents were fundamentally ignorant and intolerant (certainly my stepfather was a bigot when it came to blacks or even gentiles), that they couldn't understand half of what was on my mind, and what is worse they were abashed at my physical presence in the house, at my height and my girth and my smells. Luckily, I had a room of my own where I could spend most of my hours, but when I was about in the house I was made to feel that I was too big, awkward and dirty for it. My mother was still, in matters of housekeeping, a loud-mouthed, belittling scold – and I was never clean enough for her, never out of the way enough for her. My stepfather, for his part, was something of a bully. He liked things done his way. He got enraged at my sister and me and shouted to the heavens when we left a light on in a part of the house that we had just vacated. He swore at us when he didn't like what we were wearing, or saying, or the way we were sitting, or slouching or walking. He liked to challenge and abuse me when it seemed I took it for granted that the home I lived in was mine as well as his. 'What is the matter with you?' 'Who do you think you are?' 'Your highness', he would call me with a laugh of derision. Sometimes he complained that I stunk. When bullying didn't do, under his breath he scoffed at me with a dismissive 'ugh'.

And so – although 'and so' seems to imply a causal sequence, and I am sure it was not so simple as that, for causes came from many directions, and effects often had lives of their own – I shut them off, my mother and Sandy. I paid as little attention to them as possible. I was upstairs in my bedroom most of the time, or outside, at school or at a friend's or at the large shopping plaza nearby, Golf Mill, or (eventually) at work, in a restaurant (first it was the International House of Pancakes; then it was the lunch room at Sears). As a symptom of my disengagement I lost interest in family meals. I don't even remember them. I can picture the dining area well enough, a section of a large long room that smelled of bleach, between a kitchen and a lounge where we watched TV, the floor of the room tiled with off-white linoleum, the dining table a white round Formica-topped affair, with brass coloured legs. The kitchen area was modern but homely, a wall of fake-wood cabinets and drawers, an olive-coloured electric stove and a matching olive refrigerator. The kitchen was always clean and uncluttered, not a knife or a cup left out. We ate at six o' clock, sitting under a small high window, next to a door that led to the cold patch of fenced-in concrete in the back that we called our 'patio', and then we retired to the lounge area, where we had two small white vinyl 'Danish Modern' couches and a moderate size TV set, and where the eating continued the rest of the night, as my mother brought out ice cream, saltines, cookies and even peanuts, and shows like *Gilligan's Island, The Beverly Hillbillies* and *The Man from U.N.C.L.E* came on. I must have spent hundreds of nights like this, with my mother, Sandy and my sister, first at the kitchen table and then at the TV, the only TV in the house for a long while. I remember the programs, comedies that seldom made any of us laugh, dramas that were never especially dramatic, yet shows which nevertheless amused … but I don't much remember the evenings spent watching them.

What I remember is being up in my room, listening to the radio. It was a small transistor radio I had, but to me it was as good as a concert hall. I sat on my bed, listening and learning, enthused and absorbed. An *alternative* was coming on, played by alternative deejays, on the FM rather than the AM. There was no telling what would come next. I remember hearing 'Light My Fire' for the first time (the short version), an ocean of sound and turbulence rushing out of an organ, a guitarist, and a drum, plus a singer who seemed to ride the sound like a fish on a wave; and Cream, another three-instrument band, doing 'I Feel Free', sounding like it was flying through the air, on wings. Then there was the San Francisco sound, the Jefferson Airplane singing angrily about what happens

When the truth is found to be lies
And all the joy within you dies …

I knew that I was not listening to great poetry, or maybe even to great music, but it all spoke to me of possibilities, of more things I couldn't get but certainly wanted, or rather of a voice already within me that said 'Light my fire'; 'I feel free'; 'I want somebody to love'. I know that one of the reasons I remember these songs so vividly is that they have been endlessly played and replayed over the past forty-five years. There has never been any escape from 'Light My Fire'. I have long since learned every single bass pedal by heart, and the organ solo of the long version, and I have tried many times, in vain, to duplicate the guitar playing of José Feliciano in his own, Latin, flamenco-inspired version of the song. But at the time, hearing these songs for the first time, I felt almost as if a new sort of religion was being revealed to me. There was a new language to hearken to. Those organ riffs, those guitar distortions, those lyrics, that banging and banging and banging. What young people like me felt at the time was not only that new kinds of words and sounds were being aired, but that a new kind of responsibility was being drummed into us: be free! And for people who played music as well as listened to it, there was still another challenge. Figure out what we are doing, the songs said, and see if you can do something better. Do something with the Doors' wall of sound, with Cream's virtuosity, with Jefferson Airplane's anger ... and do something better.

Alone, in my room, I listened and thought about doing better ... even though the idea was stupid. For there I was, a companionless adolescent, and I wasn't able to write anything anymore, and even if I did I would have no one to play with, and no one to listen to me. And even if I had all those things, I was in dull, homely suburban Chicago. And anyway ... but this is how depression thinks. I was looking for ecstasy. I was finding only the ordinary, the repellent, the false and the oppressive, except that I was also finding these promises from afar over the radio waves, these musical prophecies of possibility, and I was still holding onto my hopes – my fourteen and fifteen and sixteen year-old hopes – that someday within me I would find a solution … only someday wasn't today and it might be never.

I suffered from insomnia. I could not go to sleep because of the thoughts crackling in my head. Sometimes, when I finally nodded off, I was immediately shocked back into wakefulness, as if an electric current had burst out of my spine and was trying to execute me, or else force me to stay alert. As I lay awake, sometimes with the radio on very low, sometimes in the quiet, I started feeling hungry. And after eleven or twelve o'clock, when my parents and sister were asleep, I would sometimes get up and sneak downstairs in my pyjamas, and start to eat. The late night snacks I took, or rather the binges I went on, are the meals I remember best from the scene of the family table in Niles, Illinois. In the kitchen, alone, under the window, next to the door, desperately quiet so as not to wake anyone, usually with a bit of reading at my side – a magazine, a comic book, a newspaper, a school book, a novel – I started on salami with crackers, on potato chips and pretzels, on several bowls of Cheerio's or Lucky Charms, whose boxes I propped beside me and on which I read again and again the nutritional information, counting up my calories, vitamins and minerals; or I went into the desserts, Danish pastries left over from the morning, or ice cream or cake or pie. Sara Lee's Cream Cheese Cake with a Graham Cracker crust was an especially favourite night-time destination. I could eat a quarter of a salami, half a dozen crackers, and a half a cheesecake at a single sitting, along with a few bites of the leftover Danish, washing it all down with a couple of glasses of milk and finishing the meal off, once I had turned sixteen, with a cigarette. My parents smoked Winston but I smoked Kent. After that, I tiptoed upstairs and crashed into the deep sleep of an adolescent without any worries .

¤ ¤ ¤

What was going on in my mother's mind I just do not know. In Cleveland she had led a breezier existence, a mother in her twenties, among other young mothers and fathers, so many of them transplanted New Yorkers, and still full of New York prejudices and appetites and a New York mischievous sense of fun. Here in Chicago she was among Chicagoans, who had their own histories, even their own brand of Judaism, and who were much more earnest. And now she was in her thirties, well past her wavy platinum blonde days (she had changed to a staid henna-red bob) and her health was not always good and her children were getting older and more difficult. Instead of a father (from whom, by the way, we seldom heard anymore) her children had a stepfather, who seemed to be doing all right with the kids but who was having trouble earning their respect and who in any case did not love them. I have imagined many times that my mother also saw through the irony of her position. Along with Sandy she impressed upon me and my sister the absolute value of having money and of doing whatever it took to acquire wealth. And she chided us whenever we seemed lazy, when we weren't working hard enough at school or taking seriously enough our need to get ahead. But we ourselves had little money, and Sandy was much more interested in playing golf and lounging about in front of the TV with a Pepsi-Cola and a corned beef sandwich than in working and collecting commissions. I have imagined that my mother perceived the problem. There was a fundamental falsity in my mother's attitude toward life, caught as she was in what Betty Friedan called the feminine mystique, and my mother knew that, at least in the mode of ironic, tacit self-knowledge. I have further imagined that a quasi-mythical quandary was at the root of the trouble. Sandy was Claudius, the assassin and adulterer, my absent father was Hamlet Senior, all but dead to me, a ghostly presence, and my mother then was the incestuous Gertrude – leaving me to be Prince Hamlet, conveniently enough, but more importantly leaving my mother to be a woman in bad faith, guilty of a crime she was incapable of admitting to, and a passion she was incapable of disowning. In actuality, I believe she felt no such guilt, and that her life had no such mythical dimensions (as nor did mine). But to understand the manifest passions with which she and I and Sandy struggled, inconsequential though they may have been, and relatively harmless, I have long believed that some latent unresolved conflicts had to be involved. And there is more than a little evidence to bear me out. My mother and Sandy took to spying on me, eavesdropping on my phone calls and going up to my room and reading my writings, including a journal I sporadically kept and the poems I still managed to scratch out. (You will recall Claudius and Polonius doing much the same thing to the Prince.) But what were they looking for? And what so troubled my mother that she would take such trouble to try to find me out? I was eventually convinced that all the pain they took with trying to discipline me, to find me out, even though in point of fact I was not given to misbehaviour, and I continued to earn straight A's and work in a job outside the home and to that extent pay my way – I was convinced that they were taking out on me what made them so angry about themselves. But it is equally plausible that I frightened them, threatened them, that I stood for a principle, a young prince of a principle, that endangered their control over life.

Again, I don't know. I lost sight of my circumstances as an objective situation. It was all but impossible for me to communicate in earnest with any adult, let alone my parents, at that time, much less to try to understand them from their own point of view. They weren't, even in a sympathetic sense, objects of attention. They were opponents.

They were opponents in a battle ostensibly fought over the most mundane of things: personal hygiene, clothes and hair-length, entertainment. There were higher principles to contest over, to be sure: apart from the Shakespearean drama of our family romance, there were issues like the positions I was beginning to take on the Vietnam War, the whole military-industrial complex that sponsored the war, led by sorry politicians like Big Daddy LBJ, and the hysteria of right-wing responses to the Cold War. I knew all the lyrics to Dylan's anti-Cold-War 'A Hard Rain's a' Gonna' Fall' and to Country Joe and the Fish's anti-Vietnam-War 'I-Feel-Like-I'm-Fixin'-to-Die Rag' and I was, in my own mind, already an outraged radical, irate at all the death and all the fear of death that apparently kept our country going. But these were not things I discussed with my parents, and in any case I am not sure that they had terribly strong feelings about them. They voted Democratic and, until his assassination, they might well have voted for Bobby Kennedy, who was running on an anti-war plank, had he been nominated for president, although they probably inclined more toward Hubert Humphrey and they certainly abhorred the radical peacenik Eugene McCarthy. But the mundane was our battlefield: the clothes I wore (since my initial fiasco on arriving in Chicago, causing me to change my wardrobe rather quickly, my clothes were always a problem for me and my parents), the length of my hair, the music I listened to, the drugs I took.

Well yes, the drugs. But the two drugs I most indulged in were approved: coffee and cigarettes. The other drug was cannabis, usually taken in the form of marijuana. It was not a drug, as I mentioned earlier, that I found particularly congenial. What little I could get at the time was weak, as much catnip and oregano as the real thing, and almost hardly worth the effort. Nor were my parents ever able to ascertain that I actually took any, for they never found any in their searches of my room. But I smoked some now and then – more in a later period than the one I am talking about now – and I learned from marijuana to concentrate. When I was stoned, when I actually managed to get stoned, the world slowed down and lost the illusion of coherence. It was fragmented into parts, and I would therefore meditate on one of its parts – the light in a window, in isolation from the house to which it belonged, or even from the lamp that was casting the light; the bass notes of a song, in isolation from the high notes and the percussion, the bass guitar itself in isolation from the regular guitar, the piano, the drums, the throb of the bass in isolation from the guitar itself, the throb in isolation from the note. I would get absorbed into that part with a kind of ecstasy. So I learned from cannabis a directive: pay attention! Even if it was only a burning mouthful of over-carbonated Coca-Cola, or the tickle of the cigarette smoke exhaled through my nose, I paid attention, and I was learning the secrets of things.

Absurd, someone might say. But for me it was like lifting the veil of Maya. Getting high and paying attention undid the irreality around me. 'If the doors of perception were cleansed', wrote William Blake, in words that would be taken up by Aldous Huxley and then by the Doors, 'every thing would appear to man as it is … '. Blake goes on to say that 'as it is' means 'infinite' – an idea to which I was not committed. But at least, I had the idea that, even if it was only a mouthful of carbonation, or a swirl of smoke, or the light in a window or the throb of a bass, you could learn to pay attention to the object and learn to intuit its reality. Just taste. Just listen. Just look.

I am fairly certain that if, at bottom, my mother and stepfather were liberal-minded and hedonistic, they never ever reckoned with the world as I was trying to reckon with it, which is to say metaphysically. We raged over the mundane. Beneath the mundane was our conflicted family romance, a struggle for authority and love waged between a mother, a stepfather and son, connected in our minds with events in the outside world, the struggle for authority and love waged on the TV and the newspapers and in the streets and the halls of high schools and universities between the war-mongers and the peacemakers, the authoritarian Establishment and the libertarian counter-cultural movement. Yet beneath the family romance, for me, was a metaphysical problem knotted up with the apparent superficialities of everyday life. What was reality and who would have control over how we perceived it? My experiments with cannabis and my inclination toward introspection had led me to believe that beneath the appearances of things was something more vital, interesting and true. And even the coursework I was doing in my mediocre school was supporting the idea, and adding to it the idea that if it was easy to mistake an appearance for a reality that was because social forces and what I would later learn to call 'ideology' wrested the power of seeing reality away from individuals, imposed their appearances on them, imposed their lies. We read *Huckleberry Finn* and *1984*. We read Emerson and Whitman and a page or two of Thoreau. We learned about the Periodic Table and the laws of genetics – and the development of scientific knowledge into the atom bomb and Nazi eugenics. (One of my nicknames at high school was 'A-bomb', and it wasn't supposed to be complimentary.) Between my parents and me there was opening a gulf not only between one generation and another, but between one way of knowing the world and another. My way was confused, a hodgepodge of intuitionism, empiricism, aestheticism, transcendentalism and vulgar historical materialism, joined with an impulse toward dissent for the sake of dissent, but at least it was a way: my parents did not have a way, and were not aware of the idea that one might have one.

A theorist in the mould of the Marxist critic Raymond Williams might say that the gap between my parents and me was representative of the new salience of 'culture' as a domain of struggle. We were not directly struggling over money or power – although money and power were always back there, in the wings, and they were of course controlling a lot of what was going on in Vietnam—but rather over 'culture'. My parents had one culture. I was struggling to be a part of another. And everyday life was a part of it as much as the Doors. Hair length was culture; marijuana was culture; *Father's Knows Best* was culture and 'Light My Fire' was culture too. But there were two paradoxes. The first was that all this 'culture' was also something to be enjoyed in one's capacity as a consumer. Even the fight against consumer society, in which I imagined myself enlisted, was waged at the level of consumption. So in many respects I was no different from my parents, even in my differing from them. And the second paradox was that, even though I imagined myself to be *against* a whole lot of things, what I was really looking for was something to *be for*; and meanwhile, all my parents could be for, since they had neither faith nor belief in anything but the illusion of their own authority, was being against me. My parents were the real nihilists. I was just a seeker with an inconsistent point of view, an insufficient number of clues, and no one to serve me as a guide. Even in my metaphysical moments, I was doing no better than working the aisles.

¤ ¤ ¤

When I turned sixteen, early in 1968, I got my driver's license, and my mother handed down a car to me, a four-door white 1962 Dodge Lancer. Before long I was going on dates, and fumbling in the front seat of my car with blouse buttons and bra straps. I made new friends, genuine companions, arty types like myself: an actor, a painter, a bass-player. At some point I got a job from a friend of my stepfather's, driving into Chicago to deliver and receive payment for baby pictures. I got to know the north side of Chicago pretty well, from Rogers Park to Wicker Park. I would drive into the city from Evanston down Sheridan Road and admire the high rise apartment buildings, built in the gutsy Chicago modernist style. I would visit neighbourhoods away from the lake shore that were ugly, lonely, and rough and try to collect money from people who, it seemed to me, had better things to do with it, but who were usually so ecstatic at seeing their baby close-up in eight-by-twelve colour lustres that they searched around their homes for spare change to pay for pictures which were taken with 'no obligation' by the photographers sent around by salesmen who milled about in hospital wards cadging for customers. I made a dollar per delivery, and if the family wasn't home or wouldn't pay I made nothing. In any case I had cash in my pocket, I had a car, and I was very quickly debouched from the confines of soul-less Niles and mediocre Maine East.

The world: it was out there, it had always been out there. And now, in spite of my parents' effort to keep me under their control and also because of their willingness, all the same, to let me roam outside of their control, I was seeing some of it, if only along the shores of Lake Michigan. (King Claudius should never have had Hamlet set sail for England, even if his intention was to have Hamlet killed when he got there.) Only I am perhaps losing my grip on the chronology of my life. Maybe it wasn't till I was seventeen that I started delivering photographs. Maybe for a long time, though I had a car, I wasn't allowed to drive into Chicago ... I was supposed to stay in the suburbs, I was supposed to keep close to the nest and work hard at school ... I really don't remember.

In the spring of 1968, when I was sixteen, however, I do remember, the anti-war movement was coming to a head. On March 31, the President Lyndon Baines Johnson announced that he would not seek re-election. I saw it on TV. 'Accordingly, I shall not seek, and I will not accept, the nomination of my party for another term as your President.' Immediately there began a new struggle for power between Humphrey, McCarthy and (until his assassination) Kennedy (I was a McCarthyite) and between deeper forces too. For with the collapse of the power of Big Daddy, the future of the war effort, of the Democratic Party, of the student movement and the counter-cultural future were all at stake. American politics was going Apocalyptic. And it would be coming to a head, at the end of August, in Chicago. The

Democratic Convention was coming to Chicago. And the word was coming that the whole hippie, student, anti-war, black power, flower power, power to the people movement would be coming to Chicago, and the whole world will be watching.

Here was something I could be a part of. Here was something that would connect me to the real world, to vital events, to interesting and important people, and of course to a cause, a cause about which I entertained no doubts, even if the cause was erratic and diffuse. The whole world would be watching and so in a way the whole world would be coming to Chicago, and I would be there.

As it turned out, my parents decided to go on a holiday at the end of August. We drove to New York, and stayed in Long Island at the house of one of my aunts. We slept in the basement, on mattresses laid on the concrete floor. One morning I woke up to find a huge gooey wet patch on my mattress where my crotch had been, the result of a nocturnal emission, and I remember my mother, my stepfather and me standing over the mattress, embarrassed, trying to think of how to clean it up so my aunt wouldn't notice. On the way back from New York, we stayed at my stepfather's sister's house in Cleveland Heights (where I slept on a real bed, shared with a cousin, and was innocent of wet dreams) and I was sitting with the family in front of a TV when on came news of the riots in Chicago. Pictures of students being beaten with billy-clubs and hauled into paddy wagons. Pictures of students marching, chanting. Twenty-seven thousand armed police officers, national guardsman and army troops, brandishing tear gas and guns pitched against no one knows how many thousands of protesters, armed with anger and rocks. Pictures of what newscasters were beginning to call a 'police riot'. Pictures of picture-takers, journalists, being accosted and struck with clubs and having their cameras ripped from them and dashed to the ground by police officers doing their job. Stories of the power struggle within the Democratic Party inside the convention centre, the Party ripping itself apart from within. Stories of the power struggle within America itself, played out on the streets of Chicago, America ripping itself apart from within.

I was supposed to have been there. And I wasn't. That is my particular story. But it was not for lack of trying. For I had tried to will myself into being there. I had no doubts that the essential cause of the protestors-to-come would be right, although I wasn't sure of some of the things I had heard about some of them, the so-called Yippies, who seemed too frivolous to me. I was certain that the Vietnam War had to be stopped, and I was certain that stopping it would require a transformation in the political culture of the Democratic Party and of America in general. To use old-fashioned but necessary language, I knew it was my *duty* to protest the War and the powers that sustained it. But duty was only a part of my motivation. There was also desire. If there was something that had to be done, there was also something that I, personally, had to become.

Students of the history of revolutions are well familiar with the phenomenon. The revolutionary moment is a carnival of collective self-invention. And in the summer of 1968 a condition of revolution nearly broke out in Chicago, as it also did, even more significantly in places like Paris and Prague. The Big No (as in No More War) is also a Big Yes. There is bliss in it, as Wordsworth pointed out long ago, even if also the first thing that comes is anger.

But what would I be, then? Or rather, what would I become? I regretted that I wasn't a few years older, that I wasn't at university, where the real action was, that I wasn't in San Francisco, where the real action also was. I regretted the fact that I was hearing so much about the counter-culture, but that in Niles, Illinois there was none of it. Yet as the spring came on I heard a deejay on the radio say something about a Be-In that was to be held in the city, in Lincoln Park one Sunday. The 'Be-In' was something that had been invented in San Francisco a couple years earlier. It was a demonstration without a demonstration. People gathered on behalf of a cause, but they didn't march through the streets, trying to rally support for their cause. They assembled in a park. People gathered to make a political statement, but they didn't make any statements. They chanted, they danced, they played.

Really, I didn't know what to expect, but I knew I had to be a part of it. And so I made my preparations. Unfortunately I did not have long hair at the time. My high school did not allow it yet. Nor did I have the kind of clothes anymore that would make me a fit participant at a Be-In, as I understood it. The modish clothes I had brought from Cleveland no longer fit me. I had grown tall and thin. The clothes I replaced them with were standard issue, fit for a conservative suburban school but not for the counter-culture. So I went shopping, looking for something that would say, when I got to the Be-In, that I belonged there, that I too *was*. In Niles, Illinois, even in 1968, however, there was little to buy, and in any case I did not have much money. I went rifling through a few thrift shops. I had no luck finding a jacket with fringe, or a wildly-printed bell bottom trousers, or a Nehru jacket or a gauze pullover Mexican shirt. But I came across a used football uniform, with white three-quarter-length pants and a matching white jersey with a big blue number on the back. The uniform fit.

I took it home and schemed. By itself a football uniform would communicate exactly the wrong message. The hippie movement was anti-sports, and so, by then, was I; sports signifying conformity and collective aggression, militarism writ small. But a football uniform worn without pads or a helmet or real football shoes, by someone who wasn't a football player, was a uniform in masquerade. It could be made to say, I hoped, exactly the opposite of what it was supposed to say. It would be strange, to begin with. It would be out of place. Context alone could change its meaning. And then some adjustments could be made.

I got a magic marker and wrote, on the back of the jersey, where a player's name could have been, 'Peace and Love', and added a peace symbol under the words:

Then I tried on my outfit in front of a mirror. The bagginess of the jersey and the pants, for want of pads, gave the uniform a nice de-mystifying droop. But still, if you looked at me straight on you couldn't be sure of what I was trying to say or be. The writing was all on the back, the front being taken up by a very large number. So I went back to the shopping plaza. I bought a head band and a medallion showing the sun to wear around my neck. I fancied that it was the Aztec sun god that the medallion depicted, but it might have been the Navajo sun god, or the deity of some other Indian group. The important thing was that it was Indian, a signifier of alternativeness and joy and also perhaps a kind of tragic sadness in the face of injustice and war:

So, I had a head band, a medallion, and a silly-looking football uniform, with 'Peace and Love' written on the back. And still something was missing. So I got radical. I took a pair of scissors and started making slits in the side of my pants. I made a slit along the belly of the jersey too, and one of the slits in my pants I ripped open slightly, as if to signify a bodily wound. And now I was ready.

The day came, a Sunday. I hadn't actually heard much about it since it was first announced on the radio, but I knew that it would be in Lincoln Park and that the deejay I listened to on the radio at midnight would be among the gatherers. So early in the day I slipped out of the house, got in my car and drove.

I drove down Dempster Street, a narrow commercial avenue, though Morton Grove and Skokie, down to Interstate 94, The Edens Expressway, and drove down 94 until it merged with Interstate 90, The Kennedy Expressway. At the merge traffic thickens, the roadway broadens (if I remember correctly) to six lanes in either direction, only to narrow again to five lanes on either side, and a two-lane Express Lane opens down the middle, which is sometimes open to southbound traffic and sometimes not. The confusion of merging and de-merging traffic is treacherous for even an experienced driver; for a novice it was terrifying, but I made my way through. From there on, the driver comes increasingly toward a centre visible in the distance, Chicago's great downtown. In the spring of 1968 the mighty John Hancock Building, angling obelisk-like up to 100 stories, and at the time about to be the second tallest building in the world, was being completed. It dominated the skyline. And it communicated a complex idea: on the one hand, even unfinished it was proudly beautiful, a monument of commerce and human potential; on the other hand, it was brutal in its design, expressing on the outside the x-form struts that supported it on the inside; it was a giant, unfinished middle finger of coarse aggressive metal, and one of the things it said to the city and the world around it, in this era of the Vietnam War, was 'Fuck'.

I drove on, as the landscape on either side of the highway became more urban. I left the freeway at Fullerton Avenue, drove west toward the lake, went past North Lincoln Avenue and Clark Street, the main commercial arteries, and slipped into the park itself. And then I realised that I didn't know what to do. I didn't know *where* in Lincoln Park the Be-In would be. Nor did I know much about the park, or how to navigate my way through it. The park is seven miles long, it has museums, a zoo, nature reserves, lakes, meadows, beaches, harbours, boating docks, a golf course, baseball diamonds and football fields. I drove about as best I could, most of the park being closed to traffic. It was, and is, a fine park, a deep green forest of a park, but it was rough around the edges at the time, with no flowers or other sorts of decorative warmth. I drove about in circles. I drove down to the southern edge of the park, where it verges onto crowded North Michigan Avenue district, Chicago's poshest shopping area, and got stuck in traffic going the wrong way. I drove back north, and found myself ending up on Lake Shore Avenue, a fast moving limited access road, heading along the lakefront back toward the suburbs. I got off the avenue, and manoeuvred my way back into the trees and the meadows, and still I could see nothing. Few people of any kind were out and about. I drove a little bit more and finally, discouraged, I headed back north and made my way back home.

I got home about two o'clock in the afternoon. I came in through the back door, into the kitchen, and there were my mother and stepfather waiting for me. My mother was sitting at the bare dining table, my stepfather was standing off to the right, near the sitting area with the two plastic couches. 'Where the hell have you been?', was no doubt one of the expressions shouted at me as I came into the house. Many more oaths and curses were no doubt hurled in my direction too. When I told my parents that I had been in Chicago, I gave them more cause for outrage. I could not of course explain to them what my purpose had been in going to Chicago, although I may have whispered something about my hearing that a festival was taking place there. But … there were no 'buts'. And when my mother got a good look at me, when she saw my football uniform, when she saw my Aztec sun god medallion, when she saw the rips in my pants and my jersey, she exploded. How could I leave the house looking like that? How could I do that to her? To *her*? Who did I think I was? *What* did I think I was? Going out of the house with rips in his pants! And there was more and more that aggrieved her, more and more …

And suddenly, in a rage, tears in her eyes and fire in her lungs, she rose out of her seat and screamed, 'I'll kill him!' She rushed to a kitchen drawer and pulled out a kitchen knife, and raised it over her head, inching toward me and screaming again, 'I'll kill him!'

My stepfather stopped her, taking the knife out of her hands. She slumped back down in her chair and cried. I went up to my room. I could say, in the end, that after that things were never quite the same in our household, but the fact is, things had never been quite the same.

Chapter Three

Unforgettable

Sometimes it would be so busy at the airport that I had no time to stop for food or drink or even a piss; I would be going back and forth and back and forth seven, eight, nine times in a row without a pause, a half hour each way, the money coming in like winnings from a poker game. Once, on a busy day in the middle of what in northern California passes for winter, having started at seven in the morning, and getting ready to wrap things up for the day, I headed back to the airport at about nine in the evening for one last trip. Arriving at the airport I learned that flights were being diverted from central California and elsewhere because a thick blanket of tulle fog had unrolled over the ground, especially around Reno and Sacramento. The dispatcher informed us over the radio that an airline would be paying limousine drivers to take diverted passengers to nearby hotels, paying full fares for very short trips. So I got ready for my last run of the night, looking forward to earning another fifteen dollars or so and going home to bed. Called in from the parking lot to the terminal, I was introduced to a family of four, who were supposed to be going on a ski holiday in South Lake Tahoe. The father of the family, a physician, tired and annoyed, let me understand that he wasn't spending the night in San Francisco: he was going to pay me out of his own pocket a fare of about three hundred and fifty dollars to take him and his family all the way to the ski lodge at South Lake Tahoe they had booked, some two hundred miles away. So off we were. I could not refuse the fare. But as soon as we left the Bay Area on the road to the mountains we were socked in by the same fog that had diverted his plane, and it was hard to see where I was going and the going itself was slow. By the time it reached eleven o' clock I was so dogged with effort and fatigue I could scarcely keep my eyes open. At one point in the lowlands of the Central Valley I was startled by the screams of passengers. I was about to plough into the rear of a slow-moving truck, it seemed. I was not actually asleep at the wheel, but I had been close to it, and they were startled by an optical illusion. A lighted overhead signpost looming in the shroud suddenly seemed to be crashing into us. We only thought it was a truck. In any case, I straightened my shoulders, clinched my jaw, opened wide my eyes and leaned forward to the wheel. We pushed on. By about one o'clock in the morning we were out of the fog and up on the mountain road between the freeway and the Tahoe basin, in my long ponderous vehicle skirting around hairpin turns overlooking steep cliffs, dropping hundreds of feet, hundreds of yards into the darkness of ravines. I was so tired, I had to work so hard just to keep my eyes open and my mind on the road ahead, that I was afraid for my life. That wasn't the way I wanted to die, crashing with a three-hundred-fifty-dollar-paying family down the side of a mountain. It wasn't the time. It wasn't the place. I had visions of my little daughter being informed that her Daddy wouldn't be coming home anymore, her Daddy was dead. But I pressed on. And even so, when we finally arrived at the ski resort it still wasn't enough; I couldn't just drop them off. I was instructed to follow a confusing photocopy of a map from the lodge to a chalet near the top of the slope. We got lost several times, once ending back at the lodge, and I was so tired by then that it seemed like someone or something else was putting its foot on the gas and turning the steering wheel this way and that, while my disembodied spirit bounced about in a space of its own. Meanwhile the wife was complaining, the children were snoring, the father was grunting. And when we got toward the top of the mountain, and stopped at a cheap wooden cabin set among other cheap wooden cabins and scatterings of pine and fir, it was clear that in addition to all the grief the very long trip had cost everyone, there wasn't any snow. The weather was too warm. At two-thirty in the morning or so I was done with them. But I had a good long drive ahead of me, some of it back through the fog. I hadn't eaten since the late afternoon and hadn't slept in a day. And the father of the family, the physician, the big shot, hadn't given me a tip. Not an extra penny for my trouble. I had earned a one hundred and five dollars for my effort, about two-thirds of what I expected.

It took me over five hours to get back to San Francisco, drop off the limo and make my way back home. By the time I arrived at my apartment it was full daylight; I had been up for about 30 hours; my wife and child were up and about and I had to ask them to go outside and leave me to rest for a while. Our bed had been moved into what used to be the dining room, so that we could give our daughter a room of her own and there was nowhere in the apartment for me to lay down in quiet unless they went out. I felt sick, nauseous and achy. I had earned over two hundred dollars during my shift, which wasn't too bad, except that in this case the shift had stretched over two days and I had been to Lake Tahoe and back and I had expected more and I needed more and I was angry: we were still over eight thousand dollars in debt. Soon my wife would be going back to work full time – she was a legal secretary – and we might have a chance to catch up, but until then our livelihood would continue to rely mainly on me, and my labours in the limousine trade, and the sicknesses I suffered as a result of them.

¤ ¤ ¤

What was I doing there? The year was 1986 and I still have nightmares about that period in my life. I fall asleep at the wheel. I wake up, and I need to go to work, but I can't remember where I parked the limo. I walk the dark streets of San Francisco, down by Ghirardelli Square, down by the parking lot on Van Ness, looking for my means of making a living, and I work myself into a panic. The car is nowhere to be found. Or else I am working my boss's car without telling him. I am driving his limo and earning money and not telling him about it. I owe him hundreds, maybe thousands of dollars. When will I tell him? How will I repay him? And then there's that cliff, high on a mountain pass on the way to Lake Tahoe, and all it would take is a little twist of the wheel to hurl me into the valley hundreds of feet or yards below, and have a stranger tell my wife and have my wife tell my daughter that I am dead …

A few years later, I would attend a forum at the San Francisco Opera House, where the philosopher Susan Sontag would have a public discussion with the dramatist Tony Kushner, author of *Angels in America*. It was not all that interesting. Kushner was not a good public conversationalist. But at one point Sontag, who was by contrast an exceptional public conversationalist, was moved to make a statement. The Western world had changed, she said, and changed for the worst. It had changed in 1975. For in that year, the liberal consensus had died. Our faith in the welfare state had died. Our belief in one another and the ideals of social democracy had died, and we were now in another kind of world, ruled by more severe principles.

What she said was supposed to have been akin to Virginia Woolf's famous pronouncement about the coming of modernism: 'On or about December 1910', Woolf wrote, 'human nature changed. All human relations shifted, and when human relations change there is at the same time a change in religion, conduct, politics, and literature.' Although the precise dating of the event was a joke, Woolf was serious about her fundamental perception, and many people have since agreed. 'Human nature', so far as it is a case of 'human relations', is subject to change, and change it did, late in the nineteenth or early in twentieth century.

Now there was the case of 1975. Again, the precise date is not entirely serious, but 1975 is as good as any to pick. That was the year when a great recession reached its low point, impelled by the oil crisis of 1973-74. It was the year after Watergate and the administration of a president (Gerald Ford) who no one really wanted. It was the year when the comedy show *Saturday Night Live* first came on the air. It was the year when, as later French historians would say, the *trentes glorieuses*, thirty years of nearly uninterrupted economic expansion and improvements in the standard of living in France and much of the rest of the Western World, would come to an end. It was a year in America of nine per cent inflation and nine per cent unemployment, the latter the highest it had been since the Great Depression. It was the year of the collapse of the steel industry and the beginning of a collapse in the auto industry, in the face of competition from Japan and elsewhere. It was the year of the triumph of conservative monetarism over progressive fiscal activism, and the spirit of deregulated laissez-faire in the American and ultimately the world economy. The value of capital would triumph over the value of daily life. It was just about the year, according to sociologist Jean Baudrillard, when the 'order of production' that had governed Western society for several centuries, had given way to an 'order of simulation', when industrial society became post-industrial society, when modernism became postmodernism, and when progress became retro, a memory rather than a hope, a fashion statement rather than a political project. The world of Reagan and Thatcher was slouching in our direction. We still had *all that stuff*. Eventually we would have *even more stuff*. But we lose our sense of being the creators of our stuff (even if that sense had from the start been something of an illusion), and we would no longer, as a society, be responsible for any of it.

For me, it was the year when my father's *schmata* business in New York went bankrupt and his second marriage broke up, after the events of which I would never hear from him again. No, not ever. It was the year when I came back from a year of studying, travelling and working in Europe (France, Italy, Greece), and when I got my first real job. I wasn't able to go on to advanced study at a university, which was really what I wanted to do, or to sit for long hours behind a typewriter writing fiction, which was what I wanted to do even more. I had to work, and though I tried to stay on the Bohemian outskirts of economic life and work part time as a language teacher, with the hope of returning as soon as possible to the Left Bank of Paris, and doing more language-teaching, I ended up with a more-than-full-time-job as an executive manager of a school, the Berlitz School of Languages in Cincinnati, Ohio. The job, which was offered to me out of the blue, and for no particular reason except that I had a degree from the University of Chicago and I had showed up at the right place at the right time, was what was commonly called an opportunity and I could not pass it up, even if it meant returning to Ohio. But it meant that, even in a mid-sized city in Ohio, I was caught in the thick of things.

After three years I had to escape from Ohio and that job and I found myself, once again, making the long drive across country to San Francisco, this time with a girlfriend from Cincinnati and with the idea of settling in Northern California permanently. There followed a long period when I worked as an art dealer in San Francisco, peddling overpriced and mediocre artworks to tourists, and then a period when I couldn't do that anymore either. Limousine driving was my salvation. I was married now to a woman from the area, I had a baby daughter, and we were broke. On my first brief shift as a limo driver I made over a hundred dollars in cash for six hours work. The economy was in a booming recovery from still another terrible recession and our company of something like twenty-five cars, an association of owner-operators, who hired replacement drivers like myself, dominated the market. I could make more money doing the mindless work of limousine driving than I had ever made in more exacting work which called upon my education and my wits, and at first it seemed like fun. After all, I could get to motor up and down the San Francisco every day, passing through urban and exurban landscapes that had never ceased to move me with their vertiginous beauty. And then I would be paid, usually in cash.

As a limousine driver I was on the outskirts again. No longer would I have to pretend that I was a middle class regular, like my clients, with the values of a middle class regular. All I had to do was shut up and drive, and open car doors now and then, or do a little witty but stupid entertaining, taking tourists on tours of the City or the Wine Country. Nob Hill. Russian Hill. The mansions at Pacific Heights. The Golden Gate Bridge. The Cliff House at Sutro Point. Golden Gate Park, where the hippies used to be hippies, and the famous Be-Ins used to take place. Or up through Marin County onto the Mondavi and the Beaulieu Wineries. The quaint dusty Napa Valley towns: Yountville, St. Helena, Calistoga. Passengers getting drunk at tastings, or else coming back telling me they don't think they like wine that much and don't know what the fuss is all about.

So I was, in my own way, a Bohemian again. But there were a couple of differences. In the first place, I often had to play the role of a menial servant. In fact, when I was playing that undignified role, obsequiously catering to an out-of-towner or even a local who needed pampering, I made the best money I could and the work, in principle, was easiest. Freelancing to and from the airport was a lot more hectic and precarious. And in the second place, even if I was on the outside I was also on the inside. From my first days as an executive in Cincinnati I was introduced into a situation I had not anticipated, and which I had never been able to extricate myself: the situation of economic need, of debt and growing indebtedness, of having to maintain a standard of living, of people depending on me to keep doing what I was doing, since they too were in economic need, in debt and trying to maintain a standard of living, and they too had people depending on them. All of us were linked inside the belly of the beast, some happily, some unhappily, some successfully, some less so, and some failing, miserably. As a limousine driver I had much less responsibility to other people than I had when I was an executive or an art dealer, but still I had more than enough of it. I had responsibility to the people I drove; I had to give them what they needed and wanted. I had responsibility to my boss and my fellow drivers and the company we represented. I had responsibility to myself and my family, and our many creditors, our landlord, our city and our state and our federal authorities. I had the responsibility to keep working the machine and I could not escape the machine, even if I didn't like the machine or doing whatever I had to do to cater to it.

The 'machine', the 'beast' – I've mixed my metaphors. And I have been arguing from the beginning that there is a still better metaphor: the supermarket. But all three metaphors are required. The machine indicates the system of production. The beast indicates the amoral brutality of the system. The supermarket indicates what Baudrillard called simulation. There I was labouring to make money and contribute to the Gross Domestic Product. There I was labouring by the terms of a system that needed me but that was ultimately indifferent to my welfare and that would swallow me up if it ever got hungry enough. And there I was trying to fashion a life by working the aisles. When I first had a look at San Francisco, coming over the Bay Bridge, I had no idea that going into the city would come to this, that I would be opening car doors for strangers and zipping along the streets and the highways in pursuit of fares, and that I would have no alternative for a long time but to keep on zipping along the streets and highways in pursuit of fares, loading up a basket that was always, if not empty, in danger of becoming empty if I did not keep loading it up. To make an escape and really fashion myself, to leave the aisles behind me – how could I do that? I had a basket to refill.

But driving a limousine was my Yale College and my Harvard. I saw social and economic life from the inside. Working the streets when other people were enjoying their leisure or gathering for expense-paid conventions, making kick-back deals with hotel doormen and concierges, hustling, becoming privy to the private lives of strangers, from international bankers to local con-men, from movie stars visiting town on a promotional tour to silly adolescents out for a prom, I was like Hegel's 'bondsman' or 'slave'. I had knowledge of both myself and the Other ... whereas the Others had neither, since they (usually) had no knowledge of me, and so no knowledge of themselves. I heard passengers tell each other, and me, secrets that should have been kept secret. I saw passengers behaving in front of me in ways they should not have behaved in front of themselves. Bankers taunted each other about their bottom lines, or lack of one. A deal for a ten billion dollar hostile takeover was massaged in the back of my limo one day. Con-men conned themselves, and sometimes me as well. Movie stars exposed their frailties and insecurities – or their admirable and outrageous ability never to expose anything of themselves at all. Adult couples, coming up from the airport together, preened in front of themselves like adolescents at a corner table at a prom – 'I own this, I own that, I have been to ___, I have spoken to ___.' Adolescents unable to hold their liquor proved themselves unable to hold their liquor. Sometimes I had people fucking in the back of my car. More frequently, I had people fucking each other over. Of course, as Hegel also said somewhere, no man is a hero to his valet, not because the hero is not a hero, but because the valet is a valet, and I was the travelling equivalent of a valet. Granted. Still, along with the un-heroics of my passengers, some of whom I have to confess were decent people, and some of whom were violent crooks, I got a good long inside look at the system itself: the machine, the beast, the supermarket. I also got to a point where I was able to start thinking about putting down my basket ... and getting hold of new and better one.

¤ ¤ ¤

Which brings me to my first night with a woman I will call Maggie. It was a year-and-a-half after my trip in the fog up to Lake Tahoe, a week before Easter, and business had been slow, partly because of increased competition, partly because of the season.

I had had heard rumours that my partner Isaac, the doughy and dishonest Israeli with whom I shared the vehicle, both of us working for his thin and honest older brother, had recently been driving a rich woman from Burlingame who had, for an evening's work, given him a tip of five hundred dollars. But on my shifts I wasn't getting much of anything. And there were those bills to pay, those debts to handle. The Easter holidays were upon us, always a slow time, and there I was on a slow day waiting for business ... but I'll stop complaining. I'll only say, I remember one day feeling a little desperate. I remember not having had that day (as I often didn't) a full night's sleep, and I remember not having felt emotionally safe. I remember sitting alone in the front seat in that long white stretch Lincoln limousine from seven in the morning to three in the afternoon still waiting for my first fare out of the airport, and worrying that I was going to go home that night absolutely empty-handed, a day gone, and a day then deeper in debt. I remember feeling myself nearly in tears. And then the phone rang, and before I was being given instructions to go to the home of that woman whom my partner had been dallying with, the woman I call Maggie.

She lived in a three-bedroom bungalow in a modest, new-built part of the old posh suburb of Burlingame. She was about sixty-five years old. She had dry thick straight grey hair and tough, pallid leathery skin. She was wearing a housecoat and slippers, and when she walked she hobbled and shuffled; there was something wrong with her legs. I had been given instructions over the phone from my partner Isaac, who regretted, really regretted, that he was unable to work that night, due to family commitments – a son playing clarinet that evening in a junior school band. Do whatever she wants, he said. Do whatever she says. Charge her the usual full fare but don't charge her a gratuity; she'll take care of that herself. Let her write you a cheque; her money's good. And above all, he concluded: *don't fuck up*. We don't want to lose this client.

Not only did she not appear to be wealthy or powerful and in need of expertly obsequious service when I first saw her; she did not appear to be sane. But the problem, mostly, was alcohol. She told me to help her as we walked from the doorway back into the house, to hold her by the arm and shoulder and prop her up as she shuffled through the narrow corridors into the dim and low-roofed interior. She mumbled confusedly at first – or perhaps it was just that I wasn't used to her way of talking yet, and hadn't learned how to follow her ramblings, her musings, her asides, mixed in with straight statements, confessions, instructions, commands. We went back to her bedroom, where she dragged herself onto the bed, careful not to expose her thighs under her housecoat, and propped herself up on a mound of pillows. Next to her side of the bed, on the floor, was a half-gallon bottle of Smirnoff Vodka; and on her night table was a pack of menthol cigarettes, a dirty ashtray, and a half-empty cocktail glass.

'Freshen this up for me, would you?' she said, raising the glass.

'What?'

'Vodka and grapefruit juice. The juice is in the fridge. Vodka and grapefruit with some ice.'

'Get you a drink?'

'In the kitchen. In the kitchen, you know. But light me a cigarette before you go. And not too much ice. Make it nice. You know ... nice!'

As I write this, trying to recollect and convey the experience, I feel a knot in my stomach. You might think all this was funny, and it was, but at the time it wasn't. It is hard for me to write about it even today; the very thought of that vodka and grapefruit juice, that cigarette smoke, those ashen thighs she kept covering up under her drab housecoat, puts me in mind of something I once was that I don't want to remember having been, and don't want to admit to, even though I know I have to. I feel the knot again of the knotted up being I had become back then, like an animal in the wild, a little mammal in the grass, on the alert. All of life was uncertain back then, a bit of a gamble, and catastrophe always threatened.

'They do this to me …' Maggie would mumble to herself when something didn't go her way. 'Who's the boss?' she would demand when she sensed any resistance from me. 'Who' – the alcohol slurring her already slurred thoughts – 'who is it … paying? Me. I'm paying. Me.'

I sat alone with her in the bedroom, fetching her drinks – each one of which she expostulated over, reviewing the ratio of the quantity of ice to liquid, of grapefruit juice to vodka, sometimes favourably (the 'nice') sometimes not (the 'not so nice') – lighting her menthol cigarettes, fetching this and that from elsewhere in the room or the house, and listening to her every now and then initiate a confession.

'She died you know.'

'Who died.'

'My sister. My sister Helen.'

'When?'

'It was … we grew up together … I hardly ever saw her … a month ago I think.'

She had me put on music, a tape recording of Nat King Cole, from the fifties, singing *Unforgettable*.

Unforgettable, that's what you are.
Unforgettable, though near or far …

'That was a song', she said. 'We used to play it. Helen and me. But that's not right. It wasn't Helen … I can't remember. It's been too long. I've gotten too old, haven't I, *Robert*.' She usually said my name that way, as if it were in italics.

I asked her if we were going to be driving anywhere. After all, I was a driver. I wasn't normally paid to sit in someone's bedroom and serve her drinks.

'Maybe later', she said. 'Later we'll go for a ride.'

'But Maggie …'

'Don't you Maggie me, now' she said. She smiled and frowned, so that I hardly knew whether she was being serious. 'Who's the boss, *Robert*? Who?' Okay, she was serious. 'You want to get paid now don't you? Maybe I should call Isaac', she said. 'You know Isaac, don't you?'

'Isaac.'

'Yes, Isaac. He's your boss, isn't he?'

'Not really.'

'Well but …' She held up a finger, wagged it, and then lost her train of thought. We sat there in silence.

'They do this to me', she mumbled again under breath.

'They do what?'

'*You* do it! You're doing it now! I'll send you home is what I'll do.'

I gulped.

'Damn you and your … You and your … You! You're a smart one, *Robert*, aren't you. I can tell. At least you think you are.'

I felt myself flexing to get up and leave, but suddenly she softened up. 'Sit down here', she said, patting the space beside her on the bed. I rose, and bent in her direction. 'Here, right here.' I sat on the edge of the mattress. 'A smart one', she said again. 'And you know what, you … you. I like the way you mix the drinks. Nice. Nice! … Let's play … Let's play some cards', she suggested out of the blue. 'You play rummy, don't you *Robert*? *Robert?*'

We were interrupted by a knock on the door, a visitor, a perky forty-year-old redhead, a woman from the neighbourhood.

'Amanda, Amanda', said Maggie. 'I'm so glad to see you. This is *Robert*. He'd got a big limousine outside, did you see it?'

'It's beautiful, Maggie, really beautiful. And you're looking very … how are you, Maggie? How *are* you?'

The two women gossiped, Maggie suddenly becoming much more animated and coherent, while I sat in silence at the foot of Maggie's bed. It turned out that the tape of *Unforgettable* we were playing was made by Amanda's son. Maggie kept thanking her for the great gift her son had given her; kept saying what a nice boy he was. Amanda kept saying nice things about Maggie and her family and the way Maggie was getting on, this in spite of the fact that Maggie was lying in bed at four in the afternoon roaring drunk, with a limousine driver in a wrinkled blue suit pouring her drinks. It did not take long to see that this woman was interested in Maggie because of her money.

And Maggie genuinely had money, it began to emerge. Her father had been a famous real estate tycoon. Maggie had lived modestly in this dull part of Burlingame with her late husband, a middle-level manager in a middle-level business, but her father had revolutionised the Northern California landscape. He had been one of the inventors of its peculiar, crowded style of middle-class suburbia, homes in white stucco cheek-by-jowl to one another on flat oversized streets. He had built its first successful shopping mall. And as Maggie's family aged since the death of her husband, as aunts and uncles and sisters and cousins passed on, she found herself inheriting, little by little, bits and pieces of the old real estate empire. With every death in the family she was a little bit richer. And in her bedridden alcoholism, Maggie was starting to show it, hiring house-helpers and limousine drivers, making a bit of a spectacle of herself, and every now and then sending the neighbours little gifts.

So therefore Amanda the redhead turned up, talking about

her boy who made the cheap cassette tape of *Unforgettable,* and not long after, the husband and father, Larry, a fat and bald little man, with horn rim spectacles and a golfer's lusty sunburnt skin. I answered the door and there he was, almost as drunk as Maggie, and I showed him to the bedroom. He stormed into it with his arms out in a gesture of enthusiasm, taking in the whole room. 'Maaa — gheee!' he shouted.

I jumped.

'Larry, my stud!' Maggie shouted back.

'Maaa — gheee!'

'Oh Larry!'

'Maggie!'

I sat there on a folding chair at the foot of the bed, not knowing where to look, what to think. Meanwhile Larry, all two hundred pounds of him, went hurtling on top of the mattress. He landed on the other side of where Maggie lay and bounced up like a medicine ball. Then he came back down and put his arms around Maggie, who laughed and cackled.

'Maaa – gheee! My beauty! My lover!'

'Let's have sex!' Maggie retorted.

'Oh yeah, oh yeah', he said. 'Oh, baby!'

The two of them on the bed, knee to knee and side to side, pretended to hump.

'Oh my God!'

'My stud!'

'My sex pot!'

'Uhhn - uhhn!'

'Uhhn - uhhn!'

Amanda was howling with laughter.

'Oh Larry', she said. 'You crack me up!'

This went on for some time. Then Larry rose from the bed panting, brushed his clothes straight, caught his breath, and started holding court about this and that. I don't remember the conversation, but Maggie was thrilled with it. I was aghast, but kept my counsel. Eventually Amanda found herself less amused than she originally had been, and intervened, telling Larry that he had drunk too much, and it was time for her to take him home. Maggie begged for them to stay, she was having so much fun, but the redhead held firm and by five o'clock Maggie and I were alone again.

In the quiet, I fetched her a drink. I helped her up to go to the bathroom. I walked her into the bathroom, where she made me wait until she was ready to have me let go of her and get to the toilet on her own. Then after a long pause, during which I waited outside the closed door, I fetched her back, got her back into bed and sat opposite her in silence.

I was puzzled. I was vexed. And I was getting paid. Apparently I was being paid to be puzzled and vexed. At one point Maggie appeared to be falling asleep. I was afraid that I myself was about to fall asleep, so I got up with the intention of splashing some water on my face and seeing if I could scratch up a cup of coffee in the kitchen, but I wasn't two feet from my chair when Maggie started and opened her eyes.

'You're not leaving me, are you, Robert?' Her eyes were wide open.

'No, I was just stretching my legs.'

'You were leaving me, weren't you?'

'No …'

'*Isaac* never left me. I should call *Isaac* here. He's your boss, isn't he?'

'I already told you no.'

'You already told me. You know what you are, *Robert*?'

(You will note this is yet another form of interpellation, though in this case interpellation was a process, a story, and it had both its successes and its failures.)

I looked her in the eye and then I looked away. The one thing I could not tell her was *who* I was. The answer to her question, in any case, turned out to be that I was her *employee*. *That's* what I was. But the look in her eyes told me that she wasn't sure whether she herself believed it. Before long I was helping her to the bathroom again. I got her out a fresh housecoat from her closet, a green and purple floral print with buttons down the front, and waited outside the door of the bathroom as she put it on. I brought her back to her bed. I sat with her on the bed and combed her incurably straggly and dry grey hair, gathering it in a tight ponytail. I helped her put lotion on her dry face. I played a couple of hands of gin rummy with her. I sat across from her as she again dozed off. I got up and fetched her a fresh drink when in a few minutes she was awake again. I must have expressed some impatience with her since I remember getting at least one more lecture from her. 'You know what you are, *Robert*?' she said. Again, I was her employee. And Maggie was paying.

'I know that, Maggie.'

'I'm *paying*. And you … you … you better watch out.'

We received some visitors. First there was the redhead Amanda and bald bespeckled Larry again. They came and went, like cats re-asserting a territory, pissing in the corners: there. Then Isaac actually showed up, bringing his wife Esther, another chatty redhead, in tow. This couple too were like a pair of cats, pissing, pissing, in spite of my evident establishment in the room. And Maggie saw through them. She especially saw through Esther, who angered her with all her talk about the poor family, her poor parents, her poor but wonderful son, playing clarinet in the band that night, though the music lessons were so expensive, they could hardly manage. Maggie let them know, first politely and then abusively – *damn it, I told you, I told the two of you!* – that she wanted them to leave. And they left, a little huffy, though Isaac was careful, indeed embarrassingly scrupulous, to kiss Maggie on both cheeks before going, and to get her to smile at him, and promise him he could see her the next day.

A fifth and final visitor appeared as Isaac and Esther were

leaving: Pauley, a very tall, muscular, dashing white haired man in his sixties, wearing a light blue track suit and sneakers, Maggie's cousin. It was Pauley whom we had been waiting for all this time. Pauley had been drinking that evening as well, and immediately set to matching vodkas with Maggie. The big man was agitated. Maggie and he kissed and joked, joked about being kissing cousins, joked about being Norwegians and Vikings, joked about all the secrets they knew about each other. But Pauley was agitated. He stood with his back leaning against one of Maggie's dressers, studying his drink, drawing deeply on his cigarettes, thinking intensely about something. Then it came out.

'Robert', Maggie said to me softly, and not at all drunkenly, it seemed. 'There is something you need to know. I am not the only one who has lost someone recently. Why don't you put the tape on again. Put it on softly.'

I hadn't rewound it correctly so it came on in mid-stanza. 'And forever more', the smooth Nat King Cole was crooning, 'That's how you'll stay.'

Pauley actually turned his back to the room. He was starting to shake a little.

> That's why, darling, it's incredible
> That someone so unforgettable
> Thinks that I am
> Unforgettable, too.

A pause. Pauley was sobbing. The main theme came up again: 'Unforgettable, that's what you are …'

'Oh Pauley, it's okay, let it out.'

'It's hard for me, Maggie, it's hard.'

He choked up, he shuddered. The big man was struggling with himself, struggling both with his grief and with his need to stay in control of his emotions.

The song ended. The bedroom filled up with smoke. My head

ached and I struggled to keep my eyes from closing. Pauley calmed down, emptied his glass, and looked away. Maggie gazed at him kindly and sighed. If this were a nightmare, I told myself, I wouldn't believe it. If this were a Tennessee Williams play and I was watching it from the gallery I would be – what, entertained, maybe, or appalled, or appalled and entertained at the same time. But it wasn't a play and I wasn't on the outside, looking in. I was in it, and I didn't like it. *I don't want,* I heard myself think, *I don't want, I don't want* … But Maggie was looking me in the eyes now, her legs drawn close together on top of the coverlet, speaking in an even, sober, and sensitive tone.

'Robert.' She said it softly. 'I have to tell you something.' She had lost her half-sister Helen a few weeks ago, she said, someone she had grown up with. At least for a few years they had grown up together. And they had drifted apart, yes, all these years they had drifted apart, but now she was dead. Dead but unforgettable. And Pauley, with whom Maggie had just about grown up with as well, had lost someone too. It was about a month ago, a month and a half. 'Show him, Pauley', Maggie said.

'Aww, Maggie.'

'Show him the picture you have.'

Pauley took out his wallet, and from his wallet removed a photo. It was a wallet-size mug shot of a young, smiling Filipino woman, maybe thirty years old, with long black hair and very bad buck teeth. Her skin was blotchy with acne. 'That was Pauley's wife', Maggie said. 'Marietta.' They had been married for about five years. The young woman had died a month and a half ago, quite suddenly, of pancreatic cancer.

'I'm sorry', I said, remembering the line from all those television programs.

'She was a beautiful girl', Maggie went on, while Pauley looked down at this feet. 'And so sweet.'

¤ ¤ ¤

At eleven o'clock we were finally on the road, or at least in the limo, Pauley in his track suit, Maggie in her purple flowered housecoat and slippers, the big fuzzy kind, and me in the blue suit I had been wearing for sixteen hours, which was beginning to cling to me in places where it was not supposed to cling. Maggie was on an alcoholic rush now, and Pauley was in higher spirits at last. On to San Francisco! A bucket of ice, a fresh bottle of vodka, and jar of grapefruit juice in tow, we were going to have a big night out. See the sights. Stop for supper. But I no sooner started the car than Maggie yelled at me to stop and come sit in the back with Pauley and her. I had to go in the back and show them how to work the fancy cassette player, and start the tape of *Unforgettable*. I had to show her how to adjust the volume. I had to pause and pour her and Pauley a fresh drink.

Unforgettable, that's what you are,
Unforgettable, though near or far …

Finally, I got back into the driver's seat, started the car and drove. But it happened again, at least half a dozen times.

'Stop the car! Stop the car!' she would yell.

I would have driven all of a few blocks, or even a few yards when it happened.

'Stop the car! Stop the car!'

In the back of the car when I joined her there she would be sweet, indulgent, demanding, and hostile all at the same time, telling me how nice it was to sit there with me and Pauley, and how nice were the drinks I served her, and insisting that I stay there till I told her to go, that I keep quiet until she told me to speak, and then all right, go, get back in the front, drive if I wanted to, drive anywhere, just go, just leave her alone. Except no! Wait! Fix the tape! Sit here! Listen!

Unforgettable, that's what you are.

Unforgettable, though near or far …

And then we would be going again. She had me head toward San Francisco, where to exactly she wouldn't say. Once in town, she had me head up Fell Street toward Golden Gate Park and the ocean, Pauley and her drinking and yacking it up in the back, a little excited by the city lights. As we approached the park she had me pull in and drive along one of the narrow lanes that twisted through the trees. It got very dark in there, and foggy, and lonely and spooky. I protested but she insisted that we go on and on to ever more remote and foggy little lanes, and at one point, there, in the thick of things, on an empty road, stop. Stop! Stop the car! Come on back here! *Robert*, come on back!

Unforgettable, that's what you are.
Unforgettable, though near or far …

Then on again we went to the ocean itself and Ocean Beach, a long wide stretch of sand at the flat western edge of the City, stopping in the parking lot half way down by the old derelict concrete promenade. Maggie had Pauley and I escort her out of the car and into the blowy bitter cold at the water's edge, the fog behind us now, stuck in the trees of Golden Gate Park, the sky black, a handful of stars twinkling in the infinite gloom, a half moon setting to the west over the ocean, picking up the wisps of few stray silver clouds. Across the Great Highway was a black gap where the Sutro Baths and Playland-at-the-Beach once had been. 'We used to play there, didn't we Pauley', Maggie said.

'On Saturdays', Pauley said. 'We'd take the streetcar down. The roller coaster, the Big Dipper.'

'The Funhouse.'

'The Shoot-the-Chutes.'

'Cotton candy.'

'Shoot-the-Chutes.'

'You said that.'

'Shoot.'

'We'd go there on dates.'

'Our first dates.'

'A bunch of kids together.'

'Under the stands together. I know what you did there Maggie, did with the boys under there.'

'Didn't do a thing. A kiss. My first kiss. But not my second. Just the one.'

'Shoot.'

'And now it's gone', Maggie said, suddenly turning bitter. Pauley and I were still holding her up against the wind, our backs to the ocean, looking at the black gap to the east. 'It's all gone. Everything's gone. They've taken it all away. God damn them! *They've taken it all away!*'

'Now Maggie.'

'Don't you "now" me. Don't you ... you've got no right. No, not either of you. Not either... Take me to the beach.'

'Maggie!'

'The beach. I want to go to the beach.'

We turned into the wind and tottered across the promenade, down the steps, and onto the sand. The ocean, full before us, cold and dark and sand-swept and gusty and deserted on an early spring night, the moon glowing over it, the waves heaving and catching the light – it never seemed so chastening to me and my littleness than it did to me that night. But for Pauley and Maggie it was something else again. For them it was agitated with memories. It resounded to the yells that Maggie hurled at it, the imprecations, the greetings, the welcoming laughs. It danced with the images of youth and sunny summers and lost loves that Maggie and Pauley emblazoned it with, the brilliant, mindless, mindlessly hopeful lost light of the forties and fifties and California's early days of post-war glory. Maggie and Pauley could see it out there, leaning precariously against one another in the sand, thinking about first dates and swimsuits and cotton candy while I shivered and turned away, holding Maggie by the arm, tears of resistance to the sharp wind rushing to my eyes. For a moment, as I stood apart, Pauley seemed even taller than he was as he held Maggie to his breast, as if proud to be able to shelter her, and fend off his own debilitating grief. 'What a time we had then, Maggie', I heard him say. But Maggie pushed him away. She was angry again. Angry at Pauley. Angry at the ocean. Angry at the moon. And soon enough we were back in the car, and Maggie was screaming.

She opened her window as I started taking off and threw a glass out the window, into the car, crashing on the road with an explosive pop.

'Now Maggie', I said.

'Don't you say a word, not a word you, goddamn it!'

I stopped the car.

'Drive on! Drive on!'

'Where?'

'I don't care, just drive, you sonofabitch!'

I pulled to the curb and stopped the car and waited and thought about what to do. For nearly nine hours I had been with her now. That made four hundred fifty dollars for the service, one hundred fifty dollars as my own share, hardly enough to compensate for what I had been through so far, but still, a hundred and fifty dollars. And as for a tip – fuck the tip. I'd just drive her home, tell her enough was enough, demand the fare, and go home and who cared? There is only so much that one could be expected to put up with. This was shit. I wasn't a slave. I didn't care how much money she had, or what her money seemingly entitled her to. I had had enough.

But Maggie suddenly softened. 'It's all right, Robert', she said. '*Robert*.' She apologized. She said she wouldn't do that again. 'Tell him, Pauley, tell him it's all right.' 'It's all right', Pauley said. Maggie said please, let's move on, there is something she wanted to see, and then we'd go to supper. She wanted to see it. *It*. With her and Pauley together. *It*. Then she pronounced the name.

So we drove on, up from the beach and into the Avenues, where the streets were wide and flat and the one and two story homes were all white and cramped, with one-car garages and miniature lawns. It was where her father had started out, building these homes, in the nineteen twenties. He had started with nothing. He had come over as a kid, on his own, from Norway. Quietly and reverently, almost piously, Pauley and Maggie reminisced about her father, and about the homes the great man had built. They had ended up themselves, as children, in the Avenues. Pauley lived in them still. There were sections – Maggie had me divert my route especially to see some of them – where the houses and the roadscapes were elegant, vaguely European in design, with a little bit of France showing through on a grey slate, mansard-like roof and the thin long windows that reached down to the floor, or a little bit of romantic Spain, with arabesque touches in the pointed arches over high blank picture windows, or the glazed tile and terra cotta mouldings around the doors. Built to charm and to last forever these houses were. 'My father always did things right', Maggie said. She herself had lived in one of these houses, with a French theme, as if her father wanted to live in his own little country chateau.

Soon we drove up to our destination, the parking lot of the shopping mall. It was the first and only suburban-style shopping mall in all of San Francisco. Surrounded by an enormous, dark and lonely parking lot, small by contemporary standards but still a mall, with one and two floors of department stores and shops and a pedestrian walkway running through them open to the sky; it sat, in San Francisco, as if an anomaly, as if a lazy, stupid square of American homogeneity slouching in the middle of a crowded Eurasian capital. The product of the genius of Maggie's father, his ability to think creatively and act boldly in the early nineteen fifties, it bore its founder's name, and for many years had been something of a San Francisco landmark. It had come to be an embarrassing landmark; for after the heyday of the urban renewal of the fifties and sixties, the mall had fallen out of fashion. Small by the standards of the enclosed and air-conditioned suburban malls that had since sprung up, and humdrum by the standards of the cosmopolitan city at whose edge it lurked, which was still accustomed to shop downtown, the mall had become less and less of a destination over the years. Shops closed down. The facilities deteriorated. The largest tenant, the old Emporium department store, had gone out of business, and little but small discount outlets and a supermarket, a Safeway's I think it was, had remained. Then the outlets shut down.

Now in the dark and empty parking lot, we sat at the edge of a ruinous construction site. Cranes loomed overhead, casting shadows into the shadows, like the skeletons of dinosaurs caught motionless and hungry in the moonlight. A good deal of the parking lot was torn up and ringed in by chain link fences. Chunks of tarmac stood piled up in mounds beside the fences, while earth diggers, at the ready, stood by to resume ploughing away at the rest of the tarmac in the morning. You could smell the bitumen in the air. Along the north bank of the mall a ring of enormous reddish refuse bins were lined up, like land-bound buzzards, in expectation of the oily leftovers of a kill.

They were taking the place apart, little by little. The mall had done its service. The vision that had given birth to the mall was obsolete, customers had deserted the place, and the mall was being dug up and disassembled. In its place, said Maggie, who was speaking softly and soberly again, would rise a modern two-level 'galleria', enclosed and air-conditioned like its competitors on the Peninsula, but better, more luxurious, its floors and stairways paved with marble, its balustrades finished in brass, its storefronts in wood and stone and stainless steel, its glassy atrium humming with natural light. Only the fanciest of stores would be allowed to open there: a new Macy's, a Nordstrom, an

Anne Taylor, an Eddie Bauer, a Banana Republic, a Mrs Field's Cookies. 'I only want the best', Maggie said. 'That's what I told them. Nothing but the best!'

¤ ¤ ¤

Then we were off again, to our final destination, a restaurant on a hilltop in Daly City, Westlake Joe's, an institution of the area since 1956 – a copy in style and service of any of several Italian-American restaurants in the City which also had 'Joe' in their name. It served charcoal grilled steaks and chops, sautéed chicken and veal and seafood dishes, a variety of pastas and salads and side dishes, and the famous 'Joe's Special', a San Francisco invention from the twenties, a fry-up of eggs, spinach, onions, ground beef, and spices that I used to order in Joe's-type restaurants in the City with friends for a late-night meal or a hangover-overcoming brunch. This Westlake Joe's sat opposite yet another suburban-style mall, a small one with a drug store and a hardware shop, and it was fitted inside the space of what is called Googie architecture, a restaurant design from the fifties with features like plate glass windows, sharp angles, and cantilevered roofs. They look like space ships. Usually they housed a 'coffee shop' so-called, an all-day restaurant serving club sandwiches and tuna melts and hamburgers with special sauce and watery coffee; but Westlake Joe's was a white-tablecloth establishment inside, with waiters done up Parisian-style in black waistcoats and white shirts and little black bow ties; the maître d' who wore a tux and acted as if he were running a fine dining establishment in the city.

We got there just a little before closing time. Maggie was a regular there, it turned out. The maître d' and a couple of waiters came rushing up as soon as we entered, uttering tender greetings. The customers at their tables looked up from their calamari rings, their veal scaloppini, their chargrilled 'steak à la Bruno'. Pauley and I each had Maggie by an arm, whose legs were hurting her now. We shuffled in, me in my wrinkled suit and day-old beard, Pauley in his exercise clothes and sneakers, and Maggie in her flowery housecoat and fuzzy slippers, a half-step at a time, with the maître d' and waiters in tow, as if we were parading with halts in the course of royal progress, giving the good subjects of the Kingdom of Westlake Joe's a chance to see the Queen come by and dispense her benedictions. But Maggie was having a hard time of it. 'Not so fast', she muttered, pulling us back. 'Not so fast. It hurts. Wait.' She refused, however, to take a place at the table up front, which would have made the progress easier on her. No, she wanted a place in the back, the large corner booth at the window overlooking the street, opposite a darkened service station and an illuminated Burger King outlet.

'Sammy', she said to the maître d', when we finally got to our seats. 'You know what we want.'

He looked at her with wet, expectant eyes, not unlike Amanda and Esther's. He was about 35-years-old, a small and handsome moustachioed man with a difficult-to-place accent, not Italian, maybe Middle Eastern or Latin American. The waiters beside him were younger, and less certain about what they were supposed to be doing, knowing only that somehow they were required, and some kind of reward awaited them.

'Champagne!' she trumpeted. 'Two bottles. And six glasses.'

'Six glasses?' asked Sammy. 'Are any others joining you?'

'Just bring us six glasses. Do as you're told!'

We looked at the menus. I was hungry but my stomach was knotted up with the stress of the day. I thought optimistically of a little shrimp cocktail, a salad with oil and vinegar, a little bit of bread.

'Do you still have those appetizers, Sammy?'

'What appetizers, Maggie.'

'You know, the one's we had last time. The fried mushrooms. And those other fried things. The shrimps. Things like that.'

'Oh yes, our side dishes. Which would you like?'

'Bring them all!' Maggie said. 'We'll have them as appetizers with the champagne. Then we'll order the main courses.'

I was not permitted to order on my own.

When the champagne came Maggie had Sammy pour out six glasses. 'Now', she said, 'I'd like all of you to have a drink with me. *Robert* you too, but only a few sips. Come on now, I want you all to have drink with me.'

Pauley was already working on his glass but the waiters hung back, not knowing what to do.

'Come on, Sammy, and you and you ...'

'Maggie, I'm not sure that we ...'

'Sure you can. Just a sip. Just take a sip. For friendship's sake. I'm *paying*.'

'Well ...'

One of the waiters disappeared and the second waiter held back. But Sammy stepped up to the table and ceremoniously raised a glass. 'To Maggie, then', he said. 'And health. *Salute*.'

'*Salutee*!' Maggie said.

I took a couple of deep sips, which burned my lips, and looked at Pauley, who was already pouring himself another glass. Then I ordered a cup of coffee. When the appetizers came – greasy clods of mushrooms, shrimps, and bits of chicken, heaped onto beds of pale shredded lettuce and served with a creamy dipping sauce – my stomach clenched up. 'Eat, eat', said Maggie. I took a couple of bites and gave up, full of remorse.

'Don't worry', Maggie was saying. 'What we don't eat we can take home. I like reheating these things for lunch. I just put them in the microwave.'

We were now supposed to order a full dinner. I ordered some pasta and a salad while Pauley and Maggie ordered steaks. Pauley went back on vodka and Maggie finished off the champagne from all the glasses. They got animated again and started to argue about something. I was on a second cup of coffee and had to excuse myself. I was tingling inside. My eyes felt like they were going to fall out of their sockets. I looked in the mirror in the restroom and saw something that surprised me: a middle aged man getting thick around the waist, dressed in that wrinkled, dirty blue worsted suit, needing a shave and a good night's sleep. He looked dangerous. His face was puffy, his eyes red and swollen. There was nothing in this has been in which I recognized myself. But he was me and he would have to go on being me. I splashed water on my face and combed my hair. I leaned on the sink and took some deep breaths, waiting for the tingling to pass. It didn't pass. I felt a sharp pain at the back of my neck. I took some more deep breaths and made my way back to the dining room, where Pauley and Maggie were picking at their food and smoking cigarettes.

'That's not the way it was', Pauley was saying, looking piqued.

'Pauley and I are talking about the past', Maggie said to me. 'I'm telling him how my father helped him. Pauley's father was no good, so my father helped him out. He set Pauley up in the business.'

'He didn't set me up', Pauley argued. 'He just gave me some advice and lent me some money.'

'Yeah, and you were such a success. A sporting goods store that's been out of business for fifteen years. And you never paid my father back. Don't tell me. I know. Pauley, who do you think you are? Whose money do you think you've been living on all these years?'

'Maggie ...'

'Such a big shot you make yourself out to be. The big man. And you can't even run a little store on your own.'

'That's not ...'

I tried to look away.

'Think about it. What did you ever do, Pauley, what did you ever do in your life that a real man would do? What kind of man do you think you are? A *man*? Bullshit. You're bullshit, Pauley, nothing but bullshit.'

Pauley smashed his cigarette into the ashtray, jumped up from his seat, and threw down his napkin. 'Fuck you, Maggie. Fuck you.'

He took off from the table and stomped out of the restaurant.

I looked down at my plate, the half-eaten linguine, the bitter lettuce.

Maggie was silent.

'*Robert*', she said. 'Go get Pauley back. Tell him I'm sorry.'

I rose almost gratefully, and left the restaurant. Outside, in the cool air, Pauley was standing on a curb at the edge of the parking lot, dragging on a cigarette, his back illuminated by floodlights, the shadow of him dancing toward the parked cars. I approached him and he turned away from me, but I went around some more to try to face him. He had tears in his eyes. He dragged on his cigarette. 'I know I haven't amounted to much', he said.

'Maggie told me to ask you to come back in.'

'She can't', he said.

'She can't what?'

'She can't talk to me like that. No one can talk to me like that.' Pauley flicked his cigarette to the ground and hugged himself. He started heaving, sighing. The light caught the silver in his hair and cast a long knotted shadow along the pavement as I stood behind him, watching him clutching himself and crying. 'I know that Maggie's in pain right now too', he finally said as his sobbing died down. 'We're all in pain. I can forgive her.'

He turned back toward the restaurant, heaved his chest, and marched back in. I followed him in to our table in the corner.

¤ ¤ ¤

The long, quiet, dark, sleepy hung-over drive back to Pauley's house back in the City, where we let him off because he was too drunk to drive himself home, and then back out toward the suburbs of the Peninsula. One thirty in the morning after the fried food and the cigarettes and vodkas and tears: a long, quiet, dark, sleepy hung-over drive back from the City onto the freeway and Burlingame and Maggie's middle class home. Every now and then I heard Maggie muttering something to herself, sometimes as if in anger, sometimes as if something amusing had occurred to her. Then she went quiet, except for putting on 'Unforgettable' one last time. The long drive until two in the morning, my eyes fending off the oncoming headlights, my hands trying to keep a grip on the wheel while my mind wandered into a dream-like state. I was biting my lower lip. A couple of times my eyesight seems to shut down. Then a kind of crack of electricity shot through me and I was sitting upright, my hands on the wheel, straightening the limo in its lane. I calculated the money I'd be making. Keeping it simple, supposing I started at three o'clock and ended at two o'clock, no make it three o'clock, that's twelve hours. Fifty dollars an hour times my take of 30 per cent left me with – what? I was too tired to calculate. I tried working with ten hours. Five hundred dollars and I would get one hundred fifty plus a tip ... All told, it seems that I could count on making three hundred dollars for the day. Not bad but it wasn't worth it. I would gladly have given the three hundred dollars back just to be at home in bed.

But by the time we had returned to her house, Maggie was animated again. She played one of her games, making it hard for me to help her out of the limo and into her house. As we got into the hallway in her house, she started acting drunk, drunker than she was, and laughing, just as when I first came in. Then she has me fuss over her as she changed clothes again – into another housecoat – and got ready for bed. She had me undo her ponytail and comb out her hair. Finally she pulled herself into bed, her legs under the covers. I stood at the edge of her bed, expectantly.

'Sit down', she said.

'Well', I said.

Maggie looked at me quizzically and taps the side of her head. '*Robert,* why don't you get some fresh ice cubes from the refrigerator and pour me another drink. And I need a fresh pack of cigarettes.'

I mixed her another drink and lit her another cigarette. We played gin rummy on her bed. I tried to complain. I said to her, 'Maggie, I'm really beat, I don't think I can stay up anymore', and she got angry, she shook a finger at me, she started muttering something, and I started trying to apologize and she said, 'Don't apologize to *me, Robert*. You can apologize to your boss. You can apologize to Isaac.'

'I told you, Isaac's not my boss', I said.

'Oh yeah, then who?'

She gave me a look, at once mean, amused, threatening, and ironic.

'You', I said, getting her drift. 'You're the boss.'

'Okay, get my chequebook and that's it.'

'Now, Maggie.'

'Don't "Maggie" me. Don't "Maggie" me, you sonofabitch!'

I backed away. Enough was enough. I was going to leave. No, I was going to demand my money and leave. I'd call the cops if I had to. I was going to get my money.

But suddenly Maggie went soft. 'I'm sorry', she said. 'Robert, just be nice to me for a little while longer. Have a seat and we'll talk and I'll write out a cheque for you.'

She asked me a few questions about myself. She was delighted to hear I had a young daughter, still a toddler. She told me she had been her own father's little girl, his favourite child, but she hadn't always done what he wanted.

'I can believe that', I said.

'I wasn't always like this, you know.'

'Like what?'

'I used to be young. I used to be young and pretty. I never

cared for sex, though. No it was no big deal for me. I was pretty wild for a while, growing up in San Francisco, and by the time I was in high school we were rich, we were rich and wild, but I never cared for sex. It used to piss my husband off. Not that it mattered. We didn't get along in other ways either. Look at this house. This is where he took me. This is where I ended up. A Paulsen and I've been living like this for all these years.'

She told me more about the family fortune and how it was little by little passing to her now. She told me about the kind of nuisance she made at the Board meetings, where she had a vote now, and at all the plans the corporation had for developing its holdings, building up its properties, selling off what it could. She told me how everyone in her family hated her now because she had all the money. But it wasn't fair, she did what she could, she gave presents all the time, she tried to help everyone out … She told me about her daughters, both of them living up in Marin County. Neither of them would speak to her anymore if they could help it.

By six in the morning she was quiet, 'resting her eyes', as she put it. I sat across from her, resting my eyes as well. Then she started awake. 'Robert', she said, 'I need another drink.'

'You already have one', I said, pointing.

'Oh, okay. We'll get my chequebook, and light me a cigarette. Now, how much is it. How much do I owe you?'

I rounded up the hours to thirteen – a tough one to calculate. 'Six hundred fifty dollars', I said.

'Six hundred fifty dollars. A lot of money. See? I'm not so drunk. Then there's the tip.' She looked at me mischievously. 'Robert I'm going to write a cheque for six hundred fifty dollars plus a tip for yourself. Okay. So where's my pen?

'You're holding your pen.'

'Oh yeah, and the chequebook. Where's the chequebook?'

'It's on your lap.'

'Oh, right. And who do I make this out to.'

I told her my full name.

'I make it out to you?'

'Yeah, and then I take my boss his share out of what you give me.'

'And how do you spell that? Is that Robert with an 'a' or an 'e'? One 'b' or two?'

I can write it out for you myself if you'd like.'

'Hey! Hey! Don't you touch this, you.' She gave me a mean look. Then she tapped the side of her head. 'I'm the boss, huh?'

'Yeah.'

'I'm the boss! ... Where's my drink.'

The phone rang. It was Isaac. Maggie spoke a few pleasantries to him and handed me the phone, meanwhile staring at her chequebook as if she didn't know what it was.

'Robert', Isaac said, 'What the hell are you still doing there. It's six-thirty in the morning.'

'Well, Maggie's been keeping me busy.'

Maggie smiled.

'Is everything okay?'

'Everything's fine. I was just getting ready to leave.'

'Do you think Maggie needs me to work for her this morning?'

'I doubt it. We've been up all night.'

'Well ask her. Ask her anyway.'

'Maggie, do you need Isaac for anything this morning.'

'Oh yeah', Maggie said, 'you tell him to come by when he's not busy. Maybe he should come by.'

'But I need to know now', Isaac said when I relayed the message. 'Either that or I need the limo back right away. I've got other customers this morning, going to the airport.'

Seeing how Maggie was delaying things I told Isaac to wait half an hour, and if I didn't show up at his home he should drive over here and we'd switch cars. 'Is that okay with you, Maggie?'

'That's fine', she said. 'I'm the boss.'

I hung up the phone and sat on the bed next to Maggie,

watching her hands.

'You look too much, Robert', she said. 'You know, I think you've got some problems. You've got some things you need to work on if you're going to be a good limo driver. I know. There are some things you could learn from Isaac. Now how to do you spell that. "A," "p," "p" - that's two "p's" right?'

This went on for a long long time. The spelling of my name, the date, the figure we'd agreed on, which by now was inadequate since we'd gone past the thirteen hours I had calculated, although I decided not to mention it to her. The tip she was going to include on the cheque, although she wouldn't tell me how much she was giving me – it went on, Maggie taking pleasure in teasing me about the money. 'Five', she said. 'A five – that's five with an "F," right? And then a "v," is that a "v" that comes next?'

We stared at each other. She frowned. She growled like cat. She wrote some more. She stopped.

'Maybe we'll do this later', she said. 'If I decide I've been happy with the service.'

I sneered, I think.

'All right', she said. 'But I don't think this pen is working. And I can't hold it right.'

I looked at her hands. She was fine. Her hands were fine. But there was anger in them, or if not anger contempt, or if not contempt a kind of cruel indifference, the indifference of the hands of a young boy when he catches a beetle and tears the legs off it one by one, and then smashes the body against the ground; or the hands of an old man when he raises a gun to his head, preparing to end it all, and then hesitates, uncertain whether he is succeeding at being cruel to himself or else rather doing himself a favour, putting himself to a final dreamless sleep, and hence not being cruel at all, just weak, helpless and old.

'I don't know', Maggie said. 'I think I made a mistake somewhere. Maybe I should start all over. What did you say, six hundred fifty?'

'Six hundred fifty', I said. 'Please.'

'*Please,* he says. *Please*. Well all right then.'

The doorbell rang. Isaac was at the door. I was free to go.

'Let me just see if I can rip this cheque out of the book. Go answer the door.'

I rose in exasperation, and started out of the bedroom.

'No wait', said Maggie. She was triumphant now. She smiled. She had utterly defeated me. I was a beetle. I was a dying and very old man. I was in need. I was in need of … kindness.

'I've got it now', she said. 'First take this. I think it's just enough.'

She handed me the cheque. I went out of the bedroom and into the hallway and then into the living room to answer the door. I paused and looked at the tiny piece of paper in my hand. She had given me a cheque, made out to me, for five thousand dollars.

Chapter Four

Wonderful Alison

I once had a thing for *Cosmopolitan* – not for all of the magazine, but for the how-to part advertised on the front cover:

'Your Sex Life Now – How to Get it Revved Up'

'How to Drive Your Man Really *Wild*'

'What Men Want – Ten Things You Should Know, Ten Things You Should *Try*'

'How to Have Multiple Orgasms – Again and Again'

'Sex for Fun and Games: What's Love Got to Do With It?'

I would never actually buy the magazine. I would only read it while waiting in the checkout lane at the supermarket. And I would only read the one section, if I could find it after leafing through all the ads and fashion spreads, where I would discover that the woman 'should play the tip of [her] tongue lightly around the back of his ears'; that she should 'set aside time for romantic interludes'; 'try out some sexy new lingerie'; 'gently massage the outer edge of his anus …'; and 'learn how to contract and contract around his shaft as if you life depended on it, and *hold on!*'

I was alone in those days. My marriage had broken up. The wealth my wife and I had accumulated because of my association with Maggie (business with her went on for a only another fortnight) had also broken up. The money had gone to creditors and then it had gone halves, since I now had to help support two households instead of one. I was living in a shared flat in the Richmond District, then in a two-room apartment in Uptown, in Oakland. Two or three days a week I took care of my daughter. Thirty to forty hours a week, mostly on weekends, I drove the limousine. Other times I went to school, first at San Francisco State and then at Berkeley, where I enrolled to earn a PhD, and where I also took on the job of a teaching assistant. I lived a life of hurried intensity, moderated only by intervals of shopping, cooking, eating, introspective melancholy, music-listening (sad Dmitri Shostakovich being my hero of the moment) and alcohol abuse. My best friend, maybe my only friend in those days, was a bottle of Korbel Brandy. Never E&J.

As for women – none. For four years I was celibate. I found that after the separation from my wife, to whom I had been faithful, I could no longer communicate with women. I could not understand them or make myself understood. I could scarcely look a woman in the eye without feeling demeaned. And yet my loneliness was terrible. My need for companionship, love and sex was like the need of a person in a frightening dream to end the nightmare and wake up, except in my case there was no waking up. I didn't know how to go about it. I didn't understand why something which had once been so easy for me, attracting the interest of an available woman, was now impossible.

Much had changed, of course. I was no longer young. I didn't have much money. I didn't have any status. I didn't have any spare time. I had started gaining weight and was developing a double chin. And meanwhile, the world had moved on. AIDS was in the picture, teaching people to associate sex with death and grief. Feminism was in the picture, especially at Berkeley, at that time in a very angry and indignant stage, so that it almost seemed criminal to be a man. S&M and B&D were in the picture, so popular among men and women, gays and straights, that whole clubs and journals had arisen to accommodate them, and it had become normal to associate sex with pain and hostility. Phone sex, something I could hardly even imagine, was in the picture: people having sex by talking about it, while miles apart from one another, people even reading books about phone sex, including Nicholson Baker's classic, *Vox*. And finally, as I was slowly discovering, the marketplace was in the picture. There in the San Francisco Bay Area, home to eight million souls, the nation's incubator of alternative lifestyles, the personal computer, California cuisine and gay liberation, not to mention the fashion for S&M and B&D, sexual activity and romantic attachment had been marketised. There were new forms of prostitution, including bondage dominatrices and phone sex operators, which had become an intricate element of the local popular culture. And there were new forms of dating, either through a service to which one subscribed or through classified ads. Finding your soul mate, or merely a sexual partner, had turned into a business. And men and women in need found that in order to move on they had to expose themselves to the cruel and invisible hand of the market.

So I would stand there in the checkout lane, studying the cover of *Cosmopolitan*, readying myself to thumb through the pages. There would be women milling about, old and young, some of them working, some of them shopping, some of them standing in line with me, some of them pretty or fashionable or both, some of them neither the one nor the other, some of them cheerful or at least not nonplussed, some of them in a daze, some of them care-worn, some of them dead-on depressed, some of them with such life and looks, in their tight jeans and sweaters and boots, that I did not wish to take my eyes away from them. Of course I had to. No staring in a supermarket is allowed. ... Meanwhile, beaming at me from the cover of the magazine was an impossibly beautiful young woman with tousled hair, a wicked smile and a slinky v-line dress open from her neck to her navel, encouraging some sort of attitude and action.

I beheld an alternative world in that magazine, so close to me that I could stick out my tongue and lick it, yet so far from me that it may well have been on the other side of the moon. What could I do? I wanted to believe that this other world was false. It was merely a simulacrum of femininity, promoted to sell the products of simulated femininity. I wanted to believe that all this commerce, founded in a mythos of personal beauty and sexual liberty was a falsehood that any intelligent person was obliged to eschew. And yet women were buying the magazine, along with the products, the cosmetics, the perfumes, the clothes, the how-to advice. Women could find something of themselves in that magazine, as well as find something that they desired. It was puzzling. On the one hand, it was puzzling because it made women as a species so remote from me, even if their remoteness was staged in a mode of heterosexual magnetism. On the other, it was puzzling because it made sex itself seem like a simulation, the adoption of a certain style, the acting of a kind of script, the deployment of a manipulative strategy. Couldn't, I wondered, a woman just *be* and a man just *be*, and couldn't a man and a woman just *be* together? My philosophy told me yes but my experience told me no. My loneliness, neediness and alienation were actually proof that my understanding of the heart was obsolete, and perhaps had always been wrong.

But how to begin, then? How to set off into that alternative world of which I had been too long unaware? I did not want a *Cosmo* girl and in any case it was unlikely that a *Cosmo* girl would have me. But I wanted . . . I would have to face up to the fact that I could never again, as I had when I was young, count on spontaneous combustion. I would need to find a style, a script and a strategy, and I would have to embrace, rather than eschew, the commerce-like aspects of modern-day love. I would have to think of myself as both an asset to sell and a purchaser preparing to buy. That would be hard. My years of celibacy hadn't coarsened me; rather, they made me into a sentimentalist. I wanted everything perfect: Romeo and Juliet, up to somewhere in Act Three. I wanted Cole Porter, in one of his non-cynical songs. I wanted . . . her. I wanted her even though, improbably, that meant that she would also want me. Maybe that made me not so different from a lot of lonely hearts out there, even the ones who hardened into cynics, or who believed that all they wanted from a partner was sex, but whether I was different or the same as others was something I had yet to discover.

So I stated rummaging through the personal ads of the San Francisco Bay Guardian. A good name for it: 'personal' ads, like the 'personal' computer. First I started answering ads placed by suitable-sounding women. I would find a brief enticement – SWF 34, interested in the arts, etc.' Then I would phone a special number, where I would listen to a recorded greeting and then record a message of my own, leaving my own number for the woman to call back. All of this cost money, of course. My phone was directly charged a toll by the minute and the amount on my bill could add up quickly. But no matter. I would leave my message and I would wait, and wait some more. Then I would answer another ad, leave a message and wait. And then another. And wait.

The waiting itself was transformative. At any moment, I could get a phone call. At any moment I could be giving a kind of audition, I could be selling a kind of product, I could be trying to close a deal and get a date... with her. I was revved up with expectation and it seemed as if my life had taken on a new shape. For something was to come. And something else, my loneliness, was to come to an end.

It turned out, however, that I was playing a losing game. Women who called themselves 'attractive' and 'sensual' or some such thing got dozens of responses. It was hard to make myself stand out – and it was very hard, after getting myself on the list, to keep myself from disappointing the woman, what with my melancholy, my incipient double-chin, and my lack of money, confidence and status. I was, yes, a limousine driver and forty-one-year graduate student, not to mention a single father. So I began running my own ads, and that turned out to be a much better strategy. In print I called myself a 'post-Marxist' and a 'sensualist' and in my recorded greeting on the phone service I spoke of my love for film, literature, art, and sometimes it worked. Every now and then a private message was left for me on the phone service by a woman who had been intrigued by my ad, had listened to my greeting, liked my voice, wanted to know what a post-Marxist was or didn't care what a post-Marxist was but guessed that I was an intellectual and an interesting person. It hadn't hurt that I claimed that I was handsome, in the mould of Robert DeNiro. By putting out my own ads, I was able to control the message, the sales pitch, even to some extent the product. And the women who responded to my ads, few though there were, were what people in sales call 'pre-qualified' customers. It could be taken for granted that they were in the market for the kind of commodity I wished to supply.

And so I began, slowly and awkwardly. I must have been pretty bad at first, even in spite of all the pre-qualification. I was hard pressed to get a good night kiss, much less a promise of another date, from any of the first few women to whom I was attracted. Some of the women, it almost goes without saying, were not attractive, at least to me. One woman I had dinner with had been mentally and physically handicapped by a car accident; she limped, she shook, her voice was wiry and she was very bitter and contentious. She would argue about the colour of the tablecloth if the subject came up. So there was no going forward on this occasion. Other women were overweight or just plain homely or dull. But then there were hopeful prospects: an Israeli woman who wrote plays; a mathematician from the Midwest studying at Berkeley. But nothing went forward. I couldn't manage.

Eventually, however, I got more comfortable with the process. I got to know how to present myself without seeming either arrogant or needy. I knew how to take interest in the woman sitting across from me in the café and assert my attractiveness. I became an asset to myself. I started noticing looks of hunger in the women's eyes. I started getting suggestions. Although it was too late, much to my regret, for me to get back to the Israeli playwright or the Midwestern mathematician, I kept running new ads and getting responses and meeting women in cafés, and I was getting very close to IT, finally. I was going to have my pick of women before long. I just had to keep at it. And then one night I met a woman I will call Alison, after the *sweete Alisoun* of the story by Chaucer. For she was no Juliet. And it all began, and not just IT, but a lot more of IT than I ever expected, actually, or could ever have foreseen. In this case I wouldn't just be working the aisles, but I would be worked over, and unworked and altogether deconstructed.

¤ ¤ ¤

When I met her, a fair-haired woman in her early thirties, the bells rang, the stars twinkled. I felt almost as if I had known her in a previous life, she understood me so completely. She could finish my sentences. She could listen to me, and listen some more, and then cause me to want to listen endlessly to her. And she was erotic. With me. For the first time in four years, from the moment I first met here, I was back in the zone. I knew where I was. I knew what I desired. And I could feel that I was desired in return. Yes, there was that feeling – where had it gone to? It had so passed out of my life that I had forgotten what it felt like. But I was remembering it now.

We got drunk in a Mission District café. We talked about Derrida and Lacan, whom she was dying to know more about, and about whom I pretended to have some understanding. She was a graduate student in psychoanalytically-oriented psychotherapy, doing research under a famous professor, but she was so tired of the positivism all about her, the fixed meanings, the literalism, the naiveté, the formulaic results-orientation of her scientifically-minded teachers and colleagues. She wanted to move beyond that. She wanted to do things with language, to deconstruct, to write, to be creative, to challenge the psychoanalytic status quo. She was so glad she met me ... We got a little drunker, and then we went back to her apartment, a walk-up studio in what had formerly been a Victorian mansion, and after talking and talking, finishing each other's sentences, remarking on how much we thought alike and felt alike, we ended up in bed. First we sat at her small dining table, in the round bay of a window overlooking a slope of the Mission District and, below in the distance, the glimmering towers of downtown. 'Oh, Bob, you are so right about that', she would say. Or, 'Oh Bob, that must have been painful for you. Or, 'Bob, that's so sexy.' Then she was sitting on my lap. 'You are really wonderful', I was saying to her. 'I can't believe I've met you. I can't believe we've made this connection.'

Our talk had soon turned graphically to sex. Alison wanted me to know that she was perverted. We were entering into something, it seemed, and as a premise of what we were entering into I had to be informed that Alison liked her sex strange. There were games she liked to play: for a starter, being given commands, being spanked, being led around with a dog leash. These were things of which I at the time, was, in practice if not in theory, unfamiliar. The language made me delirious. I was shocked and afraid – this was it, finally, this. I didn't know if I would like it. I didn't know if I could do it. Yet I was also aroused, provoked and entranced. I was hungry for it, wasn't I? I was ready for it, wasn't I? Alison sat on my lap and talked sweetly about bondage and semen. I sprang up and carried her into bed.

It was a mattress on a low platform in the corner of the room, against the wall, and we were on it with our clothes off, grasping at one another. In fact the sex was not perverse; we just rolled around naked for a while. And it was not so successful. My orgasm was painful, so disused had my apparatus become. I don't believe that Alison came at all. And the whole performance was amateurish, almost as if neither of us had ever done it before.

But it was sex. Sex! And sex with this wonderful Alison. The words of the Cole Porter song sprang to mind: 'From this moment on …' I had made a new beginning. *From this moment on.* 'No more blue songs', the song continued in my head. 'Only hoop-de-doo songs!', the song said in a bit of a joke. 'You and I babe … riding high babe.' This was no time for Shostakovich! It was time to swing! I lay there on her bed, naked, listening to her breathing beside me, and I blushed at the momentous change that had just come over my life.

As for the poor quality of the sex, I did not allow myself to be disappointed. I was experienced enough, from an earlier life, to believe that good sex would come; the important thing was that I had linked with someone, wonderful Alison. Everything that was supposed to come from these things would come, I supposed. That we had met under the bizarre circumstances of the classifieds, that we had gotten aroused by talking about Derrida and Lacan, that one of us was supposed to be perverse, that the other one of us hardly knew what the hell he was doing when it came to perversity, that we had from the outset entered into a quasi-commercial transaction of desires and desirabilities, on the level of verbalized desire and desirabilities yet also on the level of the crudest spoken and unspoken needs – none of this disturbed me. I assumed that 'You and I babe' was sure to be the next step. For that, I believed, was how things worked out. In a matter of weeks, however, I discovered that I was utterly mistaken. In spite of our extremely intimate conversations, I didn't know much about Alison at all.

Initially, because of my busy schedule – childcare, limousine driving, graduate school – we rarely saw one another, our relationship was mainly lived on the phone. But our phone conversations were scintillating. I had never been able to talk to a woman, on so many levels, so intimately and heatedly before. We had had one evening of awkward kinkiness, together in her apartment in the Mission, and one real evening of erotic fabulousness, at my apartment in Oakland, after I had cooked her my specialty of the time, spaghetti carbonara, heavy with parmesan and egg yolk. Our lovemaking this time was not quite kinky but it came close and it was exciting. But then came a party at her apartment, with lots of guests, food and wine and sexual innuendoes. Alison wore a vintage gold lamé dress she had bought in a second-hand store with a matching gold lamé turban. Her legs were bare. She professed to be showing me off to her friends, but she also told me to play the game of ignoring her, to flirt instead with the other women in the room. 'That will really turn me on', she said. 'The more you ignore me the more I will want you.'

So we had a good time. I flirted with other women, sort of: I was not really very good at it. In spite of her admonitions, I flirted with Alison herself: at that I was better. Then, when all the guests had finally left, we went to bed together, clothes off … and she refused to have sex with me. 'I can't, I can't', she said. We had sex anyway; I had persisted. But it was no good afterwards and that was it; she would never have sex with me again.

She explained herself the next morning. She told me she had 'issues with intimacy'. She told me that she was damaged. One day, while in college, back on the eastern seaboard, she discovered herself naked, crouched under a table. She didn't know where she had been. She didn't know how she had gotten there. But she knew something was wrong. She found a telephone, and brought it back to her place under the table, where she huddled in fear of she didn't know what. She dialled her father at his office, got on the phone with him and found herself saying, 'Daddy, you incested me. Why did you incest me?'

She had suffered a psychotic break, she said, and then had gone through a schizophrenic episode. It had taken her years to recover from it, including a prolonged stay at a mental hospital. Technically, now, after years of therapy, she was diagnosed as a 'schizoid'. Similar to those troubled people featured in R.D. Laing's *The Divided Self,* she frequently felt detached from her body, from her personhood. Sometimes it seemed to her as if her selfhood was floating about, hovering over her, or being absorbed into the walls of a room. Yes, there was something sexual about her condition. She was often obsessed with sex, and just as often alienated from it. She seduced colleagues, teachers, friends, the boyfriends of girlfriends, and more often than not had sex with these individuals only once. Just once. She couldn't do it more than once. Otherwise she felt as if she was being crushed, smothered, annihilated. She had not had a real boyfriend in years. And she sometimes found it difficult to stay in physical contact with people even in everyday situations. She had difficulty working in the same room as others, especially if they were men. It was either possession or nothing at all. As for me, she had thought it might be different. But it couldn't be.

She said this to me sweetly, not sadly or regretfully but rather as a parent might tell a child a bedroom story. And so we did not break up with one another. Instead we entered into a compact where I would be the man in her life, or at least *a* man in her life, and she would be my ... it was not clear what. We tried sleeping together once again, without having sex, and she was very pleased with the experiment, waking up all smiles. But for me it was torture. All I could think about while I lay awake at night (for I could hardly get to sleep) with her lying beside me was her womb, and how I wanted to enter it. I explained that to her, angrily, the next morning. And so there was unpleasantness between us, though we tried to resolve it. We set about developing a kind of relationship that was both erotic and chaste, altogether on – since we could be so intimate with each other when we talked – and yet altogether off, since the real intimacy between us would be taboo.

I tried to go my own way, to move on, to forget about her ... supply your own cliché. But I couldn't keep away from her. Nor, I believed, perhaps wrongly, was Alison capable of keeping away from me. I remember getting phone calls from her at five in the morning, at eleven o'clock at night, at any time of the day or night at all, where when her voice came, giving me a little 'Hi Bob ' as a greeting, all loving, I felt myself tremble with pleasure, like a little boy. And she would go on, at five in the morning, or eleven o'clock at night, or any time at all, talking to me with her sweet, high-pitched voice, discussing anything and everything that had come into her head, communicating with me as if we had been companions for decades, and I would stay on the line with her for an hour, responding. Oh yes, I was convinced, she really loved me. And of course I was completely aching in my love-longing for her. But who was she, really, to me? What was I longing for?

I do not think I ever really found out the answer to either question, which only made the situation all the more infuriating. When I tried to break off with her, she told me there was nothing for me from which to break off. When I tried to get back together with her, she told me how happy she was to hear from me again, how much she had missed me. But we were just as often apart as together. There were weeks at a time when we were out of communication with one another, and I was despondent, waiting for her to call. I had begun moving on, in fact, not in fantasy, in my erotic life. Since meeting Alison, newly invigorated, I had dropped twenty pounds. I had started exercising. I had become reacquainted with the power of my body. And women appreciated that. They also appreciated the fact that, largely because of Alison, I had learned to talk about sex, to be frank and open about it, to reach beyond the vulgar indirectness and passive aggression that was the normal male paradigm for my generation and go straight but respectfully and cheerfully into fantasy and passion. In this world of single people in tatters, where social life was useless, and everything was at least symbolically for sale, what was needed, apart from effective marketing, was diplomatic directness. You had to own up to what you really wanted, and to what your interlocutor wanted too; you had to find a language for this thing the two of you wanted, and a way to express it, to make it sound out and to make it heard. Alison had taught me how to do that. And so, bizarre though my education had been, and bizarre though this new world of classifieds dating always was, I rediscovered myself sexually. I went through a renaissance. But I couldn't really have any affection for the women I was with. They weren't Alison. And it was Alison I wanted.

In the midst of all this, during a period of being off again on again and then nowhere with Alison, I moved back to San Francisco, taking an apartment I couldn't afford, in a neighbourhood close to my daughter and her school and nearer to my job with the limousine company … and only a few blocks away from *sweete Alisoun* in her Victorian mansion. The Mission District was the place to be in those days; it was the San Francisco's new Bohemia. And there I was. Alison was at my new apartment the moment I moved in, but not to help with the moving or the unpacking. No, even while the two guys I hired for the job were unloading my possessions, Alison came up to the flat to talk about her plans for the two of us now that I was living in her neighbourhood. We were going to be writers together, she said. I was thinking, I don't know about this. I was thinking, Alison, what I really want to do is sleep with you; just listening to you speak, just looking at you turning your glance in my direction makes me burn. And I was thinking, let's put the bookcase over there. And the front room will be the bedroom, looking out over Lapidge Street, a narrow one-block lane of Victorian cottages and Edwardian apartments, at the end of which was a huge 'Woman's Centre' with a fantastic, brilliantly coloured and drawn 35-foot tall mural on the theme of woman's heroic suffering painted on the wall facing my window. And I was thinking, thank God I am back in San Francisco. And above all I was thinking, this woman is selfish, oblivious, crazy, and I love her and I can't live without her. And there I was, with her, the moving men needing my attention but Alison monopolizing all of it, going on about how fine it was that we were living so near to one another. We were going to be very close from now on, she said, touching me on the wrist, and write together. She was going to help me break out of the prison of my intellectualism (a prison in which I was not so sure that I was confined). She was going to help me find the emotional centre from which real creative writing emanated. And in return I could help her. I could provide the orderliness her own writing lacked. We could even write stories and essays together. She had an idea for one. Wait till I heard it. And never mind the other stuff. What she and I had together, she claimed, was far more important to her than what she would ever have with a lover. The two of us, that would be something. The writer's life. And of course now I could start helping her again with that business we had set up together, the phone sex business.

A phone sex business. That had started a few months earlier. She had mentioned it to me once in passing, an idea that she had come up with, approved by her psychotherapist, a business she was sure she could succeed at, for who was better at talking dirty than she, and who better at talking on the phone? She could stay at home, work on her dissertation, and take phone calls now and then. The details of getting it set up, of establishing a 900-line with the telephone company, of receiving payments and running ads were a challenge, though. Maybe I could help her.

I knew right away what a shop of horrors I was being seduced to involve myself in. On one level, I was just being asked to be a friend and do her a favour. The business itself, as we were worldly people, was a thing indifferent. It was a harmless scheme for making money. But on another level I was being asked to be her pimp. I was to be the man who would protect her from the cruelties of the marketplace, and the depredations of filthy-minded paying customers. I was to be her telephone Mack the Knife. Yet on still another level, I was being asked to be wild with her, to be ultra-hip with her and, in our own secret way, *épater les bourgeois*. What could be better than for otherwise respectable would-be academics to throw themselves into the underworld of the sex trade, and laugh about it? And then there was the main level, the main event: I was being asked to enter into a sexual relationship with her, where the sex would be virtual and I was to play the role of virtual voyeur. I was being asked to be let into the world of her sexuality in the only way she could let me in, making me the non-participating observer in an endlessly revisited, oedipal triangle, where Alison would be the mother, her telephone Johns would be the father, and I would be the schlemiel.

I did not fail to help her, though. We struggled together with the phone company and its billing system, and the fact that, although so many 900 numbers were in the sex business, we were not allowed to declare that we were in a sex business, and had to come up with some other official rationale. We struggled together in designing her ads, with devising a seductive persona and come-on line, and in getting the ads placed and making them stand out. A whole page of the Bay Guardian was already devoted to ads for phone sex. How could we compete? We came up with a persona, Lola. Alison would be Lola. We came up with a handful of ad designs, with different pictures – silhouettes of a woman and her lips or legs or behind or stilettoes or handcuffs – and different messages. Eventually we settled on using a rival weekly paper, based in the East Bay, which was cheaper and had fewer sex ads. I visited their office near in an industrial park in Oakland, near Emeryville, and sat across a desk from a shy young woman in jeans who might well have been one of my composition students at Berkeley. I handed her copy: some kind of crude silhouette in black with a caption saying something like LET LOLA BLOW YOU, NOW, or I'M LOLA AND I'M HOT, or even LOLA'S A BITCH AND SHE WILL TEACH YOU TO BEHAVE! I am approximating. There was not much eye contact exchanged between me and the newspaper employee, but we soldiered on together, completing our transaction, letting the world know about the availability of sexy, nasty Lola, at a dollar a minute.

Alison and I discovered that certain ads worked, and other ads didn't. The bondage and discipline ads were what worked best, and so, we decided, B&D would be Alison's specialty. Alison would teach her clients how to behave.

As for me, I had no use for phone sex, especially the pay-for kind. But Alison, giving instead of receiving, considered herself a star. Lola was attracting a following. She had learned to work a rhythm with her customers, to build up the eroticism slowly but intensely. The worst problem was having men hang up on her prematurely, as soon as they came or felt confident that they were about to come, to hear that CLACK! of finality before the process was really finished. CLACK: it could be quite awful. All that work, that build up, that mutual development of trust, that sense of an ending, prematurely cut off with a CLACK. But she had learned to keep the interest of her callers, and she had learned how to make men come to orgasm slowly. She had even learned – but for someone like her, with her skills in empathy and the art of conversation, this was second nature – to befriend her clients.

But the game was not just a game, and the business was not just a business. Just as in phone dating, the game and the business came with a cost. In this as in any area of life, you are not what you think you are but rather what you do, and Alison was doing phone sex for money and I was pimping for her, and even the illusion of playacting sometimes dropped out of the picture. 'Even the illusion', I say, as if this was an unfortunate by-product, but maybe going behind the illusion, finding the real underneath the imaginary business we established at a dollar a minute, had always been the real point of the exercise.

First there was Max. With a young man named Max, Alison actually started up a real relationship. Having developed a friendship with him over the phone, she one day, quite coincidentally, in a movie theatre in Japantown, heard his voice behind her. And so for a few months, long-haired black leather rock scene

Max became her 'boyfriend', a genuine if sporadic and difficult 'boyfriend'. It drove me crazy, thinking of her with Max, of Alison who was supposed to be unable to have a boyfriend telling me she had one, and even telling me about her sexual escapades with him. It broke up quickly but I suffered the whole time. The illusion was not supposed to have been violated. And yet she didn't seem to get it. She seemed to take pleasure in having violated the rules, in having allowed herself to mistake a John for a boyfriend, in throwing herself into a fantasy of coupledom and ironically taunting me about it.

And then there was Nick. At that time, a while after the business with Max had imploded, Alison and I had fallen into something of a routine. On evenings when I was free she would forward her incoming phone calls to my phone and spend the time with me. I would make her dinner. We would drink some wine. Then we would watch TV together, or do homework side by side, until the phone would ring, and she would answer, and go to work.

I initially went into another room while she took the calls, but she liked being on the phone with the guys while I was sitting in the same room with her – my bedroom-den – so I could hear what was really going on. She still thought it was funny, this phone sex business. She thought the fantasies of the guys she was talking to were worthy of case study write-ups in prominent psychoanalytic journals. She thought some of them were giving her (or me) material for short stories. It was all about the unconscious, this business of orally supplemented masturbation. Freud was right. When she answered the phone, and it turned out to be one of her phone sex calls, she would direct me to sit down, and she would look at me deeply, deeply in the eyes. And as we sat some six feet apart face to face, Alison in a small art deco wooden chair I had bought at a garage store, me on the edge of my bed, she would lower her voice almost to whisper, and smile, and touch her hand to her cheek, and looking me in the eyes tell the stranger on the other end that she was a blonde, that she was five foot six, that she was wearing silk panties and a bra and real silk stockings, that she loved performing fellatio, that she loved her caller's voice, that she was getting wet just listening to him, that she wondered what it was he wanted to do, that she would do anything with him, just tell her, just say the word. She was ready to obey, although of course, she being Lola, she was also ready to command.

But Alison eventually became friendly with another caller, the man from the East Bay I am calling Nick. Nick was not an intellectual, or even a hipster like Max. He was a plumber, and he had a son who he was raising on his own. One day Alison told me that she has struck up a relationship with this caller, a sweet man. She had learned her lesson and she was not going to try to meet him in person. But she valued the time she spent talking with him. Sometimes, she called him back from her own phone, so that Nick could talk at length with Alison for free. They talked about Nick's son. Alison gave a therapist's kind of advice to him. One day, Alison announced to me, she had decided that she was in love with Nick. 'You're not going to go through with this again, are you?' I asked.

'Why not?' Alison replied.

'You told me you wouldn't. You told me you realized you made a mistake the first time.'

'But this time it's different.'

'How is it different?'

'He's not like Max. He's not like Max at all or anyone else. He doesn't have fantasies like the others. He just likes to talk.'

'He just likes to talk? No sex?'

'Of course we do sex. But Bob, you won't believe it, the sex we have, it's so sweet. When he comes he tells me he loves me.'

'He what?'

'He tells me he loves me.'

'And he pays you for it. Or are you doing freebies again?

'No, he pays. But he's always really nice. And he's a plumber.'

'A plumber.'

'I think I'm going to marry him.'

'You are not.'

'I am! Why can't I get married? Why can't I be like everyone else? I'll move out to ____, I'll help him raise his son.'

We had a conversation like this several times, and each time I couldn't tell when she was joking with me and when she was serious. She was so cheerful when she talked about her man in the East Bay that I was sure she was being ironic. Or at best (or is this at worst?) when she spun out her fantasies of living as a plumber's wife in a boring suburb, I believed that she was only trying to hurt me. She had to keep pushing me away. We were so dangerously close sometimes, she had to do things to make me angry and keep me at bay. But then again, the more I pressed her on the subject the more earnest she became. 'I *am* going to live a normal life!' she asserted. 'I *am* going to get married!'

Of course, she hadn't met the guy yet. But she insisted he was the real thing.

'I'll show you', she said.

'You will not.'

'No, I really mean it. I'll show you over the phone.'

And so she showed me. She arranged a phone date with him. Eleven o'clock at night, on a Thursday. She call-forwarded her phone and came to my apartment for dinner. We had a pleasant evening. I had mixed emotions. I was with her in my small apartment, the lights turned low. She was wearing a flimsy dress. Her legs were bare. She was going to have me listen in to her calls from an extension in another room.

A pleasant evening. Dinner and wine. Jazz on the stereo. And then the phone rang, and after a few words she motioned for me to go into the other room and pick up the extension.

Stealthily I picked up the phone.

They were talking about his son. They were talking about a

problem Nick had with his son, who wasn't doing well in school.

This Nick had a voice, like Alison's, with a vaguely southern lilt, though perhaps that was a California outer-county thing. He spoke slowly and thoughtfully, as if he were chatting with a call-in radio show host.

'I'm sure you'll work this out', Alison was saying. 'You always do.'

This went on and on, until I noticed that Alison was doing all the talking. She was showing me that she had a real relationship with this guy, that she wasn't just his telephone whore. She talked about adjustments. She talked about friends of hers who had similar problems. She was reassuring, familiar, concerned, and sweet. And Nick was hardly saying anything at all. He was just making little noises acknowledging what she said. 'Uh-umm … uh-umm.'

'I think it's really nice the way you look out for him', Alison said.

'Umm …'

'You're always thinking of him first.'

'Uh!'

'You're not like, you know, so many others, who just …'

There was not only the occasional umm and uh, but something else in the background, a kind of squishing noise.

'You're thoughtful, Nick, even if other people don't appreciate it. Do you know what I mean.'

'Lola.'

From the squishing and the umming and uhing the conversation took a sudden turn.

'What?'

'Lola. Tell me.'

'Tell you.'

'Tell me something else. Talk to me. Tell me what you're doing.'

'What I'm doing.'

'What you're doing.'

Alison's voice dropped down a pitch, and went soft.

'You know what I am doing.'

'Tell me.'

'I'm touching myself.'

My heart skipped a beat.

'I get wet when I talk to you, Nick.'

'...'

Her voice was low and soft now and her southern accent was gone. Alison had vanished and came up reborn as Lola, sexy, desperate, mesmerizing Lola, overcoming her self and her caller with desire. 'I can't help myself', she was saying. And it seemed so convincing, as if she really couldn't help herself. 'I find my hands wandering', she was saying', and I could imagine her hands wandering. 'I've got my bra off' – the bra! – 'and I'm feeling my breasts.'

I listened in rapture. Rapture as if I were caught up in clouds, on my way to the afterlife. Rapture as in pain, my body being ripped apart. Rapture as in ecstasy. Rapture as in disgust and contempt and anger and sorrow. 'My hand is moving down', I could hear Alison saying. I could feel my own hand moving down. There was no denying the hypnotic power of Alison's language, or the erotic effect it was having both on Nick and me. But it was a taboo effect. I loved it and I loathed it. I was fascinated and appalled. I could not help but feel humiliated by the whole thing. Alison was spitting in my face; she was turning her wrath on me; she was taunting me with the spectacle of what I would never have. Not again, not after I had raped her, in her view – for so she now came to regard that evening in bed when she refused to have sex with me and I insisted – not after I had allowed myself to become her pimp, not after I had allowed myself to become her eunuch, would I ever have what I wanted from her again. I was so angry I could shout. And yet I hung on.

'I've got those panties on, Nick, the ones with the open

crotch.'

'The open crotch', Nick gasped out. Yeah Nick! It was him at the end of the conversation, not me.

The business got imaginative. There was touching, smelling, licking and cooing, a sticking in of fingers, a grasping of buttocks and thighs, a swirling of tongues, a sucking of extremities, ejaculations of pleasure and appreciation, of orders given and orders received.

'…', said Nick.

They talked about taking their clothes off. They took their clothes off. There was more licking and sucking and then there was spanking and biting and fucking. There was even kissing, hard deep kissing, followed by more spanking and pain and ejaculations of submission and exasperation and utter, unconditional yearning.

'Oh Nick, please stop! Stop!'

'I can't stop, Lola, and I won't stop! I'm hurting you, now, and you can hardly stand it.'

'Give it to me, Nick.'

I was embarrassed. I was in the wrong place at the wrong time, and that even if no one knew I was there – though in fact *someone* did – what I was doing was shameful, and even worse than shameful. I was being shamed. But I couldn't let go of the receiver. My hand was in a sweat about it, I was clenching it tight, while wishing I had never got started on this business. This business! We are not talking about marketization anymore, about buying and selling on a cold an impersonal exchange. We are talking about terror. And yet underneath it all – the shame, the tension, the terror – I still hoped, felt, required, demanded, insisted that the phone conversation, unbeknownst to this Nick, was really a performance for *me*. This wasn't just Alison showing me what I could never have. It was also Alison giving me sex. This was Alison giving me the only kind of sex she could give me.

'Fuck me', Alison was saying. 'Fuck me, fuck me, fuck me.'

And then the exchange started coming to its natural conclusion. Expressions of 'oh' and 'umm', expressions of moaning and groaning and more moaning and groaning, words having been lost into the whirlwind, and then words coming back out again: 'I'm coming. I'm coming.'

'Come inside me, Nick', Alison said. 'Come inside me. I can feel you. I can feel you all hot and big and you're going faster and faster.'

'I'm going faster', Nick managed to blurt out. 'Faster, faster, I've got you I've got you.' And then finally: 'Oh Lola. Oh Lola, I LOVE YOU!'

CLACK.

¤ ¤ ¤

The CLACK, I confess, came as a surprise. This was something new. From early on in my erotic life I had learned that the moment after climax was as crucial as the climax itself. That was the moment when, after having been totally absorbed in what was happening to your own self, you returned to acknowledge the other. But here the situation was reversed. For Nick the caller seemed to have been totally absorbed in acknowledging the other *during* climax. When it was over, he in effect rolled over, tumbled out of bed, left the room and left the building. 'So much for you, you chump', his CLACK seemed to say.

Maybe this was the crucial difference between now and then, between the time when love and sex were mediated by social life and the time when they became mediated by an economic system. It was all about the *exchange* now. It was all about giving and receiving at the level of an exchange, my capital for your capital, my acknowledgement of you in return for your acknowledgement of me. Once the exchange had been conducted to a satisfactory conclusion, the connection between the parties concerned was dissolved, completed with a CLACK.

I did not of course believe this, for among other things I did not want to believe it. But there I was, having had the truth and the terror of it shouted into my ears. Meanwhile, I had to come to grips with an odd contradiction. For on the one hand, I had been treated to an impossible experience. At the age of forty-something I had been transported back to the primal scene: mom and dad going at it, getting violent in front of me, and paying me no mind. On the other hand, the scene was over and it had exposed itself to me as a sham. This was not real passion, or even real violence. This was not mom and dad. This was not an ongoing thing, an arrangement of life – mom, dad and child – that would keep on going and going, and that even after death would never stop going. This was a simulacrum. It was phony and it was finished. And now, perhaps, for even in my terror and my humiliation I was able to hope, I could move one. I could really have Alison again. Couldn't I? Why not? I was no longer the depressed, bloated, demanding celibate I had been when I first meant Alison. Alison had changed me. Alison had brought me into a new state of being, where once again I could be connected with others; I had gone through my renaissance and I could be a man. And she was here with me, wonderful Alison. Nick had hung up on her and still, she was here, in my apartment, late on a Thursday night. If only my shame could go away, I could be with Alison as the man who never went CLACK, the man who never let go, the man that, unlike anyone else in the world, actually *acknowledged* who she was. Alison, not Lola, my woman, not my fantasy and my dollar-a-minute whore.

She came running up to me after the phone call, in fact, with a broad knowing smile. A smile of collusion, I thought, for think of what we had just been through together. Think of our impossible intimacy just now, what I had heard her say, and do, and pretend to do. Look what we have done!

But I didn't have it right.

'You see, Bob?' she said. 'You see? Nick! He *really loves me.*'

Chapter Five

Winners

It was Marion's idea that we go camping for a month. I had never spent a day camping, that is, pitching a tent in the countryside somewhere and actually sleeping in it, in my whole life. I had driven a few times past isolated campsites in California, in the Sierra Nevada. Under the gaudy sun, at the side of trickling mountain streams and white water rivers, in the midst of a forest of live oaks and pines, a bright low nylon dome would be fastened to the earth like a temporary shrine to the local gods. The campers themselves, handsome bare-legged young people, could be seen lazily frolicking with the spirits of the place, dipping their feet into the water and humming. I could see the charm of that, although I had no idea how to go about doing such a thing, just like I had no idea how to go fishing or build a natural fire and I had, the older I got, become more and more attached to the comforts of indoor plumbing and corner liquor stores.

But Marion had grown up in the Lake District of northern England, where camping was as customary as sausages, and she had all the equipment: a big complicated tent with two separate sleeping areas and a sort of living room in the middle, cooking gear, sleeping bags, special chairs and cushions and forks and knives, a double air mattress with a deluxe two-handed standing air pump. Camping, she assured me, was all about comfort now, and one camped in parks with toilets and showers and electrical outlets and clean running water. It was almost like staying in a hotel, and she was sure that I would like it. The goal of our trip was not so much to draw ourselves closer to nature, in any case, but, as Europeans, to draw ourselves closer to civilisation. Camping would be a means for inexpensively exploring the landscapes and cityscapes of France, while enjoying the summer sunshine and eating and drinking as much as we could.

It was the summer of 2007 and I was feeling flush. The idea that in a short while the world economy would implode, that Europe and America both would be succumb to a Great Recession and that I too would eventually suffer the effects of it, was for me inconceivable. For the past three years I had enjoyed, for the first time since the 1970s, the benefit of stable, gainful and ostensibly permanent employment, and I had received good pay rises each of the last two years. The pound sterling reigned supreme that summer, so that along with my pay came the bonus of a powerful exchange rate vis-à-vis the dollar and the euro. My book on food and culture in early modern Europe, meanwhile, had come out to favourable reviews. I had met Marion and we had quickly moved in together and then married. I had inherited a small amount of money (unfortunately in American dollars) after we met, enough that I could put down a ten per cent deposit on a townhouse in the city centre of Lancaster, take out a subprime interest-only mortgage on the property and furnish our home nicely, and I could move in with Marion and her daughter Sara. The three of us could enjoy a semblance of middle class comfort and security, even if doing so involved spending a lot of time, as it were, working the aisles. At this point in my life I was ready to acknowledge my own responsibility for the misadventures I had gone through up to then, along with my chronic poverty and underemployment. I had long since gotten into the habit of blaming my troubles on *them* – *them* being largely the state of the world, and all those people who, unlike me, had some power in making and maintaining the state of the world, including all those people who had played a part in denying me employment at all those places where I had applied to be employed. There were a great many of those people. Now I was willing to consider that it had been my own fault if I was unable to adjust and flourish, that maybe capitalism was not all that bad

– maybe, in its social democratic version in Europe, it was the best we could hope for – and in any case, after kicking against the traces most of my adult life, it was time to allow myself to move forward and run with the coursers.

So we were off, again, to France, though this time for a full thirty-one days, and this time in a year of exceptionally wet weather. We were going to explore historical sites I had hitherto missed: Fontainebleau and the chateaux of the Loire; the city of Sancerre, site of a terrible siege in 1573, which I had already written about, even though I could not quite picture Sancerre in my mind; the ruined fortress of La Rochelle, site of another deadly siege, in the 1620s; the old vineyards of Bordeaux, where since the middle of the nineteenth century wines had been ranked according to a byzantine system of *crus*, first through fifth, and of non-*crus*, many of them ranked in other ways – *Bourgeois*, *Supérieur*, *Grand*, not to mention a variety of overlapping regional, *terroir* and *négociant* designations that also served to rank the wines – taking into account such apparently odd criteria as the height of the plot of land in which the grapes were grown and the depth of the cellar in which the wine was aged. We were also determined to spend some time on the Atlantic coast, and sunbathe and swim and sip Pastis with ice and water in cafes whose terraces overlooked the ocean, open to the breeze. Hopefully the weather would settle by the time we arrived.

So, on we went. I quote from Marion's journal:

Left home at about three pm fully loaded with camping gear. Working on the assumption that if I wasn't sure if I needed it, then pack it anyway as we probably would.

Home by the way is Lancaster. And we were heading south to Dover where Robert (my hubby, lover, friend, etc.) and I were planning on staying the night and catching an early ferry the following morning.

As to be expected in the north during the supposedly hottest month of the year……yep, it was pissing down and that followed us all the way to Dover. It was a sign of things to come.

We headed south via the M6 hoping that the earlier closure due to exploding gas bottles and thoughts of terrorism had been resolved and we wouldn't have any delays. Because, lets face it, us Brits do not like anything coming between us and a good time or a destination that includes sunshine!!!

Anyway the earlier delay had been sorted so we were on our way. We had a steady run south using the M6 and then the M6 toll road to get around Birmingham and a quick run to the M1. Once on there we made it on to the longest ring road in the land of ring roads, the M25. Actually I think it's a twenty-first century roundabout with London in the middle instead of flowers and sponsored by ___ on it. So we're making our way around the roundabout carefully keeping our eyes open for the signs for the M20. No mistakes. Later we arrived at our destination, Dover …

A modern version of a very old journey, the beginning of an English person's Grand Tour. But for me it was also a Proustian search for *le temps perdu*. (What it was for Marion I will leave readers to decide for themselves.) I had spent nearly a year in France in 1974-75, mainly in Paris, and it has been the best nearly-a-year in my whole life. From the moment I alighted from the Métro station at Odéon, on the Left Bank, I experienced what so many other innocent Americans had experienced before me. A thunderbolt. I felt the pain of the shock. I looked about myself a second time and I was better. Apparently there was another way to arrange one's priorities in life, another way to organise space and time and the life of the senses, and here it was – Paris. You felt it in the smell of the air, the roar of the diesel-fuelled traffic and the bustle of the pedestrians, almost all of whom seemed to have very high cheekbones and impeccably fashionable clothes: you felt it in the curls and waves of the stony old architecture and the flashy modernity of the boutiques on the ground floors, bulbous stainless steel facades beneath the old wrought iron balconies; you felt it in something as complicated as the warrens of the Louvre, where you could get lost into ancient memories, and in something as simple as the crunch of a freshly baked sweet baguette, bought in any of the hundreds of *boulangeries* you encountered on your walks, slathered with earthy *pâté de foie* bought from a *charcuterie* counter open to the street, and washed down with a harsh but intoxicating *vin ordinaire*.

Lancaster of course was no match for this, but Lancaster, as I have already said, was okay. It too was built of stone and smelled of diesel fuel and rain, and it had its cobblestone streets, its ancient history and its warrens. But from the moment I arrived I saw that just as I was taking a big step forward into my future so I was also trying to recover something I had long ago lost: that original feeling of being on the other side of the thunderbolt. And so, this time with Marion, I was going to France again, to experience parts of it that were new to me, thirty years later.

Arriving by ferry from Calais we made our way south on motorways that were in much better repair than the roads in Britain or for that matter in most of the United States – nice wide smooth landscaped roads running through rolling green countryside. We stopped at a luxurious toll road concession where we were able to get a fresh salad and a glass of wine and dine at a window table with a view of the woody hillsides and the highway. We were back in civilisation indeed, twenty-first century version. Unfortunately we then had to leave the nice toll road for the free ring road around Paris, where we caught our first glimpse of the other side of modern French life, traffic jams and traffic crises, hodgepodges of roads joined irrationally together at awkward angles to accommodate the benighted sprawl of this, the second largest conurbation in Europe. It was very confusing and even dangerous and I was on the verge of going into a panic when we finally found the bypass from the motorway heading south into the provinces, and the traffic that had been pinching me on all sides for over an hour suddenly fell away. We were driving along a wide open road toward a campsite in Boulancourt, a village on the edge of the Essonne River, outside of the town of Malsherbes. The skies were menacing and every now and then a drop or two of rain hit the windscreen and fouled our view of the scenery ahead.

Off the motorway, at last, and driving along two-lane country roads lined on each side with poplar trees, I felt both relaxed and little bit lost. The sky was darkening and the hour was getting late. On one stretch of the road, meandering through green fields where some kind of vegetable was growing, I espied a supermarket, an Auchan. Shouldn't we stop there and pick up something to eat and drink? I asked Marion. No, she insisted, let's get to the campsite first, with a stubborn authority which I could not protest against. So on we went, all the way into the old town of Malsherbes, looking for the turnoff to Boulancourt, and then, when we didn't find it, back in the direction of the supermarket, looking for the turnoff to Boulancourt, and then, still not having found it, back toward Malsherbes. A light rain started to fall and then eased up and the sky lightened. I stopped at a small service station on the way toward Malsherbes, which had a kiosk that sold snacks and automobile accessories. Entering the kiosk, weary with travel, walking up to the middle-aged lady who sat behind the counter, I let it all out. 'Je suis perdu!' I exclaimed, not using the best French expression for the idea I was trying to convey. I am lost, I said. The woman started and looked at me with sorrow, as if to say, with her bleary eyes, 'What I am to do about that? You are lost. We are all lost. We have turned our hearts and minds away from God and there is nothing we can do for one another anymore.' Fortunately, there was a customer in the kiosk besides myself, a middle aged man with an athletic build. And when I explained my situation, my frustrated attempts to find the turnoff to Boulancourt, the man explained,

'Ah, that is because the turnoff to Boulancourt is closed. But I can show you a detour. I live that way and I can show you if you follow me.'

He got into his car and we followed him in our own car past the closed turnoff, which we could now espy, along a narrow road through forest and wheat fields, and then took the hint from him when he blinked his turn signals at a cut-off road to the right. We found ourselves on a dirt road bumping through a very green meadow, and then into a forest, where we came upon a better road, isolated homes, a bit of a village, and a sign toward the campsite we were aiming for. Another bumpy road took us to the gates of a compound. I alighted from my car to get the attention of someone in the office, so we could be let in, register, and move on to our campsite. No one seemed to be around. I stepped off the road and into the campsite lot and several inches of mud. My fine black casual loafers, bought in London, were nearly sucked off my feet by the muck. I stepped carefully, but by the time I made it across the lot to the office water had seeped through to my socks and my shoes were ruined.

Eventually I found the owner of the facility, who let us drive into the compound, registered us, showed us the toilets and showers – they were at the edge of the mud lot – and led us down a rutted lane through the wet grass and tall green hedges to where we could park the car and set up our tent. We passed a small number of caravans, parked along the hedges – ugly vehicles, not so much shrines to nature as refugees from trailer parks and shanty towns. I felt like I had arrived not in the wilderness of my dreams but in the suburbs of my nightmares. To have come all this way, in order to camp out surrounded by homely caravans and 'caravanettes', as Marion calls them, closed in by hedges – well, three years in Europe had already spoiled me, I expected nothing less wherever I went than either the picturesque or the impressive, I was cranky from driving and hung over from the adrenaline of expectation, and this was after all my annual holiday, of course I was childishly disappointed. But we found a spot isolated from the other residents of our designated area, there not being all that many campers in this weather in any case, and started to unpack.

Lo and behold [writes Marion] as soon as we got out of the car yep, it started to rain! So I'm in a bit of a quandary do I carry on and pitch the tent or do I wait and see if it stops raining? We carry on. Robert has no idea about putting up a tent. I'm a bit self-conscious about it, as I can feel myself being watched by our neighbours in the caravan nearby.

After a bit of a struggle, we get the outer tent up though Robert isn't really helping and I'm getting noughty with him for not knowing what to do. He suggests going hunter-gathering as it was getting on and all we had was basics like tea and coffee.

That agreed, Robert pulls more gear out of the car and heads off, leaving me to finish off the tent. I get the inner tent up and then set about making it cosy for when Robert gets back to try and make up for the rain which was by now quite heavy.

'Cosy', she says. I drove back to the office and found the owner, asking him where I could find a shop to buy some food. 'We have a shop just down the road', he said. 'But unfortunately, on Tuesday afternoons it is closed.' Aren't there any supermarkets nearby? I asked, thinking about the one we had passed. 'Closed', he said. But what am I to do, I asked. 'There's a small grocery in Malesherbes that might be open. You head into town, you take your first left, then another left and then a right …'

Not believing him for a moment, I got back on the main road and headed toward the supermarket. When I got there, some fifteen minutes later, I found that it was closed. It closed for business every weekday night at seven, a sign outside the front door informed me. Some supermarket, I thought. I headed toward Malesherbes, arrived in the quaint old town and made some lefts and rights and I found nothing. So I headed back in the direction of the supermarket. Espying the service station where I had previously stopped for directions I pulled in and entered the kiosk. There was almost nothing there fit for consumption but it was my last chance. I bought a couple of cans of Heineken's beer, a bottle of cheap Rosé d'Anjou – always to me among the very worst wines in the world, cloyingly sweet – a large bag of potato crisps (*à l'ancienne* boasted the package) and a bar of Swiss chocolate with nuts.

So I returned to our tent, having been gone for about an hour, and like a cat showing off a dead mouse he had caught under the stairs I unabashedly laid out my horde, my cans of beer, my crisps, my chocolate, depositing them at the feet of my wife with catty pride. Here was our first gourmet meal in gourmet rural France. I was greeted with good-natured derision. Yet Marion meanwhile had arranged the tent with the considerable care. On one side, in a separate compartment, she had stored all our belongings. On another side, she had set up our bed, having inflated it by the hand pump and laid out our blanket and pillows and a little battery operated reading light. In the middle compartment she had set up a small folding table and a couple of folding canvas chairs. But the flap of the middle compartment was open like a patio door to our little patch of nature. She had arranged the tent so that we looked away from the caravans and hedges, and looked straight into the trees and the creek that ran past the grounds. 'We'll sit outside for a while and have some wine and relax', Marion said, not knowing perhaps how bad cheap Rosé d'Anjou can be. So we set the chairs outside, poured our drinks, and it started raining again.

At first it rained lightly and we tried to hold our position. Then it started raining heavily and we had to go back inside and close the flaps behind us. Marion lit a lamp but it was dark and cramped and the rain beat upon the tarpaulin like a joyless drummer. I sat there drinking beer and wine and nibbling on potato crisps trying to get drunk and mollify the gnawing in my stomach. Subject to claustrophobia, I felt as if the world was closing in on me. It was very cramped in there. There was nowhere to look. Two beers and half a bottle of wine were hardly enough to slake the cravings of an accomplished drinker like myself, nor was half a bag of crisps enough to gratify my adult hunger. Though I knew intellectually that the situation was comic and would be over soon enough, I felt, in a word, as if I were *perdu*. The wind and the rain howled and thundered. It was getting cold inside. The words from *King Lear* came to mind:

> Blow, winds, and crack your cheeks! rage! blow!
> You cataracts and hurricanoes, spout
> Till you have drench'd our steeples, drown'd the cocks!

I felt, irrationally (but of course 'irrationally', for what other way is there to *feel*?) that I was about to be sacrificed to the elements. I wanted to go home. I wanted to be anywhere but here. 'He that has a house to put his head in has a good head-piece', says King Lear's Fool. But I had no house just now, just a cold, loud, dark and cramped tent. They had directed King Lear for shelter toward a 'hovel', but the hovel made him think of how vulnerable every human being is, and potentially how forlorn.

> Poor naked wretches, whereso'er you are,
> That bide the pelting of this pitiless storm,
> How shall your houseless heads and unfed sides,
> Your loop'd and window'd raggedness, defend you
> From seasons such as these?

In an intellectual climax Lear asks, at the sight of a poor naked beggar, exposed to the extremity of the skies, 'Is man no more than this?' And he says to the beggar, 'Unaccommodated man is no more but such a poor bare, forked animal as thou art.' And that's what I was now: an unaccommodated man.

I mentioned none of these reflections to Marion. For Marion was dismayed. She had tried so hard to make our outing into a seductive occasion. I kept quiet, playing the stoic, and so, after the snacks and the alcohol were gone, we stripped off our clothes, changed into our nightwear, got into the sleeping compartment, and lay down to sleep.

The air mattress was completely deflated.

Marion tried to pump it up again and I tried to pump it up again and we both tried to pump it up again but it was no use. The mattress had a leak in it.

We lay down on the plastic sheeting, feeling the hard cold wet and uneven ground beneath us, and tried to ignore the battering of the wind and rain against the tarpaulin just above our heads. Hugging one another, uncomfortably, we tried to get to sleep.

The next morning when I awoke, the rain had stopped and I was alone. Then I heard Marion pottering about in the next compartment. She had gone out earlier in search of the shop that had been closed the day before, a short walk from our compound. It had a small *boulangerie*, it turned out, and Marion had done the customary French thing; she had bought us a couple of croissants for breakfast, and a small baguette. For a visitor this is always a remarkable feature of life in France, the *boulangerie* that is always just down the road, with some regional and neighbourhood variations selling always the same things, the croissants and the baguettes, the flans and fruit tarts and *palmiers*. Even in the biggest cities you can still see swarms of people, male and female, old and young, toward breakfast, lunch and dinner time, walking their baguettes home from the shop, as if they were carrying their wounded pet toy terriers home from a stay at the vet's. Here we are, *ma petite baguette*, we are almost home. Marion had done the walk, and she had boiled some coffee and was setting our little table with a proper French *petite déjeuner*. I got up feeling as if the right side of my body had been crushed overnight by a steel girder, bone by bone, and as if my left side had decomposed into mulch. Before long it was raining again.

We decided then and there, as we consumed our croissants in the rain, that our first priority that day was to buy a new airbed. One with an electric pump, I added, having struggled through the misery with Marion of trying to inflate our useless mattress with what turned out to be a useless but obstinate foot pump. We would head in the direction of Fontainebleau – where else? It was the biggest town in the area, apart from Orléans to the south. But before we allowed ourselves the luxury of sightseeing, we would find a store where an airbed could be found. It ought to be easy, said Marion, for the French are great campers, they have camping stores all over the place, just like in Northwest England …

Well, in a word, no, they don't. But as we motored along at the edge of a forest under finally dry if dull skies we saw a billboard advertising a Super U, a French supermarket, which is actually often (I believed) a French hypermarket, selling just about everything that can be sold and, once bought, stowed in the boot of a family-sized car. This Super U was in Montargis, a town south of Fontainebleau which sounded interesting in its own right. We followed the road signs to Montargis and the Super U in the town, leaving the forest for fields of sunflowers, sugar beets and grain. Marion checked a guidebook. Montargis was a town of about fifteen thousand, with roots in antiquity. In the Middle Ages it thrived. It had a chateau and a fine old church and lots of canals in the town centre, making it a kind of 'Venice of the Gâtinais', and it was famous for its saffron production and for praline.

The road to the Super U took us higgledy-piggledy through the countryside and then brought us right into the centre of town. Montargis was nice – I think that's the right word. Nice. Typical of provincial north central France, it was a quiet labyrinth of low stone and stucco buildings with shuttered windows and grey zinc mansard roofs, crowded together along narrow streets and jagged plazas. We did not see any canals. But more surprising, we hardly saw any people. The weather had lifted and the sun was beaming through the scattered clouds overhead. We came into what appeared to be the central commercial district, and there were shops lining the narrow streets, but very few people about. We did not see any food shops in the district, no bakeries, no butchers, no fish mongers, no greengrocers, no fruit stands. Instead there were travel agencies, real estate bureaus, clothing boutiques and thrift shops and, again, very few people about. Travelling to the end of a main commercial road, we came to a broader avenue where once again a sign pointing the way to Super U. We followed the road out of the city centre, underneath a viaduct, and into an area that resembled a Parisian *banlieue,* or rather any *banlieue* anywhere in France, with dull white rectangular high-rise apartment buildings lining wide pedestrian-free, largely treeless streets. This was Corbusier country. It was not a town anymore: it was just a place where a lot of people, geometrically, resided.

We found the Super U, a great big grey box of a store, and parked in a very large car park festooned with streetlamps, which was empty but for about fifteen cars. As I stepped out of the car I saw a man in his twenties walking by. It was about eleven o'clock in the morning. The man was leaving the store, making his way alone across the empty parking lot and out toward the treeless street and perhaps the apartment blocks beyond, carrying in his right hand, with solicitude, a single baguette.

¤ ¤ ¤

I was beginning to see that I needed to think more about the idea of consumption: about how my own life was determined by patterns of consumption, by expectations and experiences of consumption. Consumerism was *inside* me now, a part of my being; it was not just an external operation to which, every now and then, I had to bend my efforts. I was also beginning to see that I needed to think more about France and consumption, and the modern world and consumption, and the role – at once utilitarian, authoritarian and totalitarian – that institutions like the supermarket had come to play in the modern world. On the personal level I saw I had a lot to learn: who I was, really, and what was out there, really. For I had led a small life, I could see. Stuck in America, stuck in my own petty struggles to survive, I had 'ta'en too little care of this', as Lear had said. *This*: who I was and what was out there, including especially what was out there for people besides myself and what I or anyone else could do about it. And on a general level it was dawning on me that I would have to compose some kind of account of life in the modern world, of where it had been, where it was, and where it was going. I needed a philosophy that was bigger than myself, bigger than my own petty needs and cares and prejudices – a philosophy capacious enough, among other things, to take the hegemony of the supermarket into account, and also one big enough to understand and promote that anti-supermarket dimension of existence I have called desire.

I could begin to think about these things because I was now, finally, in a position of safety – apart from sleeping in a shitty tent on the ground, in the rain, I mean, for that was only temporary. I had accomplished the Aristotelian condition of being 'sufficiently equipped with external goods'. For the past three years, that is, in Europe, I had done pretty well accommodating myself. I had put an end, I thought, to my impoverished nomadism, and I had escaped the worst excesses of what Phillip Roth once called the American Berserk. For me that meant not just the craziness of the American imagination, its violence, its apocalypticism, its hypocritical bible-thumping, but also the wacky landscape of American material life – the forests of fast food joints, the shrill skies of unending commercial come-ons, the lofty mountains of fat menacing automobiles, obstructing the horizon. What we had in abundance in Lancaster instead was pubs.

It was especially gratifying to think that my nomadism was over. It had begun early on, with that first migration from New York to the Midwest, and I hadn't seemed able to put a stop to it. Even during intervals, like my long time in the San Francisco Bay area, I kept moving from one residence to another. I lived in south Pacific Heights, Russian Hill, Haight-Ashbury, Glen Park, central Pacific Heights (where I lived during the Maggie business), the Inner Sunset, Inner Richmond, Uptown Oakland, Grand-Lake Oakland, and then, as in my period with wonderful Alison, back in San Francisco, in the Mission District. I didn't like moving but I couldn't help myself. My circumstances kept changing – my jobs, my funds, my loves – and in any case I was always restless. After leaving San Francisco for good I had kept moving too, though less and less out of restlessness and more and more out of necessity. Cincinnati, Ohio, Ann Arbor, Michigan, Birmingham, Alabama, Washington D.C., San Diego, California, Chicago, Illinois (to stay with my widowed mother for a short while), Middletown, Connecticut ... I moved, and then I moved again. And every time I moved away from home, I lost: books, spices, musical instruments, tableware, lovers, friends. A ritual of self-renewal would then be repeated, the purchase of a new dish drainer, a towel rack, spices. I would start to acquire books again. I would buy a picture for my new walls. I would look for new friends and make symbolic purchases – invitations to dinner, to coffee, to nights on the town – in order to acquire them. Sometimes it was hopeless. I departed from San Diego with fewer friends than when I had arrived, and many fewer goods, and I departed from Middletown with even less. I was a never-has-been in America, a misfit that no one wanted to see around, and I was also an always-has-less. I even left behind me some paintings I had made in my art-dealer days in San

Francisco, large post-abstract canvasses in acrylic that I was stubbornly fond of and that I had dragged around with me for fifteen years. A couple of them my sister in Chicago kept – and then partly painted over, so that the colours of the canvases would match the colour of her sofas and rugs, and would have as little to do as possible with the intentions of their original creator.

But now, I imagined, I was settled. I had come to a stage in my life that was *once and for all*. I had purchased my last new dish drainer. And this trip we were taking around France, with a tent, was not the journey of a pair of nomads but rather the modern parody of nomadism, leisure travel, tourism – something new to me, since I hadn't been able to do much of it before. A real tourist, I had read in a book called *The Tourist*, was someone who tried not to be a tourist. That was me, and Marion too. But still, we were tourists. My real travels were over. I was aware that I was now trying not to get somewhere, to arrive and be done with it, but to get *something*, or some *things*, out of my trip, to acquire the commodities of experience. That I also wanted to *learn* while travelling, to find out more about France and (since I was about to write a book on the subject) the culture of gastronomy, was a mitigation. Though knowledge is not incompatible with the consumption of commodities, it is a categorically different, and knowledge seemed to be my main motivation. I was trying to *discover* while I travelled. But still, I was a tourist. And that meant, too, as the author of *The Tourist* (Dean MacCannell) says in a more recent book, *The Ethics of Sightseeing*, 'To say tourists go in search of pleasure and happiness is only to say they seek repression and displacement of painful memory'. So I was seeking, if MacCannell is right, to repress and displace (I won't speak for Marion here). I was seeking *not to remember* even as I was *going back over* the France of my youth and thinking about returning to my thunderbolt moment. But when, at the campsite, King Lear showed up, and when, the next day, I saw the lone figure of a man in a parking lot clutching a baguette, as if he were still in the France of yesterday, only in the guise of a bronze statue of a tortured walker in the abyss by Giacometti, I realised once and for all that I was no longer in the France of yesterday, or even my own yesterday, and I saw that I would have to do a lot more thinking than I had anticipated. For once, moreover, I had the leisure and security to do that thinking. I wasn't in a survive-or-die frame of mind anymore. I could attempt to be dispassionate and objective.

¤ ¤ ¤

We never found a camping store or a hypermarket that first day in the region of the Essone and the Marne, and we had a second night on the hard ground, in the rain. But the next day, after an interesting meal of pikeperch in the restaurant quarter of old Orléans, driving out of town, we came upon a huge Carrefour Hypermarket, where we were able to buy a new airbed and pump. After two nights we were finally able to enjoy some comfort. 'We have both slept well for the first time since arriving and it was wonderful', Marion announces in her journal. We were also stocked up with supplies, including a hoard of eau de vie and wine, and our bellies were full. It was still very damp, and even Marion had had enough of camping for a while, so that it was decided that at our next destination, Sancerre, we would stay in a hotel. I worried about the expense, but I was relieved about the dry warm bed that awaited us. So was Camper Marion. We were on the road again, and ready now to do some serious wine-tasting and food sampling and history-learning, navigating through the heartland of France: Sancerre and onwards through the Loire Valley, then to southern Brittany, then to the Atlantic Coast and the Bordeaux region. Even the weather was cooperating with the lifting of my mood, although, according to her journal, Marion was of two minds about it: 'We left the site under a sunny sky and I'm thinking bloody typical, we're going to stay in a hotel, we're stuck in a car and the sun comes out and starts splitting the trees.'

Unfortunately, I had to be of two minds about it too, not because of the sun but because of what we had seen several times already: lovely old town centres which had been eviscerated of their permanent daily food stores, since instead all the main daily shopping had been moved to supermarkets outside the centres. The lone Giacometti man, striding along the empty tarmac, with a baguette in his hand, stood for me as an icon of what seemed to have happened in small town France. I won't go so far as to claim what that icon by itself suggests, namely that the crowd of the market-going communities of France had been entirely replaced by a population of lonely shoppers. For the situation is more complicated than that. Among other things, weekly markets are still common in much of small town France, and the government helps subsidise them. Moreover, in economically successful towns, the city centres are thriving as leisure districts. At the very centre of most of the towns we visited sat the restaurants and cafés, with terraces open to a central square, or else tucked away in subsidiary alleys just off a main square. There were often also, if the town was large enough, a permanent central public market, with butchers, fishmongers and the like. Montargis, in fact, though it doesn't have a permanent site for it, has a twice weekly general market in one public square and a once-weekly market for produce in another. But still the main commercial business in towns like Montargis is conducted in supermarkets and similar big box institutions. On the periphery of any town large enough to merit such development, including early in our travels the historic towns of Orléans and Bourges, one will find one or more an obscene rings of big gaudy boxes, cloaked in rendered cement and corrugated steel, painted in loud colours and sign-posted with forests of illuminated plastic overlooking broad and treeless car parks, offering food, drink, house supplies, appliances, furniture, electronic goods, clothing, gardening supplies, toys, hardware, housewares, building materials and motor vehicles for sale. Carrefour, Conforama, Mr Bricolage, Darty, Intersport, Peugeot-Citroen, or one of their few competitors, like Géant, Castorama, Brico Depôt, Electro Depôt, GoSport, Renault, accompanied, inevitably, by a McDonald's and perhaps also a Quick Burger …

They are ugly, these peripheral commercial strips. There is no design to them, apart from being on the periphery. They are meant, like wild flowers in a wasteland, to attract the needy in search of honey, and they are successful, but not because of their beauty. They attract the needy bees because they are the only beings, in the wastelands of the car parks, and in the towns as a whole, with pollen. The shops inside the city-centres have been forced out of business. So in provincial France no less than, say, Connecticut, urbanity has been turned inside out. Capitalism since the 1960s or 70s has said to the populations of the West: 'We will continue to provide you with goods and services, in fact we will provide you with more goods and services than ever, we will provide you with things you haven't imagined yet and don't yet know you need to be provided with, and we will make them available at prices that for many of you will be easy to afford. But in return for the bounty we bring to you, we demand this, that we no longer feel compelled to come to you, and rather that you come to us. We will build our boxes in the wasteland, and the wasteland will bloom with us. What happens to the towns and cities we and you abandon is not our concern.'

There are other costs as well, familiar enough to thinking people in the West: the de-skilling and proletarianisation of the commercial workforce, and with it the corresponding lowering of wages, benefits and career opportunities for great swathes of the population; the outsourcing of manufacturing and essential service jobs to developing countries with much lower wages; the degradation of the natural environment, since access to essential goods and services now require more automobile trips, and more automotive-based infrastructure; the degradation of the urban environment, as traditional urban centres give way to centre-less sprawl. In a lot of America, the transformation is complete. I have driven though towns in California and Kansas that are essentially shuttered ghost towns, a few miles down the road from a thriving Wal-Mart, which nowadays will have not only its own food and clothing for sale but also its own bank on the premises, its own insurance company, its own dry cleaning shop, everything but its own mayor. When I lived in the centre of dull, wealthy, compact Middletown, Connecticut, population 47,000, in order to buy a television set (a twenty-inch Panasonic) I had to drive eight miles along winding state roads, over to a wide, horrid, treeless, pavement-free commercial strip of big box stores, fast food joints and traffic delays in Cromwell, Connecticut, in order to alight at my nearest Wal-Mart, set like a concrete burial mound within a huge asphalt prairie of parked cars. In rural France the situation is more complex, since town and village centres going back to the Middle Ages have been preserved. And I really can't say in fine detail what the social and economic consequences of the triumph of hyper-capitalism has been; I don't know enough about the country. I do know, though, that between 1975, when I left the France of my youth, and 2007, when I was travelling with Marion through the countryside, the commercial landscape was revolutionised, without much discernible benefit for the majority of the people in France – incomes have not improved, lifestyles have not improved, social mobility has not improved – except that there is a lot more *stuff* for everybody to ogle and own.

France has even become a leading worldwide exporter of the degradation. Carrefour, the second largest retailer in the world, has operations in twenty-four countries: Albania, Algeria, Austria, Belgium, Bulgaria, Brazil, Bahrain, China, Egypt, Georgia, Germany, Morocco, India, Indonesia, Iran, Iraq, Jordan, Kuwait, Taiwan, Saudi Arabia, Oman, Pakistan, Portugal, the

United Arab Emirates. But it is wrong to think of France's Carrefour as a singular character in a drama, bent on reproducing itself hither and yon, for Carrefour is only one point of play among many in a worldwide system. In fact Carrefour has *entered and exited* a number of countries, creating structures that were then sold off and retooled (or abandoned for tax purposes) by other conglomerates: Chile, Czech Republic, Hong Kong, Japan, Mexico, Russia, South Korea, Switzerland, South Korea, the United Kingdom. What the world has been facing since the 60s and 70s is the sexless reproductive force of capital itself, which has no characters, only impersonal structures and brands. Carrefour, Tesco, Sony, Kraft, IKEA, CBRE Commercial Real Estate Services, the Westfield Group, the Accor Group, Pepsico, HBSC, AIG, BPCE, AXA. It does not love you, this system. But it provides you with things, as long as you go to it, as long as you seek it out and patronise it, although of course there is almost no alternative but to go to it and take what it has to offer, and there is no alternative either but to buy into the lie of the inauthentic materialistic hedonism on offer, the pursuit of goods for the sake of not pursuing oneself.

I often thought about this when I was in the midst of my economic struggles, living in places like Cincinnati and Middletown — that I worked hard, or, even worse, that I worked hard at finding work to work hard at, and all that was available to me in return was *this,* this degradation, this ugly, metastasised homogeneity of streetscapes, services, goods and debts. I knew that it could be different if you were wealthy and the good sense to live in Manhattan or La Jolla. It could also be somewhat different if you resided in a bohemian hotspot, like the Mission District in San Francisco. I had hoped it would be different in Europe, and it was, except that now, as I got to know Europe better, I saw that it wasn't all that different, and that even great historic towns in the heart of France were enveloped with the cancerous extravasation of global trade. But the point of course is that this worldwide metastasis of capital is what *pays for* Park Avenue co-ops and seaside homes in La Jolla. Or rather, that's one of the points. For another point is that, with all that morbid tissue enveloping you, still, you who do not have a co-op or a villa, you have to live. And you can't help wanting *this,* or what *this* wants you to want, even amidst the degradation.

¤ ¤ ¤

In America, during my days in San Francisco, I learned to become what could be called a scavenger consumer. Once I was no longer an aspiring member of the middle class, I lived, as it were, on the leftovers of the middle class, picking through the remains like a drunken buzzard. I got my clothes in places like Marshall's and Ross-Dress-for-Less, off-loaders of fashions from previous seasons. I bought food and wine and liquor that was on sale, that was closing out, or that was sold in bulk, or otherwise packaged as being unaccountably low in price. For a long while I drove a car that was some twenty-years old and more, a rusty boxy little Datsun B-210. I lived in dodgy neighbourhoods, renting cheap apartments at the edge of decent neighbourhoods. And once I became accomplished at being a consumer of this type, I was perversely proud of myself. The scavenger consumer imagines himself as a kind of trickster. Every time he lands a close-out Liz Claiborne jacket at 60% off, or a remainder bottle of Kendall Jackson Sauvignon Blanc for $7.50 instead of $9.99, he thinks that he has triumphed. He has beaten the system. Of course, he hasn't. But he thinks he has, and he is encouraged to do so by the very system he thinks he is beating.

In the seventies corporate America discovered that there was a 'market' of and for scavenger consumers, and created a superstructure for it, even to the point of manufacturing merchandise specifically for it. 'Outlet' stories proliferated, selling not just off-loaded goods but also goods created to be sold as if they were off-loaded. The Big Box stores got into the act. They created 'clubs' – Price Club, Sam's Club – where for a membership fee the customer was privileged to purchase luxury items in bulk, as if they weren't luxury items at all – or rather, as if they were genuine luxury items for suckers only, who shopped on the high street, to which category tricky club members no longer belonged. In Europe, there also opened the 'discount supermarkets', Lidl, Netto and Aldi, stores where customers served themselves off of delivery pallets, and of course IKEA, where customers loaded up their own delivery pallets. Everywhere in the affluent West it was the same. Of course, there had always been different levels of consumption for different social classes, different shops for different buyers in the industrialised West. But now a system was in place to encourage losers to feel like winners.

The scavenger consumer raids the outlets, the clubs, the discount supermarkets, the crazy halls of IKEA, rummaging through the simulated bargains that corporate retailers have excreted for their use, and the scavenger thinks that he comes a cropper: he's got the twelve-pack of Boston-style baked beans, the new-model low wattage portable loudspeakers, the bentwood foam cushioned and sinuous lounge chair, for a lot less money, he thinks, than he would otherwise have spent, if he hadn't spent so much time and effort buzzing around and seeking it out among the efflux. I used to think of myself, living in Northern California, proudly, as a connoisseur of cheap wines: not Gallo or Sebastiani but Rabbit Ridge, Woodbridge, Bogle. I was so damn smart. I bought four dollar made-in-Italy frozen pizzas along with the reduced price California wine from Trader Joe's. I got my books from second hand shops on 16th Street. I started buying my fruits and vegetables from Latin markets on Mission Street, where produce rejected by the supermarkets for being too small or misshapen was resold at a lower price. I was so damn smart. When I moved to Lancaster, England, my choices were more limited, so dominated by major corporations was the retail world of our little city, and so little was our city. But still, I could go down to Manchester and get my jeans for £10 at Primark, or a pair of designer-label Oxfords for £50 from T.K. Maxx, a subsidiary of the American company that also owns T.J. Maxx and Marshall's ... and in Canada a leading 'off-price' clothing retailer called – and I am not making this up – Winners.

When affluence finally seemed to have arrived, for Marion and me, though I still retained the habits of the scavenger consumer, I began thinking about the quality of things as well – real 'quality', whatever that was, and what it would mean to possess it. There are few limits to the desires we can entertain for material goods, of course, except the limits of the material itself. Even if you are not affluent, and have no opportunity to become affluent, if you are a Westerner you are likely to have many desires for goods and services that seem plausible to you: that lakeside house in that country, or that BMW 510 with tan leather seats and extra trim. After all, other people have these things. Even if you don't see it much in your neighbourhood, you see it on TV, or you see it in *other people's neighbourhoods,* like maybe where you work as a gardener. You can envy these things, of course, and resent them, but the normal response today, it seems to me, is not to be envious but rather to be charged up with what the critic René Girard called 'mimetic desire'. Instead of envying the rich you emulate them, on the cheap.

And so, even if it means shopping at T.K. Maxx and buying a pair of half-priced shoes that don't quite fit, since you are emulating the rich and you have a bit of quality on your feet, you are a winner. And the goal is to keep on winning. You may be able to engage in *reverse snobbery* sometimes, so that what you have, what you have won in the great contest of shopping, would seem to better than what in any case you would not have been able to win had you desired it. Instead of the lobster, I will have the gurnard – a very underrated fish. Instead of cashmere, I will wear acrylic – much more practical. But this is compensatory bad faith. It may be possible not to be aware of the differences in the quality of things, and not to know that lobster and cashmere are better than carp and acrylic, but once you know, or at least once you are capable of emulating the knowledge, the desire and the possession, there is no escape. You're in. You have to live. And you know the difference between one way of living and another.

For my part, I soon came to appreciate the difference between material goods as *stuff* and material benefits as *equipment*. You could, for example, if you were stupid, look at your home as a miscellany of stuff – rooms, a sofa, pillows and the like. But that is not what a home actually is. A home is a material enterprise that equips you for living. The same can go for other kinds of goods – clothing, cell phones, automobiles. These things equip you for living in a certain way, and if you experience mimetic desire for a certain kind of suit or phone or car, it is because you want to be equipped for life the way you can see other people are equipped. Of course, the choices are overabundant and the choosing can be vertiginous. And so we try to fashion niches for ourselves, lifestyles and standards of taste. We try to put limits to emulation by presuming that there is actually an end-value to our behaviours as consumers, even though the end-values are not of our own choosing. My way is the best way because it is mine ... even though I know that it would be good if I could live better.

But what way is the best way, then? This is not a question that people have been asking very much since the 1960s. You find yourself in life, at a certain point ... here. And you make do. You adapt and you adopt. You find a niche where you can seem to be coming out a winner.

Yet when affluence seemed to have arrived, Marion and I were unsure of our limits. We were unsure of what we should aspire to, or why. That was another reason we took our trip to France.

¤ ¤ ¤

Sancerre is a hilltop town overlooking rolling vineyards to the north, west and south and the Loire and the lowlands of Pouilly, another wine-making area of fame, to the east. One of our guidebooks compared it to the picturesque wine-towns of Chianti: its vertiginous views, its bunched-up houses with red-tile roofs, its cobblestone alleys, its moderate climate. It is missing something, though. The town, on its hilltop, is lacking a frame. Up until 1573 it had been encased by high stone ramparts with skyscraping stone lookout towers on all sides. From a distance it looked like a fairy tale. After the siege of 1573, when the city surrendered to the Royal Catholic forces, the ramparts and gates of the city were demolished, and so now, viewed from afar, without a wall around it, the town looks naked.

If I were a postmodern novelist, I would interpose scenes of my visit with Marion to the city with scenes from its belligerent past. The ironies would be interesting, if not terribly profound. There were Marion and I, going from *cave* to *cave*, learning about the wine and having a great time, and there, in the past, was the story of a brutal siege, where the population was starved out after having been surrounded and bombarded for five months. In the end there was nothing to eat in the town except rats, wood and leather. Only the wine, which the city had been making since Roman times, remained. King Charles IX of France, the monarch in charge during the Saint Bartholomew's Day Massacre of the previous year, and still very much in charge along with his mother Catherine de' Medici, required tribute from the demolished and emptied city, and in lieu of cash accepted 2000 litres of Sancerre.

If ever one is tempted to bemoan what sociologist Max Weber originally called the disenchantment of the world, and to decry having to live in what he called the 'iron cage' of modernity, one should remember what it was like when the world was still enchanted. When life was still universally governed by the magically ultimate ends of religious faith, it was possible to fight to the death over the ends of religious faith – or to find oneself and one's family starved to death as a victim or martyr. The most famous part of the story of the siege of Sancerre is a case of cannibalism, where a winemaker and his wife were said to have eaten 'the head, the brains, the liver and the viscera of their three-year-old daughter, who had just died of hunger and languor.' Jean de Léry, the Protestant minister who reports the incident, complained that the couple ought to have been able to hold out another day at least, for they had some vegetable soup with them, along with wine. But they had been overcome by a 'inordinate' appetite, for which they themselves were to blame. They were quickly executed by the town's authorities, to make an example. When Shakespeare had King Lear think about unaccommodated man, he was thinking in part about 'man' in a post-sectarian context, about 'man' reduced below the level of ultimate ends and religious faith, the bare-forked animal reduced to the imperatives of survival. And he has Lear hint at the idea that this 'man' is what ought to replace in Western thought the religious idea of the ultimate end. 'Man' should be the object of our care.

Marion and I discovered a tight-knit community of 1700 souls, not particularly well equipped to receive tourists but dedicated to the making, the storing, the promoting, the selling and the enjoying of its wine. We attended our first French wine tastings and lessons in the science of oenology. We learned how one wine was ready to be drunk and how another needed another six months of aging first, and marvelled at how the wine tasters could tell the difference. The emphasis, to my surprise, was on the *objective* qualities of wine. We weren't overwhelmed with information about phenolic compounds and the advantages of malolactic fermentation, but we were educated in how a sip of wine interacts with different parts of our mouth because of the different kinds of receptors in the mouth and different chemicals in the wine. We were trained to smell a wine for overtones of lychee nuts, or grapefruit or blackberries or violets or cocoa or nutmeg or sage. In blind tastings we learned about the differences in the mouth between red, white and rosé, between wines that were young and wines that were old, between wines that had been aged in oak and wines that bottled without oak-aging. The wine makers of Sancerre were eager to explain to customers like us why the wines of Sancerre were so exceptional – even though, of course, even the best Sancerre wines cannot compete with the very good wines of regions like Burgundy and Bordeaux. The answer was in the soil, above all, soil that was dominated by clay, limestone, marl or flint (it is different in different parts of the region), but the answer was also in the slant of the sun, the water table level, the climate-moderating influence of the Loire and of the forested areas to the west, the age and health of vine stocks. The answer, too, was in the winemakers themselves, bound together for generations in an enterprise full of family rivalries and corporate quarrels but united in the idea of Sancerre itself – Sancerre as a brand, in the textbook marketing sense, Sancerre as an *appellation controllée,* in the French system of *appellations,* and especially Sancerre as the name of a way of life nourished by its inhabitants.

I should mention, however, that Sancerre has no public market, and to go grocery shopping inhabitants of the hilltop town have to descend by car or bus down a long windy road to a Carrefour Market at the bottom, a market which the town has to share with its valley neighbour the town of Saint Satur.

Anyway, though on the one hand a form of salesmanship and hype is inescapable as one wanders through a town and the countryside of a place like Sancerre, so there is also a real form of commitment to what is at once a way of life and a thing, the wine. And it is always to the wine and its objective qualities that one's attention is drawn. You like it or you don't like it, yes of course, but nobody really wants to hear about likes and dislikes. One wants to hear if the wine is 'fruity' or 'structured', 'open' or 'closed', 'florid' or 'earthy', worthy of aging or ready to drink. One wants to know what is *in* the wine and how it got there. Even quality is discussed as a characteristic of the thing which can be empirically demonstrated. In any basic tasting, the acolyte is given a range of wines to taste from the thriftiest to the best (and most expensive), and again and again, on the basis of the comparison as one graduates from one wine to another, one finds that the best (and most expensive) is in fact the best. All the other wines seem to have been leading up to it. All the other wines seem to have been missing some things which the final wine triumphantly delivers: a balance and a depth, a smoothness and a complexity, a surprising delectability.

Then of course comes the buying decision. You can't taste, unless you want to risk being impolite, without buying. The good news is that the wineries and *négociants* and even some of the local shops sell the local wine at a price much lower than retail: 'chateau price' some people call it. So there and then, in Sancerre, Marion and I started taking notes and buying, a little of this and a little of that, choosing from among the different price points, sometimes getting the really cheap stuff and occasionally the really good stuff, until we had actually accumulated a great deal.

Our hotel situation in Sancerre was not the best – a musky dump with exceptionally bad food, cooked from boil n' bags. Nor would our accommodation be free of ups and downs for the rest of the trip, as we alternated between camp sites and cheap hotels. We were never free of a sense of our material limits. Again and again we had to battle the weather, the hard ground, the patter of rain, the uncomfortable smell (when you are trying to sleep) of wet soil and fungus, or the rough roar of morning traffic passing just behind the hedge over our heads, spinning wheels along the rough pavement. Every hotel room we allowed ourselves to enter was a palace of dry warmth, quiet and cleanliness, even if they were often cramped or rustic or simply modern and basic and bland. There is a great variety in the standards of living experienced by travellers, and in France, when you enter a town, you experience that variety at once. You have to make a choice of where to stay, according to what standard of living, and it is clear what the consequences of your choice, and the imperatives that drive that choice, actually are. One star, two star, three star, or more: it is an admirable system, this rating of hotels in France, and guidebooks usually offer good supplementary information, so that when you get somewhere you know what you are going to get, for how much and why. But the rationality of the system, so admirable, is also an expression of the class divisions that organise the society from which and into which the tourist travels. Travelling like we did slaps you in the face with class division. You may ignore it, resent it, or take comfort in it, depending on who you are, but there it is: it is your world. For us, as I have said, it was a constant reminder of our material limits: we could go just so far in experience, and no further: we could find and satisfy desire just so far and no further. We didn't mind so much that we were in two-star hotels because at least they weren't campsites. But we couldn't eat in a lot of places we would have liked to eat, and that did disappoint us.

And what did it all mean? It couldn't mean nothing. Just as it couldn't mean nothing that French towns were nowadays ringed with nightmares of retail development, so it couldn't mean nothing that there Marion and I were, looking for pleasure, and confronting our limits. It couldn't mean nothing, for one thing, because although Marion and I have our idiosyncrasies, and although we belong to one social class or cultural class rather than another, with one set of tastes and inclinations rather than another, we were, in the basic form of what we were doing – *going on a holiday, travelling, sightseeing, eating and drinking* – doing what millions of others are doing, living as millions of others are doing, and *living for* as millions of others are living for. *Living for*: that is a principle difference between an animal and a person. A person lives for. And what were Marion and I living for, just then? Well, we were living for the pleasure of it (and so also surely to repress and displace) but also to learn our limits in the pleasure of it, and to learn not only our limits but what would be beyond our limits if we didn't have them, what we would *want* and *need* and *crave* if we were capable of them.

Of course our limits were not just about commodities. For the fact is that as dreamers – because for all our other qualities and failures both Marion and I are this: we are dreamers – we were looking for a system. We were looking for a system of experience. We were looking, in the end, for a home, a destination that, when you got there, was the last destination at which you felt you needed to arrive.

¤ ¤ ¤

Marion and I turned away from the Loire as we got past Tours and went up toward the regions of Morbihan and Finistère. Then we came back down the coast to La Rochelle and the Charente-Maritime, until we arrived in the Bordeaux region. For a week we stayed at a campsite next to a beach on the Atlantic Ocean, about 30 minutes drive from Pauillac, the heart of 'Left Bank' Bordeaux wines, and then we went down to Bordeaux itself, and then back toward the Atlantic to enjoy the Côte d'Argent: the seaside town of Arcachon and the great sand dunes to the south. We turned back east and slowly passed through the region of the Dordogne, including a stop by Moncaret to see the chateau of the sixteenth century writer Michel de Montaigne. Then we hurried to Clermont-Ferrand and, to cap off our trip, we stopped in Lyon and the wine towns of Burgundy.

The weather was clear and warm during most of the last half

of our journey, though I recall a pretty fierce rainstorm one night when we staying in the campsite, under a canopy of towering pines, on the Bordeaux coast. In any case, we found ourselves worrying less and less about the expense of our trip. We were already over budget, and there we were, in France, with all these delicacies to try: the *fruits de mer à la marmite* in Vannes, in Brittany; the *cuisses de grenouilles sauté à l'ail* and the *raie au beurre noire* in Saint Michel Chef Chef, a seaside town in the Loire Atlantique; the *gambas à la plancha, sauce madère* and the *huitres aux saucissons* in Arcachon; the *bar en croûte de sel* and the *foie de veau grillé* at a restaurant in Bergerac called, counter-intuitively, *L'Imparfait;* the *pied de cochon* and the *quenelles de brochet Lyonnaise* in a *bouchon* in Lyon. And there was always the hope, for Marion, that still one more restaurant before us would serve a house-made *tarte tatin* for dessert, and she would ultimately come face to face with the bright Platonic Idea of apple pie. The hell with the budget.

It is hard to express the joy we had in eating these meals together, along with the wine of course, or of simply tooling through the countryside with the stereo on, listening to Bob Dylan, and thinking where we would next stop, try our next bottle of wine or our next example of the local cuisine. The sociologist Max Weber inveighed against the modern 'sensualist without heart', imprisoned by his own sensuality to an economic system over which he has no control, but Marion and I, it seemed to me, had heart. It occurred to me that these meals would have been pointless, and hardly even much fun, if Marion and I weren't enjoying them together. The communion was essential: looking into each other's eyes and clinking glasses, digging into our dishes with a steady collective rhythm, taking our bites together, feeling the atmosphere and communicating with the staff at the restaurant together, and letting the taste of the food and the heat of the wine work on us together. It occurred to me too that the food we had could not have been as good as it was if the people making and serving it did not feel so connected to the food, connected to it as an expression of where they were and who they were and the values they wanted to stand for. In the huckster worlds of the United States and the UK there is plenty of room for scepticism and irony about these things: the restaurant is a commercial enterprise, the business of the restaurant is to make money, and everything else is whatever sells, including the *fashion* of the restaurant, one of the features of its fashion being that inescapable thing, *cuisine*. But here, in provincial France, there was plenty of commitment and belief. It was a belief in a way of living.

Driving along, in our 2003 5-door marine blue Nissan Primera SE ('Nice car' said a Frenchman to Marion, as we drifted on the ferry across the Gironde from Blaye to Paulliac), on smooth roads, we listened, as I said, to Bob Dylan: Dylan was a compromise, because I wouldn't listen to a lot of her favourite rock, and she wouldn't listen to a lot of my favourite jazz. We decided to rediscover Dylan together. We listened especially, again and again, to *Blood on the Tracks*, an album edgy with sadness, anger, bitterness and uneasy humour, inspired apparently by Dylan's break-up with his first wife: we listened, thrilled, knowing that those emotions were also ours, but not for now. For now we were living in a different key. We stopped at as many wineries open to the public and town-sponsored *maisons de vin* as we could. Some of the winery owners were self-conscious and defensive, a little embarrassed at having to sell their wares to the public. Others were open and the enthusiastic. They told us their life stories. They showed us around their grounds. They showed us the grapes on the vine and inveighed against the wet weather. And no matter where we went, we bought. We bought with a memory: after the wines of the Loire, the wines of Blaye and of left bank Bordeaux with place names like St.-Estèphe, Médoc, Haut Médoc, Margaux or just plain Bordeaux Supèrieure. We crammed the boot of the car with cases, and then more cases, always thinking of the places where we had been and the people we had met and the tastes we had had and the tastes we would have in the future, when we got home. We bought reds, a small number of whites and even rosès, wines that the people of Mèdoc liked to call Clairet. We moved on from Bordeaux toward Lyon with the boot of our car starting to drag, and our clothes and camping equipment bunched up in the back seat. The countryside fell around us, whistling against the doors of our car, while Dylan was screaming in anguish,

> Idiot wind, blowing through the buttons of our coats,
> Blowing through the letters that we wrote.
> Idiot wind, blowing through the dust upon our shelves,
> We're idiots, babe.
> It's a wonder we can even feed ourselves.

And then we were in Burgundy, buying up white wines, for the most part, spending most of our time in Côtes d'Or. We got some Meursault, one of the queens of the white wine world, but we also bought some Côtes de Beaune and Côtes de Beaune Villages and a few bottles of Chablis and some generic Bourgogne Blanc and Bourgogne Aligoté, along with a few reds from Beaune, Nuits St-Georges and Marsannay. Marion kept finding room and more room in the car. We had cartons of wine in the back seat now as well as the boot. Our gear was piled up to the roof and my rear view mirror was useless. The car was riding low to the ground. But how could we not stop buying? When would wine this good ever be this cheap for us again?

By the time we got to Calais, our final stop before taking the ferry back to England, our car was so overloaded that I had to be cautious about turns, and our mileage had dropped from about thirty-eight miles per gallon to something like twenty. The money we had saved on wine we were paying back again in petrol. But still we roamed the streets to get some last bottles of Calvados and Cognac and Beaujolais and rosé from a region we had skipped, Provence. Over the month we had gone over budget by about 2000 pounds sterling, and still we were shopping. Still we were eating well too. Though Calais is a town with little charm – much of it makes you feel like you're back in suburban England – our hotel was on a busy street with plenty of restaurants, and we found an excellent one, recommended by our *Guide Michelin*, serving *cuisine classique*. In fact, it was called *Histoire Ancienne* and the menu was unimaginative and I forget what we ate but it was really really good and we had a nice bottle probably of Brouilly with it, followed by a glass or two of Calvados and now we were even more over budget but it was our last day in France and by now ... well the hell with the budget.

The next day, bleary-eyed, we drove off to the ferry, and by the early afternoon we were back in England, heading along the motorway north. By midnight we were home, back in Lancaster, back in our comfortable, dry warm house. By our count, accomplished the next morning as we emptied our car of luggage, camping gear, and booty, in addition to about a half dozen bottles of spirits, we had brought back – somehow, impossibly I would have thought, given the dimensions of our car – twenty-seven cases of wine, that is one hundred sixty-two bottles: red, white and rosé, cheap and dear, wine to drink now and wine to keep, wine that was fruity and wine that was structured, wine that was common and wine that was rare, wine that smelled of perfume and wine that smelled of the earth, wine that was ready to drink and wine that warranted years of keeping, wine from the Loire, from Bordeaux, from Beaujolais and Burgundy and even Provence, and all of it ours, ours to drink and share with friends. It was a little sad being home after a thirty-one day holiday, and alarming to think how much money we had spent, but no matter: looking at the boxes of wine stacked up in our hallway, our arms around each other, Marion and I felt like winners.

Chapter Six

Beyond Confusion

I visited England for the first time in the spring of 1993, while I was a graduate student at Berkeley. I was still in the thrall of my obsession with the woman I have called Alison, but I was getting toward the end of it. Somehow. I got a grant from the university to go to Italy for a conference and then to England to do research for my dissertation at the British Library. Italy was as I remembered it from a journey twenty years before – a big red balloon of a country. That's not how Italians themselves would describe it; many Italians are bitter today; the young people are leaving; they have been leaving for years, in search of opportunity. But for me, as a visitor, it was a big red hot air balloon, what with the easy hospitality I encountered everywhere, the food and the wine and the architecture and the art and the hilarity of the street life. I got high on Italy, again. England, however, was different. England was business. England was work. And England, I felt, might be home.

Not that I imagined, at the moment, that someday I would actually move there and prosper. But it seemed, in London, where I spent almost all of my time on this visit, that I already knew my way around. I didn't need a map or a compass. I could just go, however crooked the streets. Down the Strand, up Bond Street, across on Oxford Street, or along Shaftesbury and down Kingsway and then around India House to the banks of the Thames, I just went. I seldom lost my way. 'What a lark!', as a certain Mrs Dalloway once said to herself in rather finer weather than I encountered. And sometimes, when I dawdled in Bloomsbury, where I was staying and working, in one of the squares, and I looked up at the stately but often very plain brick buildings surrounding me, and the budding trees struggling for height, I felt like I was in the centre of the universe. I still do, sometimes, when I visit the area, even though I know that the impression is false; it is only an effect of the imperial style that the city adopted long ago and of the bracing chill in the air.

But what was I doing there? My life had been stripped of metaphors by that point. It was just itself and I was trying to survive. Or rather, I was trying to find a way out. I cannot say that I felt imprisoned or caged or lost in a labyrinth or a fun house or a marooned on a strange and hostile planet; there was no figurative shape to my predicament. But I was trying to find a 'way out' to the extent that, once I found it, I would know that I was surviving. Something had gone wrong in my life and I had to find a way out of this wrongness.

Once, when I still driving a limousine for a living, I dropped off a couple of elderly ladies for lunch at the Stanford Mall, in Palo Alto. I had some time to kill and unusually, since I was out of narrow busy San Francisco, I had a safe and quiet place to park. So I left the limo and wandered into the mall and eventually found myself at a bookshop. I needed something that would divert me while I sat perched in the front of my limo, waiting for customers, not something too difficult or over-involving but not something stupid either. So I purchased a copy of *Lives of the Modern Poets*, by William H. Pritchard. It was a study, modelled after Samuel Johnson's *Lives of the Poets*, of nine early twentieth-century figures, from Thomas Hardy to William Carlos Williams. It was a very old-fashioned study, I now know, a bit naïve about the nature of literature and criticism, more eager to praise or blame than to understand. The book was innocent of what is called the 'hermeneutics of suspicion'. But I enjoyed it and I went one by one through Pritchard's stories of the lives of these poets, illustrated with excerpts from their poems. At home, as it happened, I had a copy of the collected poems of Robert Frost, so as I read about the life and works of Frost I also dipped into Frost's verse. That I had the time and energy to do this was itself unusual. But this was a period shortly before my meeting with the woman I call Maggie, and I was already driving less than I had before, Thursdays through Saturdays (though putting in very long days), while earning more money, and I had more spare time on my hands than I had had in years. By Tuesday, after a Sunday and Monday of recovery, I was rested and alert again, and my time was free. It must have been on one of those Tuesdays or Wednesdays that I was home alone, my daughter being away at day care, my wife away at work, with a space of about thirty-six or twelve hours ahead of me before I had to get back in the saddle of my limousine, and I was reading through *Lives of the Modern Poets* and thumbing through my edition of the poems of Robert Frost. I still have that edition, yellowed now, a paperback with a pale green cover showing trees in a fog, dating from 1975, in my office in Uppsala, Sweden. Pritchard alerted me to a poem called 'Directive', which begins,

> Left home at about three pm fully loaded

and which ends,

> Here are your waters and your watering place.
> Drink and be whole again beyond confusion.

I knew right away that I had found a poem that expressed something I needed to see expressed. 'Back out of all this now too much for us …' There I was alone, relaxed, alert. I was thinking, reading, responding. I was me, trying to deal with the excess of my existence. That information came to me unexpectedly. I was me, trying to cope. Like the time I was stooped on my tricycle, at the age of three, in Euclid, Ohio, I was me, trying to figure things out. And I – I, the I and me that I was – wanted to drink and be whole again. Or rather, this 'I' wanted to read poems about being overwhelmed by life and drinking redemptive waters and being whole, and it wanted to read criticism about poems that were on this subject. This 'I' did not want to drive a limousine anymore, and this 'I' would do something to put an end to it. This 'I' would go back to school.

So by the spring of 1993 I was a graduate student in good standing at Berkeley, earning grant money and teaching money and also borrowing money from the federal government to make ends meet, and I was in London, in Bloomsbury, doing research at the British Library. I was not going about my business in London in the spirit of 'I am me', however. I could not avoid the feeling that there was something false about my situation. The economics of my situation was false. Even with the grant, I could not really afford this trip. Even with the federal loans, I was financially under water, and when the loans came due my finances would only worsen. (The money from Maggie was long gone too.), And far from being 'me', I was rather a stranger to myself, trying to escape from the wrongness of myself by pretending to be something I wasn't: an emerging scholar, writing about a world he did not belong to, representing a famous institution. Instead, in my depths, I was a man in sorrow, a stranger to himself, and a worried man to boot. How would I survive? I should never have come to London, I told myself. But there was no alternative except to come to London.

For several years, possibly from even before the day when my marriage broke up, in 1988, I had been living in anguish. A musical refrain went through my head at all hours, a refrain without any notes, just words and a cadence reiterated as if in search of the notes of a song:

> What shall I do with my unhappiness?
> Oh yes, and what shall I do with my unhappiness?

It was like a coarse wool blanket enveloping my head, shading my eyes, obscuring my vision, bundled at my neck, hot and scratchy on my shoulders: my unhappiness. On the one hand, I was weighed down by certain undeniable objective facts: that my life had gone awry, that I had allowed myself to enter a loveless marriage and then allowed the marriage to deteriorate and collapse and caused myself to be alienated from my daughter, that I had failed to find a career to pursue, that I was financially and spiritually hard up and I was getting older and weaker and had all but run out of chances. This business of being a scholar was a desperate sham. On the other hand, I was weighed down by unhappiness itself. I had lost my ability to adapt. I had lost my ability to be cheerful. I had lost my ability to give or to achieve and, except for my feelings for my daughter, to love. I had instead acquired an ability and an inclination, quietly, to hate. And what could a man, stuck in loathing – first for himself, and then for everyone else – ever do, whether for himself or for others?

When I met Alison, in 1992, my condition changed. From heavy depression I went to delirious joy, and then from joy – as soon as the relationship turned sour, and I got caught up in an obsession about it – I went to anxiety. Anxiety is the other side of depression. Depression is a blanket you can't toss off. Anxiety is a fog that you can't get out of, even as oncoming vehicles, unseen but speeding toward you, are threatening your life. Sometimes you can just scream, or go dizzy with inertia. The crash is going to come. The best you can do is reach for something to medicate and blind yourself with – in those days, for me, that cheap California brandy, a bottle of which I kept next to my bed, and from which I drank all night as I lurched from drowsiness to wakefulness again and again.

Depression and anxiety. They are frequently diagnosed today as a binary syndrome, a 'disorder' with two equally unhappy symptoms. When I was especially depressed, as in the days before I started dating again and met Alison, my anxieties were often dulled, hidden or repressed. I was too sad to worry; sadness was worry enough. When I was especially anxious, as in the days after Alison, my sadness was as it were postponed. I had a more immediate *something* irrationally coming toward me, and I had to act, quick – through flight. Sadness was irrelevant at such a time. But often, I felt a little bit depressed and a little bit anxious. And meanwhile, somehow, I had to go on and live.

But there was no metaphor. I have described depression and anxiety metaphorically, and to the extent that I understood my condition I recognised the metaphors that could be attached to it. But being in London, just being there, doing research – there was no metaphor for that. It was just something I had to do because I could do it, and because it might help me survive.

I was going to the British Library, reading as many books and pamphlets as I could from what is called the Thomason Collection. Between 1640 and 1661, a bookseller and publisher named George Thomason endeavoured to collect every single item of print published in London at the time, along with as many other works he could get a hold of that were published in the provinces or abroad. These were the years of the English Revolution, a time when the censorship of the press was effectively abolished, wars of ideas as well as wars of arms were raging, and the people of the country had a lot to say, in print, to one another. The shape of the future was at stake. The collection contains over twenty-two thousand items and all of them were stored in the British Library, along with easily accessible photocopies, bound in volumes you ordered from a cage. I was trying to sample items I could not find back in California, dipping into the texts trying to get a sense of who was writing what, for what purposes, trying to grasp what I was calling the 'discourse' of the period. I only had ten days. I did not have a computer. Laptops were something new and rare. I took a spiral notebook and a pencil and wrote feverishly, transcribing and summarising. Luckily, I had a good idea of what I was looking for: works whose authors, in the midst of the conflict that had split England apart, were thinking about ideal societies, imagining what it would be like if England, or some other place – a remote island, or even a colony on the moon – was entirely happy, vigorous and just.

There was no irony in my historical researches. That is, it was not absurd that a man in my condition, alienated from the world, recovering from one emotional collapse and on the edge of another, was studying the impulse toward imagining an ideal society. There were precedents in this. The great seventeenth century recluse Robert Burton, in his *Anatomy of Melancholy*, included in that work – written, he said, to keep his own melancholy at bay – an extended 'Utopia of Mine Owne'. Melancholiacs can be idealists; their idealism is one of the things that make them melancholiacs, and vice versa. And in any case I was not doing this research in order to find a way to promote utopianism. I thought of my project as an engagement with tragedy. The story of utopian thinking in the seventeenth century in England – and that's what I was doing, it became clearer and clearer to me, not producing an analysis but writing a story – would prove, in my hands, to be a tragedy. It would be the story of a great and necessary failure. For in the end, utopia would lose, the Revolution would come to a halt, the idealistic imagination would peter out and savage pragmatism would triumph. Whether or not that was the correct interpretation of the seventeenth century, finding the means of this interpretation – though with an open mind, since after all facts had to be respected – was one of my motivations in heading into the reading rooms of the British Library. And writing this dissertation, and the book that I would eventually construct out of that dissertation, writing this tragedy, in other words, became for me a task demanding completion, a task taking precedence over any other. It was one of the things that kept me from trying to kill myself.

So ... London, and the British Library, and evenings spent

wandering the streets, looking for somewhere cheap to eat or to drink, diving into bistros and pubs. Wandering the streets but never getting lost. Discovering Fitzrovia, a well-lighted neighbourhood of restaurants and bars and the rich and the poor, once a neighbourhood of writers and musicians, on the way between Bloomsbury and Soho (a place where a character in Saul Bellow once said that one could be happy forever.) Trying the Indian food (and usually being disappointed). Looking at the girls, hoping to meet someone. Learning pub etiquette in the pubs. You drank beer there, mostly, not the brandy I kept trying to order, to the befuddlement of the bar attendants. And you always said 'please'. And you were patient. One night I went to see Harold Pinter performing in his own play at the Comedy Theatre, *No Man's Land*, where one of the characters, drunk, pronounces at the end that he and the rest of them are 'in no man's land. Which never moves, which never changes, which never grows older, but which remains forever icy and silent', and his interlocutor (played by Pinter) concludes the play by saying, 'I'll drink to that'. I left the theatre unhappy. Another night, I talked one of my co-residents at the pension house where I was staying to go out for, yes, a drink at a pub – back in Fitzrovia – and chat up some girls. We succeeded in meeting a pair of young good-looking nursing students, who weren't interested in anything from us but a little bit of conversation. I went on and on, in my cups and desperate to have something to say and make an impression, about how nursing was a terrific profession, and how nurses in the United States made a lot of money. The young women let me know that they weren't sure how terrific their future profession actually was, and that in the United Kingdom nurses were not paid all that much. They named a figure. I said it couldn't be. I said that in America nurses earned at least twice as much, just to start. They thanked me for the information and soon went on their way – wandering off, as women in London do, and as women in urban America in the early nineties almost never did, alone, into the dark streets, without feeling at all endangered, and certainly feeling (as they assured me, getting rid of me) without a need for male protection.

I meandered through this great old West End of London seeing what to my eyes was clearly a superior civilisation to the one I had been confined to all these years, the American one, California-style, and yet ever annoyed at what seemed wrong about it. For example, that nurses weren't paid so much. Or for example, that those young women doomed to a lifetime of ill-paid worked seemed resigned to that fact, seemed to accept their fate with dull equanimity. For example, that in 1993, after over a decade of Thatcher and Thatcherism the infrastructure of the city was coming apart. Pavement stones came loose everywhere you went. Paint was peeling. Tiles were falling. The buses were old, smoky and gummy inside. The people seemed ill-dressed, wearing wrinkled, ill-fitting and colourless garments, and they seemed unhealthy to boot, with bad complexions, poor posture and stringy hair. Dowdiness seemed to be the rule of thumb – a condition not just to tolerate but to aspire to, as if it were a matter of pride to look distressed. When you walked into the old British Library, with its great old wood-shelving-lined circular reading room, you could smell the plumbing. You could smell the plumbing in pubs and restaurants too, not to mention the rotten pension house where I was staying. A century of shit had clogged up the bowels of the metropolis, and nothing was being done to clean it out. The food in most places was appalling and it was impossible, in 1993, to get a decent cup of coffee.

I observed all these things with a mixture of sadness and contempt. Of course I had no right, or at least no need, to observe them with sadness and contempt. I could have been dispassionate. But in my condition, when anything that did not match my hopes or expectations was a catastrophe, I was angry at it. As if the crumbling pavement by the streets or the decrepit plumbing in the library or in the pubs or the bad coffee in the breakfast hall were a personal affront, I was indignant. How dare the city be like this! I was even angry at Harold Pinter. How dare a man as successful as him, as rich and famous and sought after and powerful and even well married – Lady Antonia Fraser was his wife, after all! – put on a play about life being 'icy and silent'? And where was the politics, from this playwright who allied himself with the radical left? Where was the drama of action, of urgency and hope for change?

It was intolerable, really. That a people could become so quiescent at their own decay. That a city like this could allow itself to become so run down, and so fatalistic. It made me incredulous. It made me dizzy. It made me take to my room in the smelly old pension house, a refuge for underprivileged scholars, where even the floorboards seemed to gurgle with intestinal gasses, and get my bottle out of the drawer, a pint of Courvoisier V.S. purchased from a cramped, dowdy tobacco shop, and drink and drink until and anger and the pain seemed to go away, and I wasn't – well, so lonely, so lost, so defeated ...

One day thumbing through a volume in the north wing of the library I discovered a hitherto unknown utopian tract from 1659, by an obscure author named John Streater. The tract was called *Government described: viz. what monarchie, aristocracie, oligarchie, and democracie, is. Together with a brief model of the government of the common-wealth, or, free-state of Ragouse*. A fellow scholar at the pension house later explained to me what 'Ragouse' was: it was Ragusa, the famous, idyllic city of the Adriatic Coast now called Dubrovnik, dating back to the Middle Ages a republic under the imperial sway of Venice. Streater described the city as an ideal state, which he thought England ought to model itself after. On my return to Berkeley I researched the tract and Ragusa some more, and put together an essay, 'Utopian Dubrovnik, 1659: An English Fantasy'. It would be my first serious academic publication.

¤ ¤ ¤

Nine years later, one dark January evening, I was in my office at the University of San Diego. This office had probably once been a storage closet. It was four feet by six feet wide. It had no windows or ventilation and stood off the anteroom to a pair of large, bright offices with views of the evergreen trees outside housing two professors who, unlike me, were either tenured or on the tenure-track. Anyway, it was late in the workday and I was apprehensive. I hadn't heard from my head of department when the second round of interviews would come for the tenure-track position in the department I had already applied and interviewed for. The job was in my field, to replace a woman who was resigning because of ill health, and whose role in the department I had already been filling for the past two-and-a-half years. I had by then already published the book on seventeenth-century utopias, with Cambridge University Press, as well as a number of articles in well-regarded journals, like *Shakespeare Quarterly*, and I was in the process of a producing two more books. Meanwhile, I had so far managed to make myself a part of the university community as to organise a teach-in, attended by over sixty students and faculty members, on the impending War in Iraq. But several weeks after I had gone through the strange ritual of travelling to the Modern Language Association annual conference, held that year in New York City, and interviewed for the job with colleagues whose offices were just a few feet away from where I was now sitting in San Diego, I hadn't heard anything. So I got up, walked down the hall, and let myself into the office of the head of department. I said 'Hi' to him with a big relaxed smile and started to sit down. I must have said something like, 'Well I am looking forward to hearing about the second interviews.' He looked down, embarrassed, and said he had just written me an email.

What? I ran back to my closet and looked at my email. I was

no longer in the running for the job. I would not be interviewed a second time. Either in the email itself or in a conversation with the head of department I had right after I looked at the email, I was told, in no uncertain terms, that as far as the head of department was concerned I would not make a very good colleague. 'Would not': I am quite sure that it was the conditional that he used.

And so came to an end a process that had begun in 1996, when I had pretty much finished my dissertation at Berkeley, of trying to get a job in American academia, a process I had begun in high hopes, with the backing of my supervisors and other advisors, a process which saw me apply for well over a hundred jobs and interview for at least twenty-five of them, maybe more, taking me around the country, from the state of Washington to the state of Maine and even down to Alabama. San Diego was the end of the line for me; there was no doubt about that. I had been popular as a job candidate when I was just finishing my degree, and popular for a couple of years more, and then I succumbed to the unwritten rule that someone who has not gotten a permanent job fresh out of the gate of grad school is, as the phrase went, 'damaged goods'. All along I had to struggle against the stream, first, in that starting at around 1996 there was a dramatic drop-off in the number of permanent full-time jobs available to humanists in American academia; second, in that I was male and white and unquestionably heterosexual, in an era when departments were striving for 'diversity' in their hiring; third, in that I was old. I had been lucky in one thing, that I never looked my age. I had kept all my hair. I still have all my hair. My hair kept its texture and colour too: thick deep sepia. It is still a thick deep sepia, with silver highlights now. My face betrayed neither wrinkles nor sags. I had no crow's feet around my eyes, or puckers around my lips. My cheeks didn't sag. By an absolute accident of nature, though my spirits might weary, my paunch expand, my teeth rot and the joints in my legs, hips and arms swell and ache, I had the face of a man much younger than myself. I was like Dorian Gray – I just couldn't show on the outside the degradation within. But still, there was no mistaking me for a twenty-seven-year-old. I spoke with the voice of a man who had experienced the world, who had raised a child, who had effectively lost a child, having moved against his will thousands of miles away from her for the sake of a job, who had had other hard licks and had experienced the fundamental disappointment of losing his youth and finding out that life would never match his expectations. I could not enter an interview for a job with what may have been the most sought-after quality from a candidate in those days: that one still held onto one's youthful illusions. And now, in 2003, in San Diego, I was fifty-one-years old. And at fifty-one I was rejected and done with.

¤ ¤ ¤

In San Diego it always feels like morning. Even at sunset, which you can see most evenings as a deep scarlet sigh over a retiring silver ocean, it feels like morning. Even in the dark of night, in the stillness, it feels like morning. The air is almost always warm and gentle, not blowing but lifting, opening its hand as if in expectation of events to come. And the events never come. It is always morning.

I arrived in San Diego, in the year 2000, in the midst of an economic boom. The San Francisco Bay Area was overcrowded, the Los Angeles area was overstretched, and so a lot of the pent-up energy among computer and biotechnology and general 'hi-tech' people were coming to California's southernmost, quietest and most conservative city. Some of the boom was home-grown, of course – but home-grown, in San Diego as in any other town of California, can mean having been in residence for ten years rather than two. In 1970 there were 1.3 million people living in San Diego County: by the time I got there, the population had more than doubled, to 2.8 million. A building boom was on when I arrived, but builders could not keep up with demand, and prices were high and getting higher. Rentals were hard to find. And I experienced again the hardship of being a newcomer, an incoming migrant with limited resources and few connections. Unlike Birmingham, Alabama, at least, where the previous year I had been turned down in my application to rent an apartment I wanted essentially because I was not from Alabama, in San Diego, like everywhere else in California, no one cares where you are from, or how long you have been there. They only care about what you have. But the competition for desirable neighbourhoods, though of course there are many different versions of the 'desirable', was fierce. I was always someone who wanted to live in the midst of things, as close to the centre of a city as possible, in a neighbourhood where I could walk to shops and cafés and public parks. There had never been many such neighbourhoods in the car culture city of San Diego, however. Parts of San Diego were being reinvented as pedestrian, urban environments when I got there, it was true, but they were being invented for the well-to-do. All over the Western world, I now know, since the 1970s urbanity was being reinvented, and reinvented almost entirely for the well-to-do. In older cities it was called 'gentrification'. In newer cities it was called 'redevelopment'. But it has almost always been a gentrification or a redevelopment for the middle class. And as an itinerant instructor in English literature, with no savings or other assets except boxes of books and a car, I didn't meet the economic threshold. I almost ended up homeless. Luckily, at the eleventh hour I had succeeded in salvaging a relationship that had begun in San Francisco with a woman working for a booming dot.com enterprise, which gave her permission to move her territory to Southern California. So I was able to cohabit and split the rent, and we got a nice if dark apartment on the edge of a wooded ravine, near enough to most of the things I wanted to be near to, including the beach, though not quite near enough to walk to any of them. I still had to drive everywhere. And in any case, shortly after we settled in together the dot.com company went bust, and my partner was unemployed, and we had to struggle to pay the rent and we lived tumultuously from paycheque to paycheque together, in anger with one another.

As the prices of food and clothing got lower in the Western world, thanks to a combination of technological miracles and globalisation, the price of real estate got higher. As incomes became more and more unequal, with the wealth of Western world becoming ever more dependent, again, on cheap labour, even while vast amounts of wealth were being created for the few, new systems of material inequality came into being. Food, clothing and, at least in America, cars and gasoline and electronic gadgets and mass entertainment were cheap and readily available, but something that someone like me would recognise as a *quality of life* became more and more a privilege of the few. A good education, good health care, good housing, good life opportunities, a safe and pleasant environment, intellectual stimulation, access to art and leisure … these things were breaking off from the mainstream of life in the West, especially in America. And the main sign of all this, for me, was that it was becoming harder and harder to find a decent place to live. As a have-not instead of a have, I couldn't compete. I had to make do with living in a ravine. It suited my bare need for shelter but it had nothing to do with my desire.

By the end of two years, my relationship having burst apart under the pressure of too many pressures, I was single again, and all I could do was to move in to a tiny, furnished one bedroom student apartment on the campus of the University of San Diego, getting it rent-free in return for being a 'tutor' of some sort to the official residents of the complex, my job specifications having never been fully fleshed out. I had spent the two years working very hard, vainly, to progress my career. I published. I taught. I invented new kinds of courses to teach: a course on terrorism and literature, for example, and another on literature and food, not to mention, for the tradition-minded, a course on the sixteenth-century lyric. I applied for jobs. I travelled to the big conferences. I interviewed in New York, in Chicago, in Saint Louis, in Kansas City, in Fort Collins, Colorado. I went to Toronto. Nothing. I was unable to get people to like me. I was unable to make them trust me. I even got a call to travel to Cambridge, England, to interview at Cambridge University. There I discovered that what was important was not convincing people to like or trust me – the British are far too sophisticated for that – but showing that I was one of them, like Conrad's Lord Jim. And of course, that was one thing I could not do, prove that I was one of them. I couldn't even imagine what it would be like to live and work in Cambridge, England. It might as well have been the moon.

And so there I was, living alone in student housing, fifty-one years old, with all my other options exhausted, being told that I would not make a good colleague. I had had some other interviews that year, but had already been turned down. It was the end of the line for me. Financially I could survive maybe another half a year, because I had saved money by not paying rent during the academic year, and I would be able to collect unemployment insurance for a while. But I would have nowhere to live. And I would have no prospects.

By that time too I had no friends but one, a professor at another university who had troubles of his own. San Diego is a town where people refrain from depending on one another, and also then from helping one another. People live far apart from one another, in their houses surrounded by lawns, as if by protective moats, and they abide by the principles of a kind of anesthetised system of self-reliance. I shall overcome because I shall not feel. Alone, I shall not feel. Nor will you. There are many destinations where people congregate around the year, the shopping malls, the restaurant districts, the beaches, but there are no common by-ways except for the high speed motorways and the lower speed, pedestrian-free, noisy urban roads. And there was no sense of community, anywhere, just of lots of houses and roads and leisure-time destinations, where people soaked up the sun, or the beer, or their post-exercise endorphin highs, and then went back to not feeling. Or so it seemed at least to me. I was never welcomed by anyone except that one friend of mine, who I had known for years before, and unfortunately his wife was at best indifferent to me, so that my welcome at his home was reduced by 50% and eventually I stopped going. Even when I arrived at my new job, at the University of San Diego, I was made to feel that no one really cared that I had arrived there. In fact, I was met with a combination of embarrassment and hostility, since after all I was a temporary employee, not a permanent one, and therefore I didn't really matter. I was never invited out by anyone from work, or except on one occasion to anybody's home. How could I be, when everybody lived so far apart from one another, and no one really invited each other out or cared for intimacy with anyone but themselves and maybe their immediate family members, lovers or sports partners? And anyway, this wasn't only affectless San Diego, a town where nothing happened; it was also the University of San Diego, a Catholic school catering to wealthy, above-average students, about half of them Catholic and almost all of them at once earnest, well-mannered, well-tanned, tight-bodied and intellectually timid. My own department was an enclave of mediocrity, most of my colleagues being professionally unaccomplished, and indeed most of them having been unaccomplished for so long that they had come to take pride in it. We were not a research university, but we weren't much of a teaching university either. We were situated on a mesa, overlooking a canyon, and from a lot of different angles on campus you could espy the glint of the Pacific Ocean. The architecture was faux-Spanish, suggesting Jesuit influence, and we were environed by palm trees and rose bushes, and you could smell the wild herbs growing along the dry slopes of the canyon – rosemary, fennel and thyme – as well as the sweet perfume from the roses and the mineral breath of the ocean. It was always morning at the university. The university strived to be at once liberal and Catholic, and it received a lot of money from Joan Kroc, the woman whose husband had founded the McDonald's Corporation. It was unquestionably the most boring place I ever worked at. And there I was, again, in year three, living in a complex among twenty-year olds who never paid any attention to me in return both for my never paying any attention to them and in return also for their never paying any attention to themselves. In June I would have to leave and I had nowhere to go.

I called an old lover, who was living in Iowa, in a small town. There was nothing she could do for me. I had started a new relationship with a woman in San Diego who worked as a graphic designer downtown. But that was no use either. She was already regretting the idea that she might get stuck with a second-rate guy like me – and now, it seemed to me, there was no one left whom she could get stuck to. I was nothing now. There was nothing to me anymore. I could not pay my own way. I could not entertain her. I could not make her happy. And at this point she, too, could do nothing for me.

I tried to reason with myself. But there were no pros or cons to deliberate over. I had no place to go and nothing to do, and I was back where I had been three years before, in Alabama, when I thought I had hit bottom. There too I had been faced, in the winter, with the prospect of not having a job to go to or anywhere to live in the coming year. And one night, as I lay awake in my bedroom, crying, wracked with anguish, I decided that I had had enough. I had a bottle of sleeping pills beside my bed and probably had enough of them to finish me off. I had only now to get up, sit by my computer, and write my last note, a note that told the world what I was doing and why, a note that explained my grievances, that pointed fingers where fingers needed to be pointed and exonerated those who were blameless, a note that asked forgiveness, a note that told the world that I had loved, and would die because I was no longer capable of loving, or of doing anything for anyone whom I might still love, a note that would say ATTENTION MUST BE PAID. But I loved my daughter and I was sorry. I got up and turned on the computer and started typing ... and realised that I was too drunk to complete a sentence. My head was reeling. I could hardly see the keyboard in front of me. So instead I called a friend – I had such a friend in Birmingham, Alabama. I called him and told him he needed to come and help me.

The next day I was in the hospital, and soon after that, since I would not let the hospital admit me, because I was too proud to so publicly signal that I had been defeated and I was sick, I was an outpatient at the psychiatric ward, talking to doctors – a trainee in psychiatry was responsible for me, since my insurance didn't cover a full-fledged doctor for psychological problems – and being prescribed two kinds of pills. The pills would take two to three weeks to take effect, I was told, so I had to be patient. I somehow had to keep working, to keep teaching and interacting with my colleagues, I had to keep living, and keeping seeing my trainee for talking therapy once or twice a week, until – well, until *something*. I relied on my friend, and one other friend, two guys who I will always cherish. We went out together, frequenting the bars at Four Corners, and talked softly. I hardly knew where I was or what I was doing in those days, only that sidewalks sometimes seemed to moving, and the buildings leaning over, and I was doing a lot of silent talking to myself. I was hallucinating my own insanity. And yet I was feeling very little. I felt like I was dead. Nothing could touch me because I was already untouchable. Then one day, about two weeks after my treatment began, I heard something strange in my head: it was music. I hadn't heard any music in my head for a long time, it seemed, but there it was, I can't remember what, a song from a record, in my head: music was possible again.

From that moment on I was a recovering depressive. I had my pills, Serzone and Trazodone, two drugs related to Prozac, and I had a new sense of myself as a precarious entity, trying to get better. It was unfair, I thought, that this story of my life, this long decline of my life, was reducible to a medical diagnosis: clinical, recurrent depressive disorder. But the doctors were right. When you came down to it, there was something wrong with the chemistry in my brain; there was something wrong with the way my brain caused me to react to stress; there was something wrong with the way my brain regulated my moods. There had always been something wrong. Think about it: that time when you were 16, that time when you were 20, that time when you were 22, that time when you were 30: days when it was still possible to hope, still possible to believe in the future, and yet you were depressed. 'I' was depressed, that is. I was nervous, melancholic, angry. A smoker (until I turned 35), a drinker, a pill popper, a pessimist, a carper, a constantly sarcastic, constantly joking, belittling son of a bitch, whose life was tolerable only because, in the midst of his anger and aggression, at himself and others, he was from time to time able to find ecstasy, the ecstasy in sex, in intoxication, in poetry and music: Mahler! The Ninth Symphony! *Das Lied von der Erde*!

And yet there were models for me of men and women who had faced far worse disasters than I ever had who had responded, not with depression, but with perseverance. I told my therapist about Christopher Columbus, whose life and work I had been studying, about how shortly after he had discovered what he considered a New World, and he was going back to Spain to tell everyone about it, he got caught off the coast of a Portuguese island, and was clapped in prison as an enemy of the state. But he kept up his spirits. He ruminated, he plotted and he escaped. Or consider the case of Bill fucking Clinton. Now there was a guy who had been dealt a lifetime of shit, from the day he was born. But he kept up his spirits. He was cheerful. Nothing could distress him and his ambitions. He was President of the United States and even after the vicious attacks on his 'character' by the Republican Party half the country absolutely loved the bastard. Whereas I, an English teacher, couldn't cope with being rejected by English teachers. Clearly, it was my fault that my life had turned out so poorly. Or rather, it was the fault of me and my brain, my stress-damaged, serotonin-starved brain, which impeded my progressing through life much like a broken leg would have impeded my running down to the street to catch up with an ice cream van. My brain.

But the medicine started working. When it was sunny outside, I saw sunlight. When music played, I heard music. I wasn't – wait – I wasn't crying at night anymore. The pills made me tired and lazy, though, and I felt bloated. So one of my medications was changed. I went onto taking this new drug in the morning and Trazodone at night and my spirits lifted even higher during the day, and at night, usually, I slept. I slept once again with the heaviness of an adolescent. I went to therapy and I started making progress, though I was still disheartened, still at a loss for how I was going to make it through. Then I got a call from San Diego, with an offer of a three-year job, with the possibility that a permanent job might come open. And then, three years later, though out in San Diego, I was back where I started.

¤ ¤ ¤

You blame yourself – but also you blame others. You hold onto the dignity of yourself – but you understand that this dignified self is slipping away from you, you fear that this self was only a mirage, and recognise that dignity depends on others, that it is something you are awarded by society for your efforts, and nobody cares about you or your dignity anymore. So maybe there is nothing to hold onto.

The thought of suicide takes hold of you, but this too gets you into thinking about your dignity, grasping onto it, losing it, or realising that you have nothing to lose. You recognise that suicide is a symbolic act. It says something loud and clear – only you won't be there to hear it. And you wonder, 'What will I really be saying? Who will I be saying it to?' A kind of revenge is uppermost in your mind. '*That'll* show them!' you think. 'That'll really show them.' You will make them feel bad. You will make them feel guilty, and there is your revenge. But you will never be able to taste it. And anyway, if you have never wanted to triumph over people this way in life, why would you want to do so in death? Or maybe, really, that is what you have wanted all along, though it has been too awful to admit it: all your life, what you really wanted was power over others, beginning with the power to make them feel sorry. But if that is the case, then you don't deserve the triumph you desire. The crime is, or will be, yours. The guilt will be yours. You will die for nothing, except for the sake of lightening the world of the burden of yourself, and of all aggression and resentment you have brought into it.

Yet there is a philosophic power to the idea of suicide. I had learned that long ago, reading Shakespeare and others: John Donne (who wrote a book ambiguously approving of suicide called *Biathanatos* in 1608), Søren Kierkegaard, who disapproved of suicide but understood it, Dostoyevsky, above all Dostoyevsky, whose book *Demons,* which I was teaching as part of my terrorism in literature course, shows a character named Kirilov killing himself in the name of the future of humanity. Albert Camus was among the writers whose reading of Dostoyevsky and nihilism had inspired me. I had no illusions about my suicide being heroic, neither intrinsically nor in the effect it might have on others, but I understood that suicide, in addition to being a symbolic act and what was commonly called a 'cry for help', was also an act of rebellion, of metaphysical rebellion. That *I* should make the decision over whether I should *be* – this was the ultimate decision. It was in that sense the ultimate act of freedom. But to commit the ultimate act meant either one of two things, both of which were suspect. Either you decided, ultimately, to live – but how did you know that you have made that decision in freedom and not in fear, in energetic bravery and not in cringing lethargy? Or, else you decided to die – but how would you be free, in the end, if you were dead, and were unaware of your freedom? What is freedom without awareness of freedom? As one character in a book by Kierkegaard puts it, 'If you hang yourself, you will regret it. And if you do not hang yourself, you will regret that too'.

The philosopher, when he thinks about his own death, has to think about motives, feelings, repercussions. He has to be suspicious of himself. But he also has to be suspicious of the world around him. In ancient Rome, when stoics contemplated suicide, they believed that taking one's own life was honourable, if one did so for the right cause. The act could be unselfish: you could kill yourself in the name of the Republic. So if you stabbed yourself in the heart, you would be a hero, and your name would be immortalised. You got something out of death, even if you were determined to get nothing out of it. In modern America, however, there was nothing honourable about suicide. Nobody admired it. People pitied it. When someone took their own life, the usual response was to think, 'That's a shame', and the very word commonly chosen, 'shame', tells the story, indicating not just that people are saddened by the news of a suicide, but that they find something dishonourable in it. In the most charitable of cases, people think that *society* is shamed when a suicide takes place. It is everyone's ignominy when Marilyn Monroe kills herself. But in less charitable cases, in most cases, the idea is that a self-murderer is a 'quitter'. We may all be shamed when one of us commits self-murder, but no one is more shamed than the self-murderer himself.

'A quitter never wins. A winner never quits.' That's what the football coach, big buff Vince Lombardi used to say. The thought was seconded once by no less a figure than Richard Nixon: 'Defeat doesn't finish a man – quit does. A man is not finished when he's defeated. He's finished when he quits.' And there, in my mind, was Christopher Columbus, in a Portuguese prison, who was not a quitter.

And I, far from being in a Portuguese prison, was in student housing, in San Diego, where it was always morning. I had a bedroom with a hard double bed, a small wooden desk and a wooden chest of drawers. I had a bathroom with a shower and a small galley kitchen, open to a living room which had a picture window overlooking the grounds toward a parking lot and a tennis court. There was no dining table, or dining area. I had to dine sitting on a narrow sofa with a tray on my knees. I had a television and a stereo and a VCR player. At night, alone, I would sit on my sofa, eat spaghetti from a bowl, drink wine, move onto fruit and brandy and watch a rented movie. When the movie was over, I usually felt more comfortable with myself, as if, on the one hand, looking at the characters in the movie talking to one another made me feel less alone; or as if, on the other hand, following the plot of the movie, whether the ending was happy or sad, really did make me experience catharsis, really did temporarily purge me of the ill humours that had been plaguing me. Aristotle was apparently right. I came back to myself somehow. But then, either with the broadcast television on – the David Letterman Show, say – or soft music in the background and a book in my hands, my drinking would have moved me into another dimension, which among other things would make me hungry again. I might get up and make myself a bowl of popcorn, or improvise a pancake, slathering it with butter and sugar, French-style. Usually, by twelve o'clock or one, I would also have downed a Trazodone or two or three, and, anesthetised, crumble into sleep.

It was no Portuguese prison. I could walk out the door. I had my spaghetti, my brandy, my TV and my pancakes. But I was in trouble. And it seemed to me that I had only choice in front of me: to choose my shame; or to put it another way, to choose the shame that I would add to the general ledger of shame in the world. Either I could go on living, a beaten man who really couldn't take care of himself, and be a shame to myself and everyone around me, or I could do the most shameful thing of all, and quit. Yet knowing that these were my choices only made the situation worse. If I had believed that there was something heroic, honourable or messianic about my killing myself, it would have been easy to choose to do it. And if I had believed that there was something heroic, honourable of messianic about choosing to live, it would have been easy to do that too. Instead there was nothing but shame – shame all around.

I gave serious thought to plotting my death. I started thinking about methods. I started imagining the unimaginable moment. I had some pills. My former girlfriend and I used to take the trolley down to Mexico, and buy sedatives illegally from a pharmacy off the main plaza in Tijuana. I still had some of those left, although they were not very strong. Clonazepam, I think they were, anti-convulsants that were also good against anxiety. I had my prescription drugs, the serotonin re-uptake inhibitors. I had some over-the-counter sleep aids. Surely, there was a way to overdose, and the benefit would be a painless and unconscious death, a death in sleep. But there were dangers. If you took too many you just might make yourself so sick that you throw it all up, and be incapacitated (and humiliated) for days after. If you took too few you might end up harming yourself indefinitely. My former girlfriend, aware of my tendencies, had told me several times that she knew of people who had tried to kill themselves by overdosing and had ended up crippled instead. Paralyzed, I think she said. Turned into vegetables with regrets. That would be worse than dying.

But what else, then? I thought of buying a gun. But I had never even held a gun before. I was averse to guns. I was averse to violence in all its forms, but gun violence especially horrified me. To hold a gun, even to enter a gun store, to pick out a weapon and bullets and buy them, was so taboo … especially, of course, if you were making your purchase with the sole desire of killing yourself … taboo, something terrible, horrible and wrong … I imagined going faint as I entered the store, or as I held a loaded gun, or aimed it at my head. The advantage, of course, was instant death, if you did a proper job, and also that burst of sound and velocity, that final bang, so loud and hard as if itself uttering a metaphysical exclamation point. That came in the instant before the instant of death. With your hand and your trigger finger and all your machinations and resolutions, with all your *thinking and doing,* fifty-one years of thinking and doing, this was IT. Would it hurt? Dostoyevsky has Kirolov claim that what keeps most people from killing themselves was the fear of pain. And I admitted to myself, I feared that pain.

And what other alternatives were left? I knew about wrist-slitting from the movies. I knew about jumping off of bridges because it was often in the news, in California; it seemed one of safest and surest ways of dying. But dying from a slit wrist was slow, you bled and you bled and you had to hold onto your resolve to die for a very long time. And as for jumping off a bridge, again I worried about the pain, and I worried about that helpless sense of suffocation under water, that helpless struggle to breathe, or even that panicked urge to survive that I imagined would come over me when I was under water and wounded with the impact of the jump and feeling my lungs collapse for want of air.

The fact was, I was a coward. I was too cowardly to die at my own hands. Or maybe I simply wanted to live? Maybe, even in deep despair, I had an unconquerable urge to live for the sake of living. To feel the earth under my feet was itself a kind of goal, and maybe goal enough, in the end. To feel the earth, to breath the air, to hear the wind, to smell the ocean, to sit in a chair and look down at my legs: that was life, and it was something I wanted, it was something I loved. Just to be sensible. Just to be aware. To hear the voice in my head. Or to hear a song that was stored somewhere in it. Ella Fitzgerald, singing 'Mack the Knife.' And if I could not be immortal, maybe it was sufficient motivation to want to see things through as far ahead as possible, to see what would happen next, and what would happen after that, and again would happen after that. It was 2003. Would I not want to be alive in 2013, in 2023, in 2033? Would I not want simply to *know*? I already knew so little. As the years went by I knew less and less. I was as little familiar with certainty as I was with hope or love. But still, wouldn't I want to be alive just in the end to know that very little bit of life that it would available to me to know? What kind of cars would we be driving in 2033? What kind of skyline would loom over San Diego Bay? Or would it all come to an end? Even if humanity was going to blow itself off the planet, wouldn't I want to be there when the blowing came? Wouldn't I want to know at least that much, that humanity had tried and failed, and I was there when it happened?

A solution was suggested to me, if such a solution was to be chosen, by an article I read about the psychoanalyst Bruno Bettelheim. Bruno Bettelheim had indirectly gotten me into trouble once at the University of San Diego. To a group of would-be primary school teachers I taught Bettelheim's psychosexual theory of the fairy tale, and when some of the students – all women – resisted the idea I got graphic. Little Red Riding Hood's red hood, blood, menstruation, the meaning of wearing a red dress today, on a date, sexual availability… Two of the students, twins, whose father worked for the university, thought that such classroom discussion was 'inappropriate' in a Catholic school, and filed a complaint against me. Maybe that was why I would not be a 'good colleague', because two entitled young women were disturbed by being asked to think, along with Bruno Bettelheim and me, about the symbolism of the colour red. I would not be a good colleague because I was capable of offending the sensibilities of privileged kids, uncertain of their sexuality but certain of their right to complain, teaching gob-standard old-fashioned psychoanalysis from a book published nearly thirty years before. (Lest the reader think that such hyper-sensitivity in those days was the province of reactionary Catholics, I should add that once, interviewing for a job at a wholly secular, prestigious liberal arts college in the Midwest, a similar challenge was posed to me before the letter. A young scholar – who has now gone on to an illustrious career at no other institution but Harvard University – asked me what I would do when the good students of his prestigious little school got *offended* by the moral outlook of an author I would probably be teaching a lot. For students there, in this age of 'diversity', were 'sensitive', he said. The author whose offensiveness he had in mind was *John Milton*.) I was fortunately spared the charge of sexual harassment, because the girls clearly stated that I did not harass them in any way; their only objection was that my language was *inappropriate*. I needed to better behave. I needed to be *disciplined, but not that much*.

But anyway, Bettelheim, a holocaust survivor whose theory of fairy tales I was teaching, as he came to the age of 86, widowed and suffering the effects of a stroke, decided to kill himself. The method he chose was to dose himself with sedatives, and then to fit a plastic bag over his head. He died of asphyxiation. And I was impressed. You add the sedatives to asphyxiation, you add asphyxiation to the sedatives. Each helps the other, and if I was afraid of the side effects and of the possibility of failure of either method used by itself, I was emboldened by the ingenuity of Bettelheim's double method. All that remained then … was to try it, if I would try it, and not worry about the year 2033.

San Diego in February. It feels like spring. It feels like morning. Temperatures in the sixties (Fahrenheit). When it rains, the rain is soft, like the spray from a fountain, and usually it doesn't rain. In my free time I would drive down to the beach and look at the water and study the horizon. I would stop at a Carl's Junior for a hamburger and a diet Coke, or to Rubio's for a fish taco and a beer. I went food shopping at Von's or Albertson's, bringing back bags (given the choice of 'paper or plastic' I often guiltily went for the plastic) of pasta, tomatoes, carrots, parmesan cheese, some Sonoma Country Red and a bottle of Korbel Brandy. I rented movies at Blockbuster's. I belonged to a gym near Point Loma and played racquetball once or twice a week. I was teaching nine hours a week, I don't remember what, it could have been Gender and Literature and/or Autobiography and/or Renaissance Drama and/or Introduction to Poetry and/or who knows what, I taught many different things. In fact, I do not remember much from that time, not in sequence anyway, and my records are gone. What I do remember is the seriousness of the moment, a seriousness that also came with a kind of hallucinatory clarity. The moment was as real as only a hallucination or a dream could be. For as I drove through the city or stopped at the beach or went shopping or played racquetball or taught poetry or drama or held office hours in my closet, I also saw that this, whatever it was that I was doing, could be the last time I was doing it, that the sand under my feet or the condiment counter at the taco shop or the aisles of beer and wine at my supermarket or the aisles of movies at the video store or the students sitting in front of me, talking with me about Aphra Behn or Thomas Middleton or for God's sake John Milton would be among my last bits of sandy beach, of condiments, of aisles of commodities, or of students sitting before me: in fact they could be the very last ones, for tonight might be the night, tonight might be the last. But that did not mean that everything became much more solid, colourful or voluminous or harder or softer or hotter or colder or more momentous. On the contrary, everything was diminished. Everything was especially vivid to me because everything was uncannily reduced, as if placed at the wrong end of telescope. I got *less* out of the world than I used to. And that was only right, since I was withdrawing from that world, it was coming to mean less and less to me, it was diminishing in order to communicate its insignificance. For what was, at bottom … any of this? The sand, the wind, the highway, the shops, the condiments, the appetite, sharpened and satiated, sharpened and satiated. A hamburger. A taco. A bottle of beer. A slice of cheese. A glass of brandy. Or for that matter a racquetball game or a discussion about a famous literary figure. What was any of that? It was all so *small*. Always had been, although I hadn't seen it that way. And what was I? I was myself diminished in my eyes. For I was the world's refuse. I was something the world didn't want, or didn't need anymore, and so I was being thrown away. Not *sent* anywhere, just discarded. And that would seem to be a judgement, a double judgement, first on my self of course, because I was no Christopher Columbus or Bill Clinton, I was a guy who couldn't persevere, who couldn't keep smiling and seducing his way to success, I was a guy who lost and lost big and couldn't imagine winning, and so allowed himself to become garbage … and second, on the world itself, or at least that world that would treat me like garbage, that had other priorities, other needs, and simply no use for the likes of me. How could there be such a world, a world that couldn't even *use* me? And that couldn't use me in large part not because of what I could or could not do – learn, write, teach – but because of what I could not *represent*. I could not represent 'diversity', and I could not put on a face of undiminished youthful illusion. I could not represent *hope*. But this was a world, of course, that was in itself hopeless in almost every way. By 2033 or sooner it might well be gone. Blown up, or succumbed to global warming, cities dying, coastal California submerged under water like an ancient algae-covered ruin. This world had an appetite, however, for semblances for hope, for figures of hope. It dined on self-deception. And I could not *feed* that to the world. Which meant, I could not *do* anything for it.

But don't heroize yourself, I told myself. Don't try to compensate for failure by pretending it is actually success. It is too late for that. The fact is … but there are no facts. Facts are dead. And there are no values. Success and failure are two sides of the same false coin, that idol you have worshipped for far too long. And as for the other values, the other false coins … even if they exist they are beyond you, even if billions find strength and delight in them, they are no use to you anymore, and apparently never have been. You are alone. Above all else, you are alone. And alone, you have no *reasons* anymore, pro or con, high or low, true or false; you have no *purposes*. You never did. Or if you ever did, they were hollow, they were wind and noise. Who were you to ever believe that you could teach young people how to *think*, or to *think for themselves*, or to ask themselves about the meaning of the colour red, or the poetry of John Milton? You never really cared about that anyway. All you ever really wanted to do was lie in bed and daydream, and write books that no one would read about subjects that no one cared about … and collect royalties from nothing. You're a sponger, you! And while we're on the subject, have another drink! I was an alcoholic.

So no, I could not try to make myself into a hero. I could not dawdle in self-deception. There was no point. Because there was no point in anything anymore.

And the days came when those job-seekers from far away places like Detroit arrived to visit our campus, to be given tours of San Diego and be wined and dined and to submit themselves for the second interview for the assistant professorship for which I had been turned down. By this time, no one in the department was speaking to me. I was all but removed from e-mail discussions. I walked the halls of the department in an envelope of silence. No one even looked in my direction. I saw one of the candidates, a dark youngish portly man standing in the hallway outside the suite of offices in which my own was located. Talking with one of my colleagues volubly, like he was the cock of the walk. I closed the door to my closet, and I started to weep. It was like visiting the earth on the day after your funeral.

And it was on a day like that, perhaps the very same day, that once again I found myself alone, at home in my tiny apartment, and realised that I would have to figure out how to kill myself. For there was one thing more about my situation that had to be taken into consideration: it was intolerable. It was literally intolerable. I could not take it anymore. It. This. Life. I had no chances anymore. I had no hope. I had no friends. I had managed to make myself despicable. I had managed to fail even in the most basic of human activities. I had failed to become part of the pattern of the lives of others, to make friends, or at least to keep them, to find love and give it. Within a few months I would not even have a shelter over my head. I simply couldn't stand it anymore. It was time to take action.

Or at the very least, it was time to rehearse. It was time to get ready. It was time to start going through the motions. The bag and the sedatives. The bag and the sedatives. I only had to take the pills in hand with a glass of water. I only had to get a bag from the kitchen. Just like that. And then my follies and my pain and anger would be at an end. I would have forced myself into nothingness. Nothingness.

But I wouldn't only be subtracting something to the world, for I would also be adding to its misery and its shame. I knew that. However little anyone really cared about me, still, there would be horror. I would be wounding, in ways incalculable, my mother, my sister, my daughter: my daughter above all, I feared. She was nineteen years old, studying at a university in New York: New York, a city I had taught her about, a city whose culture, I had impressed upon her, rightly or wrongly, was *our* culture, hers and mine. This was who we are, I had insisted: descendants of immigrants who had alighted in New York a hundred years ago, and who become part of the same world as the Gershwin brothers, as Leonard Bernstein, as Alfred Kazin, author of the memoir, *New York Jew*. New York Jews one and all. Part of something big, wondrous, world historical. Twentieth century New York. At least, that was my side of what I had passed along to her. Or rather, that was the myth of myself and our ancestors that I preferred to pass along, in spite of the fact that her mother was a Californian, and she herself had hardly ever been anywhere in her life except for California, and I myself hadn't lived in New York City since I was two years-old. My daughter arrived in New York, to begin her studies, taking up in her own way, and for her own purposes, the myth I had passed on, almost exactly a year after 9/11.

She was living, in fact, in student housing, not too far from where my father might be residing. My father, who I hadn't heard from in twenty-eight years, who could have been alive or dead, as far as I knew, but who had a somewhat unusual name, the same name, as I found out on the Internet, as someone who was residing in an apartment in a neighbourhood in lower Midtown New York that I knew him to have been fond of, to have resided in before … my father who if he was alive did not know that he had a granddaughter … did not know that his son who was a published writer and a failure … did not know that his son was in agony, wishing for him, wishing for his daughter, wishing for himself …

I cried and I drank and I cried and drank some more. My stepfather was dead. When I was sixteen I hated him. Now I mourned him. My mother was alone. She was provided for, mainly. She lived among friends. She didn't need me, I had nothing to give. My sister was okay, with a family and a good job. She didn't need me. Never had. Or so, at least, I had always told myself, maybe wrongly … And in any case, in sum, your Honour, if may: I was the only one who was not okay. I was the only one who had lost the ability to persevere. Because I would *not* persevere. I couldn't. I wouldn't. There wasn't enough of me *left* to persevere.

I drank my brandy and felt myself going into hysterics. I was heaving with agony. Maybe the students next door or upstairs could hear me, but who cares? Let them know what it sounds like for a grown man to cry, to bellow, to self-destruct. It was all over. I just had to figure out how to do it. How to do it. Do it. The pills and the bag. The pills and the bag. But who needed the pills? I was already drunk enough. Or maybe I was still uncertain. Maybe I still didn't have the guts to go through with it. Maybe I needed to rehearse. Maybe I had to be sure of my technique.

I got a plastic supermarket bag from out of the kitchen. I got a double bag, just to be sure. White and soft, supple yet strong, the classic California supermarket bag, designed for foreclosed desires. I sat back down on the sofa and took another drink of brandy. I put the double bag over my head and held it tightly around my neck. I was crying. I was in pain. But I had to feel my way around the situation. What it would be like. What it was like. For I was doing it. I was crying and heaving with my hand clutched around the bottom of the bag, clutched harder and harder, and the air was out of the bag, I was feeling what it was like not to be able to breathe. I was hot and wet. I could feel my own spit sliding over my face as the airless bag was sucked against my skin, my forehead, my cheeks, my nose, my mouth. I was in the dark and it was hot and wet and I was trying to breathe but couldn't get any air. And I was there, there … there where the death could come on, without any pills to help, without any pretence of only rehearsing. I was there and I couldn't breathe but I was struggling for breath, my lungs hurt, my lungs were demanding something from me. But I would persist, at least in this. At least in one thing I would succeed. I would get through this instant, and the next instant, I couldn't breathe but I was struggling for breath, it hurt, I was under water, pedalling with my feet, trying to get up to the surface, the air, I had to breathe …

I let go of the bag and my face was hot and wet and I recovered my breath. That was it then. I was too afraid of the pain. Or maybe not the pain but the meaning of the pain. Something in the whole of me refused to feel the meaning of the pain of death.

Chapter Seven

Personnummer

In Sweden, you need to have a number, a *personnummer*, which is something like a social security number only more indispensable. It is connected with everything you do as an official resident of Sweden, from receiving medical attention as an infant to paying taxes in your old age. You get one at birth, if you are lucky enough to be born in Sweden, and the number encodes your birthdate, your gender, your place of birth, and so forth, all by a simple algorithm.

In Sweden, moreover, to get paid for doing a job, you need to have a Swedish bank account. Sweden is a cheque-less society. Your employer could not write a cheque even it wanted to. Sweden is even on the way to becoming a cashless society, and your employer would not be able to pay you in cash either. It has to transfer the funds into your bank. But in order to have a Swedish bank account you have to have a *personnummer*, and in order to have a *personnummer* it helps to have been born in Sweden. Otherwise you have to make certain applications, and jump through the inevitable hoops of the circus masters of the Swedish bureaucracy.

I tried jumping through the hoops, but it was no good at first. So the office manager at my new place of work, the English Department at Uppsala University, contrived for me what is called a 'temporary' *personnummer*. With that I was able to open up an account with the same bank as my employer, and receive my pay.

Once my permanent *personnummer* came through, however, the problems started. How could I be the person paying the bills from an account with *personnummer* 62xxxx-xxxx, when I had claimed to the company to whom I owed the bill that I was a person with the *personnummer* 52xxxx-xxxx? Who was I now? As for applying for credit, it was utterly impossible. 52 did not equal 62; nor did 62 equal 52. Payments I made for legitimate bills got sent back. Credit card applications were turned down, and late fees kept showing up on my monthly statements.

So one day, after a number of phone calls and exchanged letters, Marion and I found ourselves on a bus to the outskirts of Uppsala. We live near the centre of Uppsala; a bank branch may be found a short walk away from us, a large central bank may be found at the very centre of the city a ten-minute walk away from us, and a major consumer exchange bank, one that actually handles cash, may be found a couple minutes farther on. But I had already tried, at each of those branches, to have a banker change my bank account number, to coincide with my real and permanent *personnummer,* and no one in any of the branches had the faintest idea about how to do it. Finally, someone in still another branch, miles away, expressed by phone that she understood our problem and could do something about it, if we came for a personal visit.

Now Uppsala is a picturesque city dating back to the Middle Ages – it's nicer than Lancaster! – with a slender stone-clad river running through it, stately colourful apartment buildings and shops and sidewalk cafes lining the river, and a bustling, pedestrianized shopping district just behind the river with hundreds of stores and services. But we had to get on a bus, following instructions from our banker, and ride through humdrum residential and ramshackle industrial districts. We found ourselves, after about forty minutes, in a development of big box stores similar to those we had seen in France on the outskirts of cities. There was an IKEA, a Co-op Hypermarket, a Media Markt, and a number of other major stores, along with fast food joints, including the pride of Sweden known as Max Burger (*Sveriges godaste hamburgare*) as well as low office buildings and a few smaller shops. The streets were wide and free of pedestrians, and there was no apparent centre to the development, just irregular grids of traffic on limited access roads and car parks where big and small stores and offices could be driven up to. It was like suburban Kansas City, Kansas, or suburban Bourges, France, only more haphazard. We arrived early in cool spring weather and tried to sit outside, but of course there was nowhere to sit. In the centre of Uppsala our bank, Nordea, occupies the ground floor of a gorgeous, ornate Edwardian office building in the central plaza, where there are benches and all kinds of street life, and it proudly blazons its corporate logo along the square, in big blue neon letters, three times. Nordea. Nordea. Nordea. Here the bank was tucked away in the car park of a low-slung office building set off a curving secondary road, jumbled among other businesses, its entrance hard to find. We leaned on the narrow sidewalk against the cold brick building, waiting for ten o'clock to arrive, listened to the drone of the traffic around us and inhaled the harsh petroleum-scented air, feeling out-of-place, wondering, annoyed, why we had to be here in this out-of-place place. But this was where the action was. This was where the banking system would adjust our accounts, and reintegrate us into the global financial order. This nothingness was my own personal Wizard of Oz, the hidden master of my world.

What else is left for me to say? It took nearly two hours for two young women, our bankers, one of whom was new on the job, to close our old accounts (we had actually accumulated a second one for Marion), and open a new one for us, with apologies all around, and then more apologies, and then with results – although we would have to wait four days before we could use our new account, and would have to make do in the meantime with the cash we had recently withdrawn from a cash machine.

An obvious lesson from the experience concerns the complexity of the system of global banking system, as Sweden among other countries has developed it, a complexity that overrides individual effort and stymies individual initiative. At least six different bankers in Uppsala and Stockholm had previously told us that they could not help us. Finally, one banker said she could, but only after undertaking a process that lasted two hours – on behalf of a non-interest bearing account that had in it perhaps ten thousand kronors (about a thousand pounds, or fifteen hundred dollars). Of course, a financial trader at Goldman Sachs can transfer millions around the world in a matter of microseconds, on behalf of people he has never met and interests of which he has little direct knowledge, and earn a generous commission just as quickly; but retail banking is at the far end of the financial universe now, especially when the customer only has one thousand pounds to fuss about. The retail customer offers up a speck of algae among other specks of algae which the huge mouth of the octopus occasionally licks off the end of a tentacle. The system is complex, and the system is cruel, and it is designed neither for the little customer nor the little banker who tries to help him, although when all is said and done those little licks of algae have a fine taste, and add indispensable nutrients to the octopus's diet.

But it is actually wrong to call any of the people who said they couldn't help, who tried to help me but failed, or who tried to help and eventually succeeded by the name of banker. They are low-wage clerks. They have no decision-making powers. They enter data into a computer programme, follow instructions, perform the functions the computer programme makes available to them, apologise and smile. (It is not only in Sweden, by the way, that I have encountered this sort of problem in recent years, but also in America and Britain: in America, at Bank of America branches in New York City, I have to say, they didn't even smile.) The clerks have no more power to think and act creatively, to participate as wilful subjects in the community of commerce, than the customer does. But to belong to this system, whether as clerk or customer – to *serve* the system, is inevitable. You need to eat. You need to have a home. You also need: means of transportation, if for no other reason than to get to from home to your job and back; access to health care and recreation, because otherwise your life will be miserable and short; means of entering into financial transactions, beginning with a bank account and a bank card, so you can access cash from a cash machine and pay your monthly bills online or make simple purchases like movie tickets (movie theatres in Sweden have ticket machines rather than box offices with human beings to greet you, and they do not take cash); an official address where you can receive bills and services and commodities by post; electricity, water, heat and light; a mobile phone, and preferably a smart phone, so you can send and receive texts and email and read the newspaper while you sit on the bus, and even, in Sweden, so you can buy your bus ticket through your mobile phone account, and display your purchase to the bus driver on your smartphone's screen; a broadband service, so you can use your personal computer and read the news blogs and watch pirated videos and stay up-to-date with your on-line 'friends' and look up stuff on Wikipedia and, most important, so you can work from home; a television and a cable or satellite television service, because without the service you can't receive any channels anymore, much less watch a programme or a movie 'on demand'. And – what else? You need furnishings and dinnerware and pots and pans and a refrigerator, a stove and a sink. And you need to be secure. You need to know that unless you or someone you encounter does something very stupid, today is going to be pretty much like yesterday. No one is going to hurt you. No one is going to take your home, your broadband, your television or your pots and pans away from you. And when there is nothing in the house to eat or drink you can go outside and within a short while find a market where just about anything you need is available at a fair price which you can pay for with your bank card or even, surprise, with cash, withdrawn from the cash machine at the entrance to the store: your oranges, your milk, your meat, and, since this is Sweden, your pickled herring, your *hårt bröd*, your boiling potatoes and your 3.5% beer. And for all this you need to be a servant of the system. With a working *personnummer* or some such thing, and a bank account with your name on it, your deposits guaranteed by the state, because the bank in itself, as we have recently learned again, cannot guarantee it and isn't even interested in doing so. All it wants is your money, and, for the sake of its want of your money, your uninterrupted cooperation. You will pay and pay into this bank, and you will have no choice but to keep on paying, because if you don't your world will be taken away from you, and there will be nothing left but bare unaccommodated you.

¤ ¤ ¤

It is good to know Swedish in Sweden. Knowing English is second best, and being a native speaker of English is second best plus, but still it comes in second. In England I was an immigrant with an accent like the characters on *Friends*. People appreciated that. Now Marion and I are immigrants in a country where we are native speakers of the nation's non-native second language – again, the language of *Friends*, along with *2 ½ Men* and *Navy CSI* – and people appreciate that too, but we are worse off than children in the nation's first language, the one that really counts: the language of Ingmar Bergman, *Project Runway Sverige*, and *Lyxfällen*, a popular reality programme broadcast from Stockholm about people needing help with their financial habits because they have overspent on luxuries and are now on the verge of going bankrupt. It can be a problem, not knowing Swedish, but we are working at it, taking free lessons, paid for by the state. How we got here is not an interesting a story and so I will not go into it, except to say that I came here to work, as well as to try to live something new, to take one more stab at finding and pursuing my desire. And here I work, and pursue my desire, along with Marion, and as I am getting old I think about what will happen when the work is put to an end, and desire will have fewer outlets, or dangers and terrors.

When I began this book, in 2007, when I had the flash of inspiration that allowed me to conceive of this book, I was operating under the assumption that my lifelong opposition to the lifeworld of modern capitalism was to some extent pathological. A psychiatrist in Connecticut who was treating me for depression explained it. First, you suffer – because of the uncooperative chemicals in your brain – from depression. Then you construct a worldview that corresponds to your suffering. You become an idealist whose ideals can never be realised. You become a radical whose radicalism is impotent. You become a non-conformist whose non-conformity guarantees that he will never find happiness. For happiness depends not just on yourself but on your relationships with others. And then you see: of course you're depressed, look how fucked up the world is today! How can any reasonable person *not* be depressed?

But then I realised I had to get better. And I did. I came close to another crisis while completing a postdoctoral fellowship in Connecticut, at Wesleyan University. I was soon to be jobless and homeless again. Yet then it came about that England welcomed me. England opened up its arms to me. England adored me. And I adored England. And in the bliss of this mutual adoration I concluded that up to now I had probably been mistaken. I had adopted a philosophy of resistance and non-conformity as a defence mechanism. In point of fact, I had been doing everything I could to make sure that I would never be happy. I resisted the world, I resisted the compromises one has to make in order to get by in the world, I resisted capitalism itself not because there was something wrong with the world, with compromise or with capitalism, but with me. Who was the dummy, the person who knew how to get by in the world, who went into business, or got a law degree, or worked in advertising or the media or any such thing as my talents who have allowed me to go into, and prospered; or the person who resisted in every which way and ended up alone, desperate and broke? The answer almost went without saying.

And in 2007, the world out there, at least from my point of view in ancient Lancaster, looked fine. The days of boom and bust were over, our British politicians assured us. Yes there was that terrible business of the War in Iraq, which the UK officially supported no less than the USA, and that terrible business was no doubt an expression of a fundamental social pathology of which I had been aware since the days of the Vietnam War. Yes there was violence, arrogance and self-destructiveness at the heart of the modern world order, and the Bush and Blair administrations gave their proof of it by rushing into a war that served no purpose but to rally the West around its own atrocious powers. Yes, there were plenty of *political* causes to support in opposition to atrocious power. But in 2007, still, it made sense to be a pragmatist. It made sense to settle down, buy a house, pay a mortgage, and be content with the little things that one could enjoy and the little things that one could do in order to make society more just, peaceful and content.

The only problem, or least the only problem it seemed I had it in me to address, apart from problems that a lot of other people were already addressing, was the matter of the commodification of everyday life. In 2007 I was happy. But I was happy in the midst of a never-ending battle against, well, the supermarket, and the supermarketisation of the world. I saw that even if I was happy, exercising my own virtues, as Aristotle put it, while being 'sufficiently equipped with external goods', I was doing so at the price of being interpellated as a consumer – that is, of being the British capitalist version of a *personnummer*. I went about the business of everyday life trying to make choices, but in fact most of the choices were already being made for me. I had very little autonomy. Nor did anyone else. We simply worked our way through aisles that we had no direct part in constructing, although the system wired us, spied on us, for input. Even if I and most of the people I knew were trying to practice an *art de faire,* in my case for example adopting a sunny Mediterranean diet in a rainy county of sausage and mash, still, I was defining the pleasure of my existence not in terms of my positive, autonomous self, but in terms of my heterogeneity, in terms of what I *wasn't.* The fact was, if I wasn't a born and bred bangers-and-masher, I wasn't a born and bred bouillabaisser either. It was all artifice. It was all negativity – combined, of course, with opportunism, for you had to grab what you could; and framed, again, by a system which was designed to manipulate me hither and yon.

I found what seemed to be the key to the problem I was facing when I heard myself saying the words with which I opened this book: *they do not love you.* In the kingdom of pleasure, I was looking for love. So, I imagined, was everybody else. And it was love, not pleasure, that was the condition of genuine pleasure. It was desire, not need, that was the condition for the satisfaction of genuine need. And how else to explain, well, me? Or the dissatisfaction I still felt, even as I picked up my organic Parmigiano Reggiano, my pasta, my beef and my two-for-the-price-of-one Piccini Chianti en route to a homemade Bolognese, and an evening with Marion and Sara around the dinner table, with Chick Corea's *Return to Forever* on the stereo playing in the background? Not a dissatisfaction with Marion and Sara and myself, but with, in general, the material means of satisfaction, a dissatisfaction with *making do,* with practicing an incomplete and negative *art de faire.*

Whatever was I really *against,* I had to ask myself, and whatever was I really *for*? And what might the rest of us be *against* in the prosperous noughties, or the rest of us for? I could try to analyse the situation as a social scientist, but it occurred to me what I had intuited was less about such objective facts and correlations as I could muster than about me, me and my drives and experiences and hopes and fears in confrontation with objective facts and correlations. Me me me. But me me me for a purpose. For what I was trying to express was something beyond the language of science and social thought. Sure, I could continue the work of others and document all the failings and depredations of the world of supermarkets. I even tried once to talk to officials at Sainsbury's, to interview them and find out what they were made of and discover what cultural as well as material objectives might motivate today's supermarket executive. No dice, of course: business executives do not, as a rule, make themselves available to the public. They are Wizards of Oz. And that is another one of the major problems today. If business is so much in control of our lives today, if decisions in the City of London can determine how people will live in the city of Leicester, or for that matter Lagos and Lahore, these decisions are opaque, and there is nothing democratic about them. The real power, the economic power that governs our lives is fundamentally anti-democratic, even if liberal democracies are good environments for that power to thrive in. But again, it was not for me to delineate all this. I didn't have the patience. I didn't have the gift. What I had, instead, was me, and the stories I had to tell.

But as I began writing, something happened. The crash came. And with the crash, like many other people, I realised that in the midst of the boom something else had been going on.

It was like the Al Kooper song, from 1968:

You know I woke up this mornin' people
the first thing I did was to look into your eyes
and in that space where I used to find so much truthfulness
there was a stone cold pack of lies

You know that somethin' goin' on

> Somethin' goin' on but I don't know what it is
> Somethin's goin' on people ...

Toward the end of 2008 we suddenly 'woke up'. It seemed that the system I had learned (the hard way) to put my trust in was 'a stone cold pack of lies'. The banks and the financial services industry had, in a word, been stealing from us. And even worse, all the cronies of finance, the insurance executive in New York, the sports shoe manufacturer from Portland, the shipbuilder from Athens, the oil rig man from Rotterdam, the oil well sheik from Riyadh, had been stealing from us. Or rather, first they had been using us, selling us their goods and services, converting us into buyers for their goods and services, and *then* they had been stealing from us, taking away our incomes, our social services, our social life. Or rather still, they had been using us and stealing from us at the same time, for using us and stealing from us was one and the same thing.

Something was going on, people – all along, something was going on. Beginning, maybe, in the year 1975 as Susan Sontag talked about it. I had lived my life, I had come to construct my identity, or perhaps my multiple identities, and I had come to maturity during the great post-1975 neo-liberal nightmare, when 'free trade' came to rule the roost, and the social contract between business, government and workers was abandoned and the radical left withdrew from public debate apart from its fights on behalf of libertarian values like 'diversity' and sexual self-expression. Nightmare is perhaps too strong a word. But I was asleep; surely most of us were asleep. Even if nightmare isn't too strong a word, to be sure, I know I need to be circumspect about it, for it is the only nightmare I will ever have had. It is the only life that I will ever have had. Me me me. But you you you as well, if you are reading this. Almost all the wealth that has been created in the West since 1975 has gone to the few rather than the many, to *them* rather than to *us*, and not just in the United States, but in most of Europe and most of the rest of the world too. And you don't have to be mean or greedy or small-minded to resent that. If it is a fundamental human capacity to create *wealth*, if creating wealth is something that we fundamentally *do* as members of a technologically advanced society, then we not only have a right to share in that wealth; but we are ourselves the wealth. By using us to create wealth, and then extracting it from us, the system, and the people who own and run the system, are robbing us not just our money but of ourselves.

From the beginning, to be sure, I understood that the supermarket was a generator of inequality. It made food plentifully and cheaply available at the cost of the impoverishment of its employees and suppliers and government services. I had worked, on a special assignment, in a supermarket in San Francisco for a few weeks, in 1983, back when supermarket workers were still protected by a strong union and were well paid, had job security, benefits and pride, and in fact when getting work at a supermarket, for a working class person, was plum. They were happy workers, it seemed to me. But now in most of America and much of Europe that happiness is gone. I understood that when I started thinking about the culture of the supermarket in the twenty-first century, and it bothered me, but I wasn't paying sufficient attention. Now I am. According to report in The Guardian from July 2011, while the chief executive of Sainsbury's was earning three and a half million pounds that year, having seen his income triple over the past few years, a full-time checkout clerk with fifteen years experience was making less than fourteen thousand pounds a year, on wages of less that seven pounds an hour. Yes, that's zero point four per cent of what the chief executive earned: less than seven pounds an hour versus more than 1500 pounds an hour.

¤ ¤ ¤

In Sweden, the big joke (on me) is Systembolaget. That's the state store that has a monopoly on all beverages of more than 3.5% alcohol by volume. Private business thrives in Sweden. There are three major supermarket chains in cutthroat competition against each other and growing newcomers like Lidl and Willy's. The banks and the railroads have been privatised during the long neo-liberal sleep. Swedish clothing chains vie with Spanish and German fashion chains. There are street venders everywhere selling hot dogs and, in the warmer months, fresh berries. But alcohol is monopolised by the state. The premise is that people's drinking supplies need to be controlled, lest the people drink too much. Until 1955 alcohol was actually rationed – married women and the unemployed were forbidden to buy alcohol, and the amount others were able to buy was proportionate to their income. But the premise since the liberalisation in 1955 has also been that Systembolaget needs to serve the Swedes as consumers in a consumer society, providing all of them, equally, with a good selection of spirits, wines and beers at a reasonable price. Since 1990 this has also meant that Swedes should be able to buy their alcohol, in most places, in a pleasant environment, with stores designed for self-service, as in a supermarket. The Swedes I talk to take pride in the Systembolaget of today– even though for a wine enthusiast like myself, the selection is stupid, dominated by overly fruity New World wines, and the prices for quality goods astronomical. Systembolaget is in effect a communist supermarket. Its profits are ploughed back into the state. Its mission is to serve the people. It is to give them what they think they want. But not too much: its mission is also to shame the people and suppress the crime of excess. In other words, the purpose of Systembolaget is at once to cater to the Swedish people as consumers and to discipline the Swedish people as citizens.

So if I left America partly in order to escape puritanism, I have ended up having puritanism showered upon my head, as if a blessing. *System* in Swedish means 'system'. *Bolaget* means 'the company'. So my local wine shop, my only local wine shop (and it is not so local, it is farther away by foot than half a dozen banks), the only wine shop in a city centre with hundreds of shops, serving a population of 200,000 people, with limited hours (it closes on the weekends on Saturday at three o'clock) is the System Company. Here the Swedish government, eager though it has been to sell off national assets like power utilities and forests, presses its knee on the throats of its people, and the people love it, for this is after all the System. And they ought to be ashamed of themselves.

Sweden has changed a great deal in the past decade or so, I have been told. Even five years ago, it was difficult to get all the fresh fruits and vegetables you see in the supermarkets today, which are not as good as the ones I used to get in Britain or America or France, but still, not too bad. The Swedes, like the Danes before them, have decided: they are going to live more like Europeans. They are going to have sidewalk cafes and restaurants with good food and drink. They are going to be gourmets. They are going to buy nice clothes, in the latest styles. They are going to be leaders in this business of design, artisanry, fashion, cookery, and the *art de vivre*. There are plans afoot, thanks to global warming, to begin making Swedish wine. Sweden will be not just a consumer society, but a *leader* among consumer societies. That is supposed to mean, in part, that workers will not be exploited, that Swedes will enhance their lives as consumers without increasing social inequality. So far the evidence is not good: income inequality is increasing very rapidly in Sweden. Moreover, although *income* inequality is still, for all its growth, much lower than the average for the developed world, *wealth* inequality is actually *worse* than in many other developed countries. It is much worse than in Italy, for example. In 2007, seventy-three per cent of the wealth in Sweden was owned by twenty per cent of the people; fifty-eight per cent of the wealth was owned by the top ten per cent.

So the evidence is not good. Maybe Sweden is en route to undermining its own famous 'Swedish model'. But still, many of the cultural and social foundations of the Swedish model remain. One of the reasons why wealth is more concentrated among the few in Sweden than elsewhere is that so many Swedes see little reason to try to accumulate wealth in the form of private property or equities. Why buy a house when you can always rent an apartment? Why purchase securities when the state will provide you with a pension? When you rent an apartment in Sweden you get a lifelong, transferrable tenure in it, paying rents controlled by the state. Marion and I have one such apartment. Meanwhile, all of the modest investments in the Anglo-American economy Marion and I were able to make went rank. Our securities invested in an American firm (their value having decreased substantially since the time we acquired them) had to be sold to pay off debts in Britain. The mortgage on our house in Lancaster appears to be underwater. That is, the house is worth substantially less than we paid for it and owe on it. We are renting it out, but we may end up losing it, along with all the money and effort we put into it. At the end of the day, not very long after my conversion to late modern capitalism and its success in transcending the old cycles of boom and bust, I find myself on the verge of bankruptcy. And I am not alone. Even in Sweden, thirty per cent of all the adults are the proud owners, on balance, of less than nothing.

¤ ¤ ¤

Political books are expected to end with ruminations about the future. But I have no idea what the future has in store. And in any case, memoirs have to do things differently. The only way a memoir can end is indefinitely, since the main subject of the text, the life of the author, hasn't ended yet. Augustine's *Confessions,* cheating, ends with a prayer about what shall be, calling upon

God, like a good masseuse, to put a happy end to our search after truth. Rousseau's *Confessions* ends more honestly, incompletely, in the middle of things. And the text comes to an end, in any case, fourteen years before Rousseau actually died. He never finished his *Confessions*, but how could he? When are one's confessions really over?

In the middle of things, I sit in front of a computer screen, either at home or at the office, and I try to think through to the present, even as it flees before me and turns into more of the past. Winter has come early this year and a foot of snow is on the ground. The temperature is well below freezing. The school term is winding down and the small city of Uppsala is quiet. Everyday life is less of an adventure than it used to be, for Marion and I have already gone to the end of what seem to be our limits in that regard. We still try new things: Marion's been working hard on producing authentic Spanish and Mexican food this year to the extent that Swedish supermarkets and speciality shops allow us to find the right ingredients, and I scour the shelves of Systembolaget twice a week or so to find something different yet good to drink and sometimes I am successful. I go on trips to give lectures or attend conferences now and then, and I bring back samples. In Bordeaux I bought some wine, including what promises to be a luscious, violet Margaux, along with a tin of cheap duck *foie gras*; in Greece (to which Marion accompanied me) I bought Ouzo and Metaxa brandy, wine from the Peloponnesus and a tin of fine olive oil from Kalamata; in Britain I bought single malt Scotch, artisanal gin and a packet of cold tablets (which are not available over the counter in Sweden). But these are not adventures. I am stocking up. I am trying to maintain a lifestyle which for now at least has reached a kind of stasis. We are where we are, we live as we live, *j'ai lu tous les livres*. From day to day we endeavour not to stretch our limits and invent new modes of sensation and conviviality but to enjoy what we have and only very delicately and playfully dream about what it would mean to enjoy something better. Someday we are sure, or at least would like to be sure, we will live by the Mediterranean Sea or else on the Atlantic coast in France or Spain, where the Basques and the oysters are, and we will spend our days in the bright weather out of doors, sitting at café tables looking patiently into each other's eyes or walking lazily along the seashore holding hands. We will go to art exhibits and watch movies. We will live like ripened fruit. Or so we hope. But that is the future, and I have no idea what the future really has in store. I know the old saying, and at this point I think I know what it means: 'let no man be called happy until he dies'.

Up until recently it really seemed to be true that my life amounted to shopping and being shopped. I had tried to delude myself into thinking that there was more to my life than that, that I was different. But even in thinking I was different I proved that I was the same as everyone else, for that was the main myth, especially in America, that everyone was 'different'. Just do it. And have it your way, by the way. I went through life making choices, or what seemed to be choices, in order to maximise what seemed to be my pleasure. But my 'pleasure' was seldom only a quick little buzz, a discrete discharge of dopamine or some such chemical in my brain, responding to the stimulus of a physiological input. It was almost always also a part of what I took to be my personal life story. Just doing it, having it my way. It was a signal of my status in the world, and indicator how far I had gone in reaching my ultimate goals in life. Even undertaken in the guise of reverse snobbery (so that it would become a point of pride *not* to consume whatever happened to be in fashion), activity and pleasure in my physical world was part of the story of my success (or failure) in everyday life. I wore corduroy jackets with tee shirts and jeans, or ate lamb, or drove a Mazda ... because. Or else my 'pleasure' was a part of what I took to be a defence against otherwise implacable misery: binge-eating, drug-taking or boozing to unconsciousness were escapes from the otherwise overpowering reality of sadness and fear. I ate, I popped pills, I drank ... because. Either way, I was trying to accomplish something excessive with my consumption, something beyond the needs of consumption. I was trying to fashion myself, and to survive in the self (however pathetic) so fashioned. Just to do it, your way, and do it now, because if you don't you collapse and die. That there might be something beyond this beyond, that there might be something like transcendent value in a practice that gave me pleasure – that was an idea I was pledged to as if an article of faith, however. First of all, there was art. John Coltrane's *A Love Supreme* did not just give me 'pleasure'. Thomas Mann's *The Magic Mountain* did not just divert me from my misery, or lull me into an opiate sense of security at the picture of the world it drew. Richard Diebenkorn's *Ocean Park* paintings did not only make me feel that I was swimming in the warm waters of *calme* and *luxe* and *volupté*. Yes, there was always the possibility that I could, egoistically and stupidly, pride myself on having discovered *A Love Supreme, The Magic Mountain* and *Ocean Park*, using these discoveries as a sign of my status in the world, a badge of honour declaring that I was just doing it, and doing it better than many others. But that is not what artworks like these were really about. There was something beyond the beyond of excess pleasure to which the artworks appealed. And secondly, there was the *art de faire* and even better the *art de vivre*, the living of life, sensual life, to its fullest expressiveness: the experience of the real as the experience of the beautiful, even if the 'beautiful' in this context amounted to nothing more than a good *tagliatelle alla Bolognese*, or a morning stroll along a cobblestone alley before the shops had opened and the air still smelled of the evening dew. I knew about this second form of transcendence from having grown up with so little of it, from having been pushed from an early age into the homely streets of suburban sub-developments and the aisles of corporate suburban supermarkets, and taught to confuse consumer choice, even from among the bland products on the shelves, wrapped in plastic and cardboard, with self-worth. I knew, in the end, that for all my delusions of grandeur, I was brought up to be petty, I was brought up to think small, I was brought up to be selfish and self-centred and it was only in these respects that I ever succeeded in life: I successfully became petty, small-minded, selfish and self-centred. (No wonder I did not seem to have the makings of a good employee.) If it weren't for the art and the example of people like John Coltrane, Thomas Mann and Richard Diebenkorn, and if it weren't for my luck in travelling as a young man and learning from the inside about European ways of life, I would never have known any better. I would not have known that it was possible to transcend, or at least to dream of transcendence and to try to live large.There were bizarre turns, some of which I have had not had the time and space to write about, like my career as an 'Art Dealer'. There were bizarre turns, too, which I have been able to write about: the night when Maggie showed me how the economy really works, the night when Alison showed me how love and lust really works, the night when I showed myself how little I myself was made of.

There I was, trying to find and pursue my desire. There I was, trying to keep going. There I was trying to bust out, to bring suffering to a conclusion, to push myself and pull, to pursue the un-pursuable in the interest of life and death. And what did I get? I got humiliated, and paid handsomely for it. Five thousand dollars. I got humiliated, and treated to the exciting, erotic nightmare of my primal scene. 'He really loves me.' I got humiliated, shown my own cowardice, my own fear of the pain of death, courtesy of a shopping bag. And meanwhile visions danced in my head, amusingly, ironically, but also seriously, about garlic, croutons and fish soup and an arm, in love, around a shoulder: as if there actually were another way of life, of sensation and desire and the means of, well, getting by, of practicing an *art de faire*.

Capitalism as we know it won't ever do it for us. Capitalism as I know it won't ever do it for me. And yet for now capitalism is the future. And we have to live. Or do we? It seems to me that we can only decide the question about how we ought to live on the basis of our answer to the question about why we ought to live. And the answer to that question cannot be, or cannot only be, fear of the alternative.

¤ ¤ ¤

I don't drink myself to sleep anymore, and I usually don't take any pills to help me get to sleep either. Several years ago, when I was still in Lancaster, I discovered that at least on some occasions I could coax myself into sleeping, usually in the afternoon, while in my office at home, after a day of studying and writing. I could *allow* my waking cares to shut down. I could *initiate* a kind of letting go: images would come into head, sometimes silly images like flashes of cartoon characters from my childhood – Yosemite Sam, Bugs Bunny, Porky Pig – sometimes serious, idyllic but again only very momentary images from my past: a day at the beach, a glimpse of sunlight through a tree. They came out of nowhere, like random electrical discharges. They lacked meaning. They had no context. (Brain scientists call them hypnogenic hallucinations.) But their innocence was their meaning. They took my mind away from itself. And from a look at Technicolor Yosemite Sam standing silently in front of me with his guns cocked, frowning under his comically huge red moustache, or from the momentary tableau of sand on a beach, the sand also saying nothing, just being, something in my mind shifted out of consciousness and into a dream – a dream which itself would say little, but still, a dream. I was asleep. And I would stay asleep, for fifteen minutes, for half-an-hour.

To let go, to sleep, to dream had never been easy for me, even as a child, and became progressively worse the older I got. My insomnia, according to the psychiatrists I saw in Alabama, was a key symptom of the type of depression from which I suffered. From a non-pathological point of view, as far as I was concerned, my insomnia was a sign, rather, that I was in trouble, that I was worried about surviving, afraid that I had not yet done enough that day to let me carry on into the future. I was like the mole in Kafka's 'The Burrow', never secure enough, even in the burrow of my bedroom, from the beast in the night that was preparing to devour me. How could one get to sleep when there was still so much to do to protect oneself? Or else my insomnia was a sign of a fear of death, a fear of going blank, which may well have in part been pathological, since I allowed the fear to obstruct my natural functioning, but which may also have been philosophical, since after all if we do not fear death it is because we are not really thinking about it.

One way or another, I couldn't get to sleep, or stay asleep, without medication. When, finally, I was able to cut back on the drinking and rely on the Trazodone that had been prescribed for me, I found that I could sleep like a champion: eight hours a night, calmly (usually), without interruption, and for much of the night deeply entranced by unconscious dreams. And I would wake up refreshed. The only problem was that I had to have my pills. Once when I found myself without my pills, I ended up awake, calm but entirely awake, for the whole eight hours of the night. On another occasion without my pills, I got the willies, and had to rely on brandy and antihistamines to get me through the ordeal. 'Don't ever leave home without your anti-depressants', my doctor in Connecticut told me. 'Get yourself a little pillbox that you can put on your keychain. You need to take your medication every day and every night and never skip it.'

Gradually, though, in Lancaster, I was learning to sleep on my own – to go off into another mental space, with Yosemite Sam and company as my momentary guides. And the day came, in Sweden, when the pills were gone, and I had to depend on myself.

It has been much easier than I expected. I have progressed. If I am not 'cured' then I have at least 'progressed'. Maybe I am even 'in remission'. I can get to sleep on my own, most nights. In fact, I have come to look forward to it. To be in bed, at night, with Marion at my side, is to be lodged in a burrow that feels like it cannot be invaded.

I go to bed now not in anxiety but in expectation. For in the sleep to come I will go somewhere. And in the minutes before, between waking and sleeping, I will have gone somewhere. The darkness about me is like the snow on the streets. I can hear nothing in it. I do not try. I am coming to rest, relieving myself of a burden, and I do not have to be logical anymore. I do not have to try to make sense. Instead, I can anticipate a dissolution: my sense of things goes dark, it divides and liquefies, it oozes and spreads, it enters and shares itself with another space of existence. But 'oozing' is perhaps too material a metaphor. I am going somewhere, my sense and my senses are going somewhere, but there is no texture or thickness or even a liquidity to the going. It is more like a draft in the air, or a dark swelling cloud, drifting. But into this ooze, or draft, or cloud comes a kind of communication. I have closed my eyes with questions left unanswered, with demands unsatisfied, with needs still unaddressed. And the questions, the demands, the needs – there is a place for them, but not where I have been looking; the answers, satisfactions, the addressings can only be found in this other site, for which I am now departing.

I had been operating, all my life, under the illusion that sleep was an interruption, a necessary but inconvenient pause in the hard business of life. Sleep was a challenge. It was a game I had to play because like it or not, the next day, if I hadn't slept well, I would feel anxious and disconnected, my thoughts would unravel, my words would sputter, I would feel as if waking existence was in itself an unbearable pain. I had to sleep and dream because my sanity depended upon it, even though the dreams themselves were often insane. Of course, I was capable of seeing that there was a truth in the insanity of my dreams. But this truth needed to be both absorbed and forgotten. I would fail to understand something about myself if I ignored my insane dreams, but I would fail altogether in my waking life if my dreams interfered with my consciousness. Sleeping was something I had to get through, even if waking up in the morning was also hard and, once asleep, something in me wanted to keep sleeping, to remain in a state of oblivion and anaesthesia.

But now I was beginning to think differently. I was inspired both by my own experience and by reading, haphazardly, into the writing of current-day sleep scientists, to complement what I had learned about sleep from Freud. I was beginning to think not that sleep was a tool necessary for waking life, but that waking life was a tool for sleep. Waking life was what gave us something to dream about.

And now, when I am oozing or drifting or swelling into the other world of sleep, I imagine that, having laboured all day, I am now going to enjoy my reward: I am going to dream. And in my dream will come a culmination of the waking day. Here will be the meaning I have been searching for. Here will come the resolution, however temporary, of the tensions of the day.

It is not always a peaceful resolution that I achieve. I frequently find myself back in San Francisco, anxiously, with my limousine, as I have said, or with my limousine missing, parked somewhere I cannot remember. And I hear the voice of my boss; I see his pinched, dark face. I owe him money. Frequently I am in the company of a girlfriend from the San Francisco days, someone with whom things ended badly. I remember the feel of her breasts. I remember the coupling of desire and dissatisfaction I felt when I was with her. I remember the guilt. Or rather, I am the guilt. I have failed a test, I have committed a crime. I have a secret I dare not tell. But the feel of her breasts, the smell of her breath, the taste of her tongue – they don't go away. They call to me. They live in me. They challenge me to accomplish something I do not know how to formulate.

For a number of years, when I was stuck in America, I dreamed of traveling to imaginary cities, or else back to Paris, the most imaginary city of all. My unconscious created cityscapes of inexplicable complexity, of twisting, tree-lined avenues mounting through rows of great sparkling edifices. The architecture of the buildings was like a living sculpture. The stone walls were liquid. I wandered through the streets looking for a friend, or just admiring the scenery, climbing steps that reached the top of hills, overlooking rooftops and balconies, towers and domes, sparkling glass constructions, angling into the sky. The spectacle was ecstatic. I was where I needed to be. I was *back* where I needed to be. The city smelled of life. My footfalls sounded like music.

Now that I am in Europe dreams like this are less frequent. Now my dreams are more likely to take me back to America and especially to San Francisco. There is a house in San Francisco I sometimes inhabit, something like the mansion in Alfred Hitchcock's *Vertigo*, only smaller and darker and crowded by other buildings. I live in an apartment in which is located a second apartment, which has been left empty. To get to the second apartment I have to open a door and mount a narrow staircase. In my dream I wonder why I am not living in the second apartment. I worry that I have not been able to pay the rent, and I think about hiding in the second apartment if my landlord comes to evict me. There is an open kitchen dating from the sixties or seventies up there, with a Formica counter and the usual appliances, but the place is dark. The floors are covered with an ugly acrylic, textured green carpet, like the one we had in our townhouse in Chicago, when I was in high school, and there is a musty smell. I dare not go there but I dare not stay where I am.

I travel between San Francisco and Oakland. Just last night I stepped on a platform that turned into a ferry. The ferry took off and I found myself clinging to the side of the platform, the ferry, a raft, moving at a quick pace into the impossibly warm waters of a non-existent river that led into San Francisco Bay. I delighted in the feel of the water, the sense of floating. I got up onto the platform. There were fish everywhere in the water (I had eaten fish that night, cod with a kind of a Basque *piperade*, prepared by Marion), and I put a hand in the water to feel them. Immediately several small fish, the size of herrings, bit my hand and clung to me with their fang-like teeth. I had to pick them off of me one by one, with the help of the other people on the ferry, including a man who reminded of the late comic television actor Jim Backus, a star in *Gilligan's Island*. We debated about what kind of fish they were, herring or pompano. Then, in the sunlight, we arrived in Oakland, at the foot of the San Francisco-Oakland Bay Bridge. But we found ourselves on another platform, a huge pile built into the water, and we were in a kind of hotel, with a large dining room overlooking the Bay. I had a child with me now, my charge. With the child, a young girl, I wandered into a room with a kind of cylindrical steam heater, used for relaxing the muscles, like something I had once seen on *I Love Lucy*, and I put the child in it. Then I realised that I had done something stupid. I opened the cylinder, which now was only about nine inches long, and the child had turned into a fish, and she was cooked. I took her out and she crumbled in my hands like tuna fish from a can. Pieces of her fell to the floor, and I tried to collect them and put her back together. What have I done?, I thought. I have killed her.

Subject to dreams like this, I cannot help but embrace Freud's original theory about the nature of dreams. I am taking something from the waking day and translating it into a deep past, by way of a desire that moves both forward and backward – a governing wish that is both progressive and regressive. And I have long thought about how a recurrent direction of my dream wishes is masochistic: I long for pain, for punishment; I long however perversely to experience the death of others, I long sometimes – for this too recurs in my dreams – for my own death, and even that pain of death which in my waking life I am unable to confront. There is no sadism in my dreams except so far as I turn aggression into my own suffering, remorse, castration or elimination.

But not all of my dreams are so patently surrealistic, or arranged like narratives, or expressive of dangerous wishes. Sometimes my dreams are more like thinking than anything else: I construct a long disquisition in my mind, trying to express a philosophic position. Sentence follows upon sentence, idea upon idea. They may ultimately be absurd: I am not sure, for I never remember them. I only remember how elaborate and seemingly ingenious they were. Or sometimes in my dreams I write stories, or follow the adventure of a film my imagination is remembering, though again I cannot remember anything about them, only that they are complex, exciting, unbelievably clever and thorough. But sleep scientists say that our brains are sometimes more active at night than they are during the day, and so the memory of cleverness, complexity and thoroughness may be accurate. My mind is in any case arranging and rearranging things. It is placing things in their categories, and then, savagely, trading them back and forth from one category to another, associating and disassociating them with one another, using a somnolent logic, or literary narrative or cinematic form to create new configurations of nonsense and sense. And this is good. This is play, mental play, undertaken within the safety of sleep. It is the play of structure. I am making my consciousness of the world of myself into a kind of game which can neither be won nor lost but only, rather, enjoyed.

So I enjoy myself at night. Or at least I challenge myself to enjoy what the night will bring. Can I accomplish this?, I wonder as I drift into sleep. Can I take what the day has given me, including all the unfinished business of the day, and all the frustrations as well as the satisfactions of the day, and make them into something whole, a dream? I don't worry that my dreams may take a bad turn: if that is where my desires go, that is where I must go. I don't worry that I may find myself in the past, back in San Francisco or Oakland, with all the unredeemed pain that I must associate with those days. Have I mentioned the Loma Prieta earthquake of 1989, and the collapse of a section of the Bay Bridge, or the Oakland 'firestorm' of 1991? No need. There are already there, in my narratives that fail to mention them, in my dreams that fail to represent them. And not to worry: sometimes my desire will have to take me back to them in one form or another. Or back to that closet in San Diego. All that is required, in the end, is that I relish, with contentment or dread, the place which my desire, treacherous desire, insists on taking me to.

Which means above all, I think, that I relish the *impulse* that transports me, that I embrace the struggle for life that animates the dream. The *struggle*: I have mentioned it before. All my life I have tried both to embrace and escape this struggle. I find myself, whether in suburban Chicago or urban Uppsala, inhabiting a lifeworld where the struggle itself is renounced, even as the renunciation itself only contributes more struggle, making it harder rather than easier to live. But what if we lived in a world designed to recognise the struggle, to accommodate and love it?

I don't know. After all, I know nothing about the future, except that capitalism will be in it. I also know, however, that just the other day, I was having a dream about which I remember nothing. Marion was awake beside me. Apparently I was turning over and speaking in my sleep. This has been happening more frequently now that I am not taking sleeping pills anymore. My dreams are apparently more voluble. My control over my dreams is apparently more tenuous. I am letting go at night. I am doing the work of desire. I come and go, I am constantly in movement. I recoil into the past, I rocket into the future. I break away from my own repressions, not to mention the repression of the world to which in daytime I am necessarily confined. I swim through the waters of non-existent rivers, I climb the stairs of non-existent cities. I arrange and rearrange the very shelves and stacks of my brain. I ride on the spinning wheels of frictionless trollies down the lanes and alleys of nowhere. And that night, though I remember nothing about it, Marion, my angel, assures me that I was travelling in my dream at a great pace, turning over, twitching my toes and calling out in the darkness, 'Yes! Yes! Yes!'

Contemporary culture has eliminated both the concept of the public and the figure of the intellectual. Former public spaces – both physical and cultural – are now either derelict or colonized by advertising. A cretinous anti-intellectualism presides, cheerled by expensively educated hacks in the pay of multinational corporations who reassure their bored readers that there is no need to rouse themselves from their interpassive stupor. The informal censorship internalized and propagated by the cultural workers of late capitalism generates a banal conformity that the propaganda chiefs of Stalinism could only ever have dreamt of imposing. Zer0 Books knows that another kind of discourse – intellectual without being academic, popular without being populist – is not only possible: it is already flourishing, in the regions beyond the striplit malls of so-called mass media and the neurotically bureaucratic halls of the academy. Zer0 is committed to the idea of publishing as a making public of the intellectual. It is convinced that in the unthinking, blandly consensual culture in which we live, critical and engaged theoretical reflection is more important than ever before.